YOUR
SPIRITUAL
POWER

JEREMY P. TARCHER/PENGUIN

a member of Penguin Group (USA) Inc.

New York

YOUR
SPIRITUAL
POWER

A Collection of Inspirational Writings

ERNEST HOLMES

JEREMY P. TARCHER/PENGUIN
Published by the Penguin Group
Penguin Group (USA) Inc., 375 Hudson Street, New York, New York 10014, USA • Penguin Group (Canada),
90 Eglinton Avenue East, Suite 700, Toronto, Ontario M4P 2Y3, Canada (a division of Pearson Penguin Canada Inc.)
• Penguin Books Ltd, 80 Strand, London WC2R 0RL, England • Penguin Ireland, 25 St Stephen's Green,
Dublin 2, Ireland (a division of Penguin Books Ltd) • Penguin Group (Australia), 707 Collins Street, Melbourne,
Victoria 3008, Australia (a division of Pearson Australia Group Pty Ltd) • Penguin Books India Pvt Ltd,
11 Community Centre, Panchsheel Park, New Delhi–110 017, India • Penguin Group (NZ), 67 Apollo Drive,
Rosedale, Auckland 0632, New Zealand (a division of Pearson New Zealand Ltd) • Penguin Books (South Africa),
Rosebank Office Park, 181 Jan Smuts Avenue, Parktown North 2193, South Africa • Penguin China,
B7 Jiaming Center, 27 East Third Ring Road North, Chaoyang District, Beijing 100020, China

Penguin Books Ltd, Registered Offices: 80 Strand, London WC2R 0RL, England

Most Tarcher/Penguin books are available at special quantity discounts for bulk purchase for sales promotions,
premiums, fund-raising, and educational needs. Special books or book excerpts also can be created to fit specific
needs. For details, write Penguin Group (USA) Inc. Special Markets, 375 Hudson Street, New York, NY 10014.

ISBN 978-0-399-16224-4

Printed in the United States of America
1   3   5   7   9   10   8   6   4   2

Book design by Meighan Cavanaugh

While the author has made every effort to provide accurate telephone numbers, Internet addresses,
and other contact information at the time of publication, neither the publisher nor the author assumes any responsibility
for errors, or for changes that occur after publication. Further, the publisher does not have any control over and
does not assume any responsibility for author or third-party websites or their content.

CONTENTS

Discover a Richer Life

THINK YOUR TROUBLES AWAY

IMMORTALITY

DEDICATION

To comfort them that mourn.
To bring light into the house
Of those who have lost the way.
To gladden the heart of the sorrowful.
To bring peace to the mind disturbed.
To fill the vacant chair and
Complete the family circle.
That the cup may again be filled with wine
And the table spread with joy.
To dry the tears of grief
And still the heart of doubt.
To bring strength to the weak, and gladness
To those who sit in lonely places.
That a new song may be upon the lips,
And a new hope may flood the soul
With peace.

These pages are affectionately dedicated to all who
would believe in eternity.

Foreword

Life is a school which all must attend. The same Intelligence being in each, it is the task and high privilege of the individual to so develop his God-given powers that he shall not remain in the kindergarten, but may, by practical use of the lessons learned in this grade,—lessons of the need of manifesting love, joy, harmony, peace and poise,—go on to each advancing grade, ever increasing in the knowledge and understanding of the One who is in all, over all, and through all. That the event called death shall be an open door to a grade beyond this plane, where he will continue to expand throughout all eternity.

Anna Columbia Holmes.

IMMORTALITY

Never the spirit was born; the spirit shall cease to be never;
   Never was time it was not; End and Beginning are Dreams!
Birthless and deathless and changeless remaineth the spirit forever;
Death hath not touched it at all, dead though the house of it seems!

> Nay, but as one who layeth
>   His worn-out robes away,
> And, taking new ones, sayeth,
>   "These will I wear today!"
> So putteth by the spirit
>   Lightly its garb of flesh,
> And passeth to inherit
>   A residence afresh.
>   —*The Song Celestial.*

>⤛⤜

He is not the God of the dead, but the God of the living; for all live
unto Him.

                                        —*Sayings of Jesus.*

"Immortality means to the average person that man shall persist after the experience of physical death, retaining a full recollection of himself and the ability to recognize others. If his full capacities go with him beyond the grave, he must be able to think consciously; to reason, will, affirm, declare, accept, reject, know and be known, communicate and be communicated with; he must be able to travel about, see and be seen, understand and be understood; he must be able to touch, taste, smell, hear, cognize and realize. In fact, if he is really to continue as a self-conscious personality, he can do so only to the degree that he maintains a continuous stream of conscious self-knowingness."

"This means that he must carry with him a complete remembrance; for it is to the remembrance alone that we must look for the link that binds one event to another, making life a constant stream of self-conscious expression. To suppose that man can forget and still remain himself is to suppose that he could cut off the entire past and at this moment be the same personality that he was a moment ago. Remembrance alone guarantees personality. Individuality might remain without remembrance, but not so with personality; for what we are, is the result of what we have been, the result of what has gone before."

"Man, then, if he is to have an immortality worthy of the name, must continue, as he now is, beyond the grave. Death cannot rob him of anything if he be Immortal."

—E. S. HOLMES, *The Science of Mind, p. 266.*

To me immortality means the continuity of the individual life, forever and ever expanding. I wish to feel, when the experience of physical death shall occur, that that which I really am will continue to live beyond the grave. I wish to feel that I shall again meet those friends whose lives and influence have made my life happy while on earth.

Most of us have as many friends on one side of the grave as on the other and we hope to see them again: we hope to talk to them, to feel their presence, to commune with their souls. With Tennyson, we all like to feel:

> Thou wilt not leave us in the dust:
>   Thou madest man, he knows not why,
>   He thinks he was not made to die;
> And thou hast made him: thou art just.
> —*In Memoriam.*

I believe that personality persists beyond the grave. And when I say personality persists, I mean that after the experience of physical death I shall know and be known. If I could not believe this I would believe in nothing in life; life would have no meaning and death could not be untimely, unless it were long delayed; it would be an event to be devoutly longed for and sought after.

Is there anyone, who, standing at the bier of loved ones, can possibly feel that the real end has come? It is useless to say that their influence lives after them. Of course their influence lives after them, but we hope for more than this; we wish to feel that they still live. How anyone can feel otherwise seems unthinkable.

But I cannot base my hopes of immortality on the revelation of anyone but myself; so far as I am concerned, nothing can exist to me unless I am aware of it. I believe in the life, the teachings and the works of the beautiful Jesus, apparently the most glorious soul who ever trod this earth; but I cannot believe in immortality simply because the Christian Bible tells me that Jesus was raised from among the dead. I was not an eye-witness to the fact. How I should love to have been! But, unfortunately, I was not. The incident is supposed to have happened nearly two thousand years ago and some mistake might have been made in the record. I do not wish to shock anyone by such remarks but I can speak only as I feel. While I believe in other men's revelations I am sure only of my own.

The poets have always sung of the immortality of the soul, and the saints and sages of the ages have told us the story of eternal existence, but I must KNOW for myself.

We have been told that immortality might mean the result of a man's life and work which he has left behind; for instance, that he immortalizes himself in his offspring, but we still ask, "What of the man?"

The idea of the acorn becoming an oak tells me nothing of true immortality for the poor little acorn is lost in the shuffle.

I am told by many that individuality might persist beyond the grave, but not personality; that is, that no remembrance can accompany the perpetuation of the individual stream of consciousness; but I am not one with such a thought.

>‹‹

I want to live and to keep on living and to know that I am I; and unless immortality means this, death means the cutting off of all conscious life, contact or recognition, and it could be truly said of the personality that it dies with the grave.

>‹‹

I wish to convince myself of my own immortality. I wish to know with a faith that cannot be shaken, with an assurance which direct knowledge always gives to the one knowing. I wish to know the Truth, that the Truth may make me free from all fear of death and the hereafter. And I feel that I do know in this way. To me the question is forever settled.

>‹‹

Here within myself, is something that thinks and knows. Here is something that knows that it IS. When I appeared upon this scene, this human drama, this thing came with me. I do not know where it came from, I do not know how it got here; but, I do know that it is here. I know that I can touch, taste, hear, smell, feel, see and be seen, know and be known, speak and be spoken to, think and be thought about, love and be loved. I know that I AM.

> Out of the night that covers me,
>   Black as the Pit from pole to pole,
> I thank whatever gods may be
>   For my unconquerable soul.
>
> In the fell clutch of circumstance
>   I have not winced nor cried aloud.
> Under the bludgeonings of chance,
>   My head is bloody, but unbowed.

Beyond this place of wrath and tears,
  Looms but the horror of the shade;
And yet the menace of the years
  Finds, and shall find me, unafraid.

It matters not how strait the gate,
  How charged with punishments the scroll,
I am the master of my fate;
  I am the captain of my soul.
                —WILLIAM ERNEST HENLEY, *Invictus.*

It seems useless to inquire why life is, for life is self-existent; and all
the poetry, wit and science of man will never fathom that which is self-
existent. God is God. "I Am That I Am." Since we are, we must have
come from this "I Am."

Strong Son of God, immortal Love,
  Whom we, that have not seen thy face,
  By faith, and faith alone, embrace,
Believing where we cannot prove.
                —TENNYSON, *In Memoriam.*

Facts admit of proof, not so with life. I feel that since I am I must have
come from a life which IS. I trust IT.

Through introspection, then, I know that I am; and by observation I
note that when death comes this I am appears no longer to be. That is,
this thing which I am appears to leave the body. The body is given
back to the native elements from which it sprang. Something will have

left it, undoubtedly. The knowing, thinking, willing, volitional, personal factor,—all that today makes me what I am will have left.

I cannot doubt that something real leaves the body; for all the physical organs which remain will be but motionless, unanimated clay. The table has four legs yet it does not walk. The piano does not play itself, someone must play on it. The ear does not hear; cut it off and it would not perceive sound. Nor does the tongue wag unless there is someone to wag it. The brain does not think. If the brain were endowed with power from on high to think, then it would think on forever. Isolate it and it will not think or ponder Truth. It is the thinker behind the brain, who thinks. There is a seer looking through the windows of the eye, who sees.

"But there is a spirit in man: and the inspiration of the Almighty giveth them understanding." Job 32:8.

Scientific research in the realm of the psychic or soul life, be it often foolish as it may, has taught us many valuable lessons in soul life and has demonstrated beyond question of doubt that many people, while in certain states of consciousness, are able to see without the agency of the physical eye, hear without the agency of the physical ear and communicate without the tongue. Indeed, every faculty of the senses has been duplicated in the mind alone. It would take volumes to provide all the data compiled by able men in the demonstrating of these facts. They may be taken for granted. The evidence leads us to suppose that the soul can operate independently of the physical instrument.

Why has nature provided us with such subtle powers unless she foreknew that we should need them sometime and somewhere? Nature is not foolish; she does nothing without an ample reason; she leaves no gap and provides for all emergencies. We have no use, in this life, for the etheric and subtle faculties of the soul which reproduce those of the physical body. I take it for granted that they are to have a use later.

> No longer half akin to brute,
>   For all we thought and loved and did,
>   And hoped, and suffer'd, is but seed
> Of what in them is flower and fruit;
>
> Whereof the man, that with me trod
>   This planet, was a noble type
>   Appearing ere the times were ripe,
> This friend of mine who lives in God,
>
> That God which ever lives and loves,
>   One God, one law, one element,
>   And one far-off divine event,
> To which the whole creation moves.
>   —TENNYSON, *In Memoriam.*

Consider the faculty of memory, without which there can be no continuity of consciousness, no real stream of personality. For memory alone links one event to another, binding all together into one continuous and logical sequence. Without memory there can be no personality. Where is this faculty? Cut a man into the smallest parts, analyze and dissect every atom of his physical being and you will never contact memory. There is something about the personality which not only performs its functions, but which also remembers what it has done, and which can anticipate future events. Where is it and what is it? It is the thing we are talking about, the non-physical faculty of perception, the thing that knows. The Knower.

And do we not all seem to remember; do we not seem to remember something 'way back?

><

Our birth is but a sleep and a forgetting;
The Soul that rises with us, our life's Star,
    Hath had elsewhere its setting
      And cometh from afar;
   Not in entire forgetfulness,
   And not in utter nakedness,
But trailing clouds of glory do we come
    From God, who is our home:

. . . . . .

But for those first affections,
Those shadowy recollections,
   Which, be they what they may,
Are yet the fountain-light of all our day,
Are yet the master-light of all our seeing;
   Uphold us, cherish, and have power to make
Our noisy years seem moments in the being
Of the eternal Silence: truths that wake,
    To perish never;
Which neither listlessness, nor mad endeavor,
    Nor man nor boy
Nor all that is at enmity with joy,
Can utterly abolish or destroy.
    Hence in season of calm weather,

Though inland far we be,
Our souls have sight of that immortal sea
Which brought us hither;
Can in a moment travel thither,
And see the children sport upon the shore,
And hear the mighty waters rolling evermore.
—WORDSWORTH, *Ode on Intimations of Immortality.*

You and I recognize each other when we pass. We understand each other as we contact each other's consciousness. Yet if we were to lay two dead bodies beside each other this could not happen; they could not recognize each other. That which talked, knew and recognized, has left the body.

And so the faculties of memory and understanding cannot be found in the body but function independently of it. There can be no question but that the soul needs the body while functioning here, else it would not have it. It needs one, therefore it evolves one. It needs all the physical instruments to properly function on the physical plane, but when it no longer desires to function here, or when by reason of sickness, decay or accident, the instrument is no longer adequate, the soul lays it aside.

Nay, but as one who layeth
His worn-out robes away,
And, taking new ones, sayeth,
"These will I wear today!"
So putteth by the spirit
Lightly its garb of flesh,
And passeth to inherit
A residence afresh.
—*The Song Celestial.*

When the soul can no longer properly function through the body, it is better for it to go. It cannot really be more than lightly connected with the body even while functioning through it. It is really separate from and has existence independently of it. The body is its physical instrument.

I have often had the experience of seeming to stand behind myself and I am sure that we all have had the same experience. We will to move, and following this volition of our thought, the body responds. When it no longer responds it is dead, worn out or useless and should be discarded.

When we pass from this plane, shall we become spirits or shall we have real tangible bodies? Well, I presume that we are spirits now as much as we ever shall be. After all, the spirit must be what we really are. But shall we still have bodies through which to function? It seems to me that we must have. I cannot think of it from any other light. We have bodies here. The soul needs something definite through which to function. If it has something definite here, why not hereafter? If the soul clothes itself in form here, and if it continues to live after the passing of the physical body, it seems logical to conclude that it will still need a body. If the soul can create one here I see no reason why it cannot create one hereafter.

But the question might be asked, out of what would the soul create a body there? Here we must realize that God's world is not limited to one plane. Science is rapidly proving that there is much more in the universe than we can see with the physical eye. I can conceive of a matter more subtle than the kind we are in the habit of handling. I think that the new idea of ether supplies a theory to fit this need and does so very adequately. From this theory I draw the conclusion that there could be a real body within the one I now have; just as solid, just as tangible, as definitely outlined, and every bit as real.

I believe that the resurrection body is within the one that we now use.

A thorough study of the topic will convince anyone that form can lie within form without interference. This concept, of course, opens up vistas of thought along the lines of immortality. The idea that we could have a body within the body, and that we are living in a universe which is infinite, suggests that there could be a body within a body to infinity. Personally, I believe this to be the case.

It seems to me that the resurrection body will be taken along with us and that it will be the result of the way we have lived while here on earth. I have no doubt that the body we now have has evolved in this manner and that the next will be a sort of continuation of this one, only more subtle. If this is true, and if remembrance links things together into one continuous stream of consciousness and form, then the future body will resemble this one, except that it will be free from disease, old age, or whatever hinders complete flow of the soul.

I am satisfied that the future, or resurrection body will be definite, real, and tangible, outlined and solid, all that we could ask for, expect or desire; a fit instrument for the future unfoldment of the soul.

> Faithful friends! It lies, I know,
> Pale and white and cold as snow;
> And ye say, "Abdellah's dead!"—
> Weeping at the feet and head.

. . . . . .

Yet I smile and whisper this,—
"I am not the thing you kiss;
Cease your tears, and let it lie;
It was mine, it is not I."

Sweet friends! What the women lave
For its last bed of the grave,
Is a tent which I am quitting,
Is a garment no more fitting,
Is a cage from which, at last,
Like a hawk my soul hath pass'd.
Love the inmate, not the room,—
The wearer, not the garb,—the plume
Of the falcon, not the bars
Which kept him from these splendid stars.

Loving friends! Be wise, and dry
Straightway every weeping eye,—
What ye lift upon the bier
Is not worth a wistful tear.
'Tis an empty sea-shell,—one
Out of which the pearl is gone;
The shell is broken, it lies there;
The pearl, the all, the soul, is here.

. . . . . .

But in light ye cannot see
Of unfulfill'd felicity,—
In enlarging paradise,

Lives a life that never dies.
Where I am ye, too, shall dwell.
I am gone before your face,
A moment's time, a little space.
When ye come where I have stepp'd
Ye will wonder why ye wept;
Ye will know, by wise love taught,
That here is all, and there is naught.
Weep awhile, if ye are fain,—
Sunshine still must follow rain;
Only not at death,—for death,
Now I know, is that first breath
Which our souls draw when we enter
Life, which is of all life center.

. . . . . .

Be ye stout of heart, and come
Bravely onward to your home!
　　　—EDWIN ARNOLD, *After Death in Arabia.*

>-<

Another question, which might engage our attention, is this. Where shall we go when we die? Where shall we take this marvelous mind and subtle body? If today is the logical continuance of yesterday, and tomorrow of today, and the next day of tomorrow, then all the tomorrows that stretch down the vistas of eternity will be a continuity of experiences and remembrances. We shall keep on keeping on. We shall continue in our own individual stream of consciousness but forever and ever expanding. Not less but ever more; more and still more.

Life is real! Life is earnest!
    And the grave is not its goal;
Dust thou art, to dust returnest,
    Was not spoken of the soul.

Not enjoyment, and not sorrow,
    Is our destined end or way;
But to act, that each tomorrow
    Finds us farther than today.
        —LONGFELLOW, *A Psalm of Life.*

But what about reward and punishment? Shall we be rewarded for our virtues and punished for our mistakes? I believe that we shall be. But I do not think of reward and punishment from any other viewpoint than that sin is a mistake and punishment a consequence. I do not believe that there is a God who either punishes or rewards. Such a concept of God creates only a human idea of the Deity, an anthropomorphic dualism, a house divided against itself. Such a house cannot stand.

I believe in law, a law that governs all things and all people. If we make mistakes we suffer; we do this right here, and shall, no doubt, do it hereafter. We are our own reward and our own punishment. Reward and punishment are the logical outcomes of our use of life. Life is a blessing or a curse according to the way we use it.

Some suffer, some are happy and some are unhappy, according to the way they contact life. No one judges us but ourselves and no one damns us but ourselves. No one gives to us but ourselves and no one robs us but ourselves. We need not fear either God or the devil, for God is Love and there is no devil.

The problem of good and evil will never enter the mind which is at peace with itself and with life. It is a mental disease and should be thought of from no other light.

If I make a mistake I suffer the consequences of that mistake. When, by reason of enlightenment and understanding, I correct that mistake I no longer suffer from it. Understanding alone constitutes true salvation, either here or hereafter.

I do not feel that we need fear anything in the universe. I am not afraid of God. I believe that God is Good. I am certain that all will arrive at the final goal, and that none will be missing. I can say with Whittier:

> But still my human hands are weak
>   To hold your iron creeds:
> Against the words ye bid me speak
>   My heart within me pleads.
>
> Who fathoms the Eternal Thought?
>   Who talks of scheme and plan?
> The Lord is God! He needeth not
>   The poor device of man.

. . . . . .

Ye see the curse which overbroods
    A world of pain and loss;
I hear our Lord's beatitudes
    And prayer upon the cross.

. . . . . .

Yet, in the maddening maze of things,
    And tossed by storm and flood,
To one fixed trust my spirit clings;
    I know that God is good!

. . . . . .

The wrong that pains my soul below
    I dare not throne above,
I know not of His hate,—I know
    His goodness and His love.

. . . . . .

I long for household voices gone,
    For vanished smiles I long,
But God hath led my dear ones on,
    And He can do no wrong.

And so beside the Silent Sea
    I wait the muffled oar;
No harm from Him can come to me
    On ocean or on shore.

I know not where His islands lift
    Their fronded palms in air;

> I only know I cannot drift
> Beyond His love and care.
> —WHITTIER, *The Eternal Goodness.*

>‹—

We waste much time and effort trying to correct the Divine Plan, and attempting to run the universe after our own weak patterns.

>‹—

I believe that every man is an incarnation of God and that the soul can no more be lost than God could be lost. I am not disturbed by the wailings of the prophets, nor the curses of theology. I believe in God and that He is Good. What more can life demand of us than that we do the best we know, and try to improve? If we have done this we have done well and all will go right with our souls, both here and hereafter.

>‹—

Theology seems to be a riddle, and too often our religions become morbid. Religion should be like the flowing river or the blossoming rose; natural and spontaneous, naked and unafraid.

>‹—

I do not believe that because we have subscribed to some creed we have, thereby, purchased a throne in heaven. I cannot feel that because we have made mistakes we shall, thereby, be damned.

>‹—

I think that our place hereafter will be what we have made it. We certainly cannot take anything with us but our character. If we have lived in accordance with the law of harmony, we shall continue to live after this Divine law. If we have lived any other way, we shall continue to live the other way until we wake to the facts of Being. This settles the whole question for me, and frees me to work out my salvation, not with fear or even with trembling, but with peace and in quiet confidence.

What may we take into the vast Forever?
    That marble door
Admits no fruit of all our long endeavor,
    No fame-wreathed crown we wore,
    No garnered lore.

What can we bear beyond the unknown portal?
    No gold, no gains
Of all our toiling, in the life immortal
    No hoarded wealth remains,
    Nor gilds, nor stains.

Naked from out that far abyss behind us
    We entered here:
No word came with our coming to remind us
    What wondrous world was near,
    No hope, no fear.

Into the silent, starless Night before us,
    Naked we glide:
No hand has mapped the constellations o'er us,
    No comrade at our side,
    No chart, no guide.
Yet fearless toward that midnight, black and hollow,
    Our footsteps fare:
The beckoning of a father's hand we follow,
    His love alone is there,
    No curse, no care.

—SILL, *Man, the Spirit.*

When we came into this life, we were met by loving friends who cared for us until we were able to care for ourselves. Judging the future by the past, and going from the known to the unknown, I find I can believe that when we enter the larger life, there will be loving hands to greet us and loving friends to care for us until we become accustomed to our new surroundings. Nature looks after everything and provides for herself at every turn of the road.

I confidently expect to meet my friends who are on the other side and to know and be known, when we shall meet. I cannot think otherwise.

It seems to me that our work in the next world will be a continuation of our work in this one. I do not look forward to a heaven where there will be nothing to do; I look forward to a place where our work will be done in greater harmony with the Divine Law, because of an enlarged understanding of it. But a place where there is nothing to do would become monotonous. It seems to me that we shall all be engaged in pleasant activities, much as we are here, but with a larger scope.

With this understanding of eternity, we can view the world war from a different light. Millions of lives were apparently snuffed out; but what difference does it make in the long run? They are all right. It is, of course, hard for those left behind, but those who have gone before are all right; perhaps they are better off than when here. We shall all go the same road, sooner or later. What difference does it make how we go, since we all must go?

The experience loses its sting, the grave its victory, when we realize the eternity of our own being. Nature will not let us stay in any one place too long. She will let us stay just long enough to gather the experience necessary to the unfolding and advancement of the soul. This is a wise provision of nature; for, should we stay here too long, we would become too set, too rigid, too inflexible. She demands the change in order that we may advance. When the change comes we should welcome it with a smile on the lips and a song in the heart.

It is human to grieve over the loss of dear ones. We would not wish it to be otherwise. We love them and cannot help missing them. But a true realization of the immortality and continuity of the individual soul will rob our grief of utter hopelessness. We shall realize that they are in God's keeping and that they are safe. We shall know that loving friends have met them and that their life still flows on with the currents of eternity. We shall feel that we have not lost them. They have only gone before.

So we will view eternity from the higher viewpoint, as a continuity of time, forever and ever expanding, until time as we now experience it shall be no more. Realizing this, we shall see in everyone a budding genius, a becoming God, an unfolding soul, an eternal destiny.

> Grow old along with me!
> The best is yet to be,
> The last of life, for which the first was made:
> Our times are in His hand

Who saith, "A whole I planned,
"Youth shows but half; trust God: see all nor be afraid!"

. . . . . .

Then, welcome each rebuff
That turns earth's smoothness rough,
Each sting that bids nor sit nor stand but go!
Be our joys three-parts pain!
Strive, and hold cheap the strain;
Learn, nor account the pang; dare, never grudge the throe!

. . . . . .

Not once beat "Praise be Thine!
"I see the whole design,
"I, who saw power, see now love perfect too;
"Perfect I call Thy plan:
"Thanks that I was a man!
"Maker, remake, complete,—I trust what Thou shalt do!"

Therefore I summon age
To grant youth's heritage,
Life's struggle having so far reached its term:
Thence shall I pass, approved
A man, for aye removed
From the developed brute; a god though in the germ.

And I shall thereupon
Take rest, ere I be gone
Once more on my adventure brave and new:
Fearless and unperplexed,

When I wage battle next,
What weapons to select, what armor to indue.

    . . . . All that is, at all,
      Lasts ever, past recall;
Earth changes, but thy soul and God stand sure:
      What entered into thee,
      That was, is, and shall be:
Time's wheel runs back or stops: Potter and clay endure.
                —ROBERT BROWNING, *from Rabbi Ben Ezra.*

Time heals all wounds, adjusts conditions, explains every fact: and time alone satisfies the expanding soul. We are born of Eternal Day and the Spiritual Sun shall never set upon its glory, for it is the coming forth of God into expression. We must give ourselves time enough to work out all problems. If we do not work them out here we shall hereafter. There will be time enough in eternity to prove everything. Every man is an incarnation of eternity, a manifestation in the finite, of that Infinite, which, Emerson tells us, "lies stretched in smiling repose."

With all these facts confronting us, we should learn to trust life. There is no power in the universe, which wishes anyone ill. Life is good and God is Good. Why not accept this and begin to live? No man need prepare to meet his God. He is meeting Him every day and each hour in every day. He meets Him in the rising sun, in the flowing stream, in the budding rose, in the joy of friendship and love, and in the silence of his own soul.

When we meet each other do we not feel that subtle presence, which flows through all things and gives color and light to our everyday experiences? In our own souls, in silent process of thought and understanding, do we not sense another presence? There is something divine about us, which we have overlooked. There is more to us than we realize. Man is an eternal destiny, a forever-expanding principle of conscious intelligence, the ocean in a drop of water, the sun in its beams. Man, the real man, is birthless, deathless, and changeless. And God, as man, in man, is man.

And so, we prepare not to die, but to live. The thought of death should slip from our consciousness altogether; and when this great event of the soul takes place, it should be beautiful, sublime; a glorious experience.

As the hawk, freed from its cage, soars to its native heights, so the soul, freed from the house of heavy flesh, will rise and return unto its Father's home, naked and unafraid.

> When death shall come
> And the spirit, freed, shall mount the air,
> And wander afar in that great no-where,
> It shall go as it came,
> Freed from sorrow, sin and shame;
> And naked and bare, through the upper air
> Shall go alone to that great no-where.
> Hinder not its onward way,
> Grieve not o'er its form of clay,
> For the spirit, freed now from clod,
> Shall go alone to meet its God.
>   —E. Holmes, *When Death Shall Come.*

⇥⇤

In adding the following lines to the Easter talk I make apologies to the muse of verse and ask my readers not to judge them from the standpoint of poetry but of the thought which they contain.

The experiences of the soul referred to are not thought of in the light of reincarnation but from the viewpoint of our advancing experiences,—experiences which, it appears to me, we all have.

I hold to the theory that man is a being of free will and volition, that he is equipped with power from on High but that he is ignorant of the fact and can only learn from experience.

It seems to me that our evolution is the result of an unfolding consciousness of that which already is, and needs but to be realized to become a fact of everyday life.

It seems to me that freedom is from within out, and never from without in.

The Journey of the Soul

PROLOGUE

In the long ago, so the sages say,
The Path of the Soul to the light of day,
Was downward bent through the Cosmic Way,
And Man emerged from a piece of clay.

But the birth of the Soul through a piece of sod
Was not a Soul born from the clod,
But was a Spark of the Living God
Come to earth to prove Itself Lord.

The purpose on which the Soul was bent,
The mission high on which it was sent,
The experiences through which it went
Were given it, by Divine Consent.

Man was directed to downward face,
To enter the bondage of time and space,
His soul within a body to place,
And back to come through the human race.

What was the reason, I hear you say,
That man should desert the Cosmic Day,
Take upon himself the form of clay,
And backward wend to the upper way?

Why should he leave his state on high
And come to earth in dust to lie?
Why should he leave his place in the sky
And enter a body which soon must die?

This is the reason, so they tell,
Why man through the Cosmic spaces fell,
Why he entered that place called hell,
And came to earth in flesh to dwell.

That God the Father, Who is One,
Wished from Himself to form a son
Through whom the Divine Life might run,
And this is why the deed was done.

So from Himself, God sent a thought
Embodied as man—with eternity fraught—
To awake to itself through the common lot,
And in free-state to heaven be brought.

In making man to be as lord,
He must evolve from out the sod,
In ignorance reach up to God,
By experience be freed from clod.

Why was the reason hidden from man,
The reason why this life began,
The reason of the human span
Through which a Cosmic Purpose ran?

The reason here is clear to see,
That the only way a man can be

Is, first to be fashioned full and free,
Then, left, to discover Divinity.

The Journey of the Soul

A beggar sat at the door of Life
And begged the gods for bread;
But no answer came from that vast domain
And never a word they said.

The beggar sat there in deep despair
And in plaintive tones he cried,
But the gods seemed busy, too busy to heed,
And begging the beggar died.

The beggar's spirit was wafted high,
And within him rose his Soul
At the thought of the gifts he would receive
Now he had reached his goal.

But the limitless space and the upper air
Contained no gifts divine,
And in vain he sought and in vain he cried,
But never was given a sign.

The Soul of him was rent and sore
At the thought of the loneliness there,
Of the emptiness of time and space,
And Eternity, grim and bare.

Must he forever wander alone
In misery, doubt and fear?
Must he forever keep going along
Through a vastness, cold and drear?

Eons and eons of time were spent
In that long search for the goal,
Endless ages of time passed by
In that vain search of the Soul.

And many and strange were the thoughts he had
In his utter loneliness there,
And many and strange were the things he felt
In his Soul, which was naked and bare.

What was the reason behind man's life,—
Was there, after all, a God?
Why was man's way one of suffering
And why the lash and the rod?

These were the thoughts the beggar had
In the anguish of his strife,
In that great battle of the Soul,
In that grim search for life.

But deep within his Soul,
As his Spirit wandered afar,
There came a faint remembrance
Of things as they really are.

A long-forgotten echo
Of a time that used to be

In a dim and distant past,
When his Spirit was joyous and free.

Of a time of Heavenly bliss,
When he, himself, was Lord,
When every wish was answered,
When he lived the life of a God.

Was this an hallucination
Of a mind that was torn and sad,
Or was it a real recollection
Of another life he had had?

And deep within, a conviction grew,
That he had lived before,
In other times and other climes,
In days that were of yore.

But why, if he had lived before,
And in a state on high,
Should he enter time and space
And come to earth to die?

And an answer came from that deep within,
From that great, Indwelling God,
"You went to earth to prove your worth,
To prove yourself a Lord."

"You went to earth for experience
In that great human school;
But while on earth you forgot yourself,
And lived the life of a fool."

And that living spark, that Spark Divine,
Arose as a lamp to his Soul,
And a voice within cried unto him,
"Return, man; reach thy goal."

"This time; go thou as a hero goes,
Not as craven, coward or fool,
But in the power of thine own might
Be thou, thyself, life's school."

So again he sought the place called earth
And through Cosmic Spaces fell,
He sought once more to gain rebirth
This time all power within to dwell.

He now did come as a king doth come,
In majesty, power and might,
He came to earth as a living Word,
He came as a power of Light.

No more to sit and beg for bread
Of gods who would not hear,
No more to walk through a dreary life
In misery, doubt and fear.

But walked as one who claimed his own,
Whose royal cup is filled,
Whose every thought is answered;
From life took what he willed.

This time no gods refused his good,
There were none to say him nay,

There was naught to hinder on the path,
No power to obstruct his way.

He learned of the Good that runs through all,
Of that God Who is deep within;
He learned of the beauty, power and peace
Of a life that is free from sin.

He learned of the Oneness of all mankind,
Of the perfect path of the Soul,
He learned of that great Indwelling Life
And the sureness of man's goal.

He learned of the peace that passeth speech,
Of a poise that knows no fear,
Of a calm that is deep and still within,
Of that Presence, ever near.

He learned that all are within the One,
Within each dwells the Living God,
And each in the other lives alway,
And no one lives by the rod.

He learned that the higher life of man
Is not by Karma driv'n,
But each has the Whole within himself,
And each, of himself, is Heaven.

Thus the great riddle of life is solved;
And the goal for which man is bound,
The good for which he ever seeks
Within man himself, is found.

So the beggar was turned into a king;
That which was lost had been found;
The lesson learned, and his goal well earned,
The now free soul, sought higher ground.

This time, as his Spirit was wafted high
Through endless time and space,
He saw a Universe filled with Life;
He beheld the true God's Face.

He saw that all Creation's blest,
All forever in the One;
For the great Cosmic Light of Love
Beheld the Father in the Son.

Epilogue

The life we give is the life we take,
And we are the life we give;
There are no Gods to say us nay,
For we are the life we live.

So, living, take; and taking, live;
And giving, get; and getting, give.

YOUR
INVISIBLE POWER

ILLUSTRATIONS

by John Arensma

I

GOD, YOUR SILENT PARTNER

We are in partnership with the Infinite Mind. The name of this partnership is "God and Company." The supreme Intelligence, the universal Creative Order, the dynamic Law and the all-perfect Presence—this is God, the Silent Partner. We are the Company. This partnership cannot be dissolved for this union was never created—it always has been and always must remain.

We are in league with the universe and this Company, with which we do business, having Its center everywhere and Its circumference nowhere—being omnipresent—is localized wherever thought and consciousness function. Wherever we place our attention, there the Company is doing business. And wherever this Company does business, there is Divine activity.

The activity of right ideas is the Father's business, and the business of the son. That is, the individual mind and the Parent Mind are one, and at whatever point we place our mental attention, at that point the firm of God and Company establishes a branch which is certain to be successful.

God and Company has no competitors. There are no other goods so perfect as those we manufacture. There are no other patterns so attractive. There is no other machinery so noiseless, perfect and efficient. God and Company, therefore, never deals with competition but always with completeness. Wherever our thought is, there this Company establishes Its branch.

Each branch carries an entire stock of the Divine Goods, and we need have no sense of a monopoly of any one of these goods. What mathematician would deny to anyone the privilege of using the principle that two and two make four? Or what musician would claim that the particular note he struck used all the harmony? For the mathematician uses the principle of mathematics and the musician uses the principle of harmony, and a principle is that which, no matter how much it is used, is neither less nor more than it was. It always refuses to be anything except exactly that which it is, and it is what it was, and it was what it is. And when tomorrow shall come it will still be that which it is.

With God and Company business is always good. To know this is to know the truth about one's business, to understand what is exactly so about one's profession, and to know what activity really means. Who would dissolve such a Divine Partnership as this? If we have a business which has no competitors and over which there is no monopoly; if we have a business that is always good, always active; if we have the intelligence to run this business; and if this business is really the business of living, then indeed we are successful.

In actual practice we must claim this Divine Partnership; we must claim that we are a member of this firm of God and Company, that the business of life is good—active, happy, whole. We must learn to counsel with this Silent Partner of ours and to accept His guidance. When we realize that our Partner makes things out of Himself by Himself becoming the things that He makes, then we shall know that no matter what undesirable facts may be in our present experience, He can dissolve them for us. Thus we transfer our burdens to this Silent Partner who has no burdens and who has no problems.

II

GOD, YOUR PERSONAL SELF

PART II

THE LIFE THAT IS WITHIN YOU

The life within you is God, whatever is true of God is true of your Life, since your Life and the Life of God are not two, but One. The enlightened have ever proclaimed this unity of good, this one-ness of man with God. For this reason many have spoken of this Life within you as both personal and impersonal. Impersonal from the standpoint that It is universal — personal from the standpoint that this Universal Life Principle is personified IN you.

This Life within you, being God, did not begin and It cannot end, hence you are immortal and eternal; that is, you can never be LESS, but must forever be MORE yourself; as this Life within you unfolds through your experience, through your gathering of knowledge and your accumulating of wisdom. Evolution is the DRAWING OUT of the God-Principle already latent within you. It is this God-Principle within you which Jesus referred to when he said, "Before Abraham was,

I am," and when he said to the one who passed from this life with him, "Today shalt thou be with me in paradise."

The God that is within you is truth, beauty, harmony and wholeness. Every apparent imperfection from which you suffer is a result of ignorance. Because ignorance of the law excuses no one from its effects, it follows that the very power which has bound you, RIGHTLY UNDERSTOOD AND PROPERLY USED, will produce freedom.

The God within you is a Unity and not a duality. The very fact that this Unity is changeless, forever revealing Itself to each, is why the God who is already within, even though He is harmonious and perfect, has ever appeared as the God we believe in. We might say that the God within, being Infinite, appears to each one of us as the God who is believed in. And we worship the God whom we believe in, rather than the God who IS. But there is nothing wrong about this, since the God who is BELIEVED IN, is, at all times, some part of the God who IS. Therefore, whatever God you believe in, provided you believe this God is already in you, must respond to you at the level of your belief. This is why it is done unto each one of us as we believe. The Principle is infallible; the practice is what we make it.

There is a great difference whether or not you believe God to be within you or outside you. For if God is outside you, how are you going to reach this God, who, not being some part of you, must be separated from you? How can you hope to unite things which are different from each other? But the God who IS ALREADY WITHIN YOU, being forever perfect and complete, needs no reunion with anyone and you need no reunion with this God, because this God already is in your every act, in every thought, in every movement, in your every plan, purpose and performance. The God within you creates every circumstance and situation you have ever experienced. You have called these circumstances and situations things in themselves, but they never have been. They have always been the fruition of your thought, and your thought has always been dominated by your belief in God, that is, ever since you have had self-conscious life.

Ever since you have had self-conscious thought, you have, by your use of the law of liberty, created bondage. Not that bondage really existed, but the possibility of using freedom in a limited way existed. You really never BOUND freedom, you merely used it in a RESTRICTED way. The restriction was not in the Principle, but in your use of It. There is a difference whether you believe in actual limitation, or merely in a restricted use of freedom. If limitation were a THING IN ITSELF you could not change it, but since it is merely an outline of experience, why not use your imagination to enlarge that experience. When you do this you will find the Life Principle within you responds just as quickly to a broader outline. The old outline was IMAGINARY only, NEVER REAL. It was like the horizon where the earth and sky appear to meet, but as we travel toward this apparent wall, we find that it disappears.

Whatever you mentally see and spiritually comprehend, you may objectively experience, for the God within you is not limited to any one experience. It is the Creator of all experience.

THE MIND THAT IS WITHIN YOU

Emerson said that there is One Mind common to all individual men, which, of course, means that the Mind of all men is the One Mind which each uses; therefore the Mind which you use is the Mind which I use, It is the Mind which everyone uses. It is the Mind of God and because the Mind of God is a complete unity, It is omnipresent. Therefore the Mind which you use and which is your mind now, is the God-Mind in you—this Mind is in all people, envelops all and is at the center of every thing. This is why it is that when you know the Truth at the center of your own being, you know it within the only Mind there is. This is why we are told to "let that mind be in us which was also in Christ Jesus." That is, the Mind which you possess at this moment is the Mind which Jesus used to demonstrate the Christ Principle. He must have realized God at the center of his being, and it is a realization of this Mind of God at the center of your being which gives power to your word.

Since the Mind within you is the Mind of God, and since the Mind of God has been in all people, then it follows that the intelligence within you understands what the great of the earth have been talking about. You already have within you an understanding, a comprehending mind. The Mind of God has no problems, no difficulties, and is never confused. Therefore, your real mind has no problems, knows no difficulties, and is never confused. It is your intellect which is confused. When you know that the Mind within you is God and cannot be confused, then your intellect becomes clarified.

This Mind, which is God, permeates every atom of your being. It is the governing Principle in every organ of your body. It is the Principle of Perfection within you. Your thought is the activity of this Principle. The Principle is perfect, complete and limitless, but your thought circumscribes Its action and causes the very Mind of Freedom to create conditions which you call bondage. As you teach your intellect to believe in the free circulation of Spirit through you, then your thought becomes a law of elimination to congestion, it purifies stagnation. Your consciousness of the Divine Presence within you, like light, dissipates the darkness. This is your eternal and true self at the center of your being. It is the Mind of God manifesting Itself in you, as you. This "you" which It manifests is not separate from Itself, but IS Itself. This

Invisible Presence is the Cause of your personality, the light shining through it.

The Divine and Infinite Mind, always desiring self-expression through you, is an insistent urge compelling you to move forward. The Mind in you is also in all people. When you recognize other people, it is this Mind knowing Itself in them. This Mind within you is timeless, yet It creates all periods of time. It is the intelligence back of every action, whether you call such action good, bad or indifferent. It is always creating form, but It is never limited to any particular form. It is in your every act, but It is always more than any or all of your actions. Even though you appear to be bound, the Mind within you is perfectly free.

Your intellect in no way limits this Mind merely because it conceives of what you call a small form or a little space. It could just as easily conceive of what you call a large form or a bigger space. In other words, your intellect is doing the best it can with the Mind within you. It reflects this Mind, but not completely. As the Apostle said, "Now we see through a glass darkly." That is, the full glory of your Christ-consciousness does not yet appear at the surface; only a dim shadow or a faint echo of It appears. Therefore you are the Eternal Mind, not caught by time, but manifesting Itself through time. You are not, then, merely a shadow of this Mind; you are really the substance of It, you are this Mind in action and the enforcement of Its Law. This Law is the Law of your Divinity, and since you are an individual, you manifest this Law in a unique way. You project this Mind through experience in a personal manner, different from all others. This constitutes your true and immortal self.

Since the Mind within you is the Mind of God, and since the Mind of God not only created everything that has ever existed, but will create everything that is ever going to be, you already have within you the ability to project new ideas, new thoughts, new inventions. Therefore, whatsoever ideas you desire, when you pray—that is, when you listen to this inner Mind—know that you are going to receive these ideas, for you are dealing with that Mind which is the Conceiver of all ideas. When you call upon this Mind for an answer to your problem, It at once knows the answer because there is no problem to It. In this way the answer to every problem already is in the Mind which you possess. "Beloved, now are we the sons of God."

THE LAW THAT IS WITHIN YOU

The Law that is within you is an activity of the Mind Principle in you. This Mind within you is the Mind of God.

All inquiry into any truths whether we consider such truth physical or metaphysical, leads to this inevitable conclusion, that the final creativeness of the universe is a movement of intelligence within and upon Itself. This Intelligence already exists at the center of your own being. It really is your own being, and the very power of imagination which you exercise is this Intelligence functioning at the level of your comprehension of It. To think is to create.

The Law that is within you is both universal and individual. Since your mind is some part of the Mind of God, there is a place within where you are universal, where you use Universal Power. That Power is Law. This Law, which is at the center of your own being, no doubt you have used largely in an unconscious way; that is, you have used It in ignorance of Its true nature, consequently, the very good which you so greatly desire, but which you have been afraid you would not gain, has been kept away from you because you have denied its presence in your experience. To affirm the presence of this good is to use the Law within you for the creation of this good which you affirm.

One of the most fascinating things which you will ever learn is that this Law, which exists at the center of your being, is creative; that you use the same creativeness which brought the planets into being, the same creativeness which produces everything that is. The Law of your life is really a law of freedom, but you have used It as a law of bondage. You must now use It as a law of freedom. All individual minds, your own included, are merely different activities of the Infinite Mind. This Mind of God is the Law of your life. When you speak. It speaks within you. Thus your thought becomes the law of your life because the Law of the One Mind already resides at the center of your being.

To think is to create. You have already been thinking and creating. Now you wish to create good instead of evil, abundance rather than limitation. You have this possibility within you, for the Law within you is set in motion by the Mind within you. The Mind within you is God, having complete authority over the Law, but you must reverse your use of this Law. You must accept your freedom, announce your liberty and proclaim your Divine birthright.

Whatever you believe to be true about God, declare to be the truth about yourself. Know that the Power within you, which is God, is the Law of Good, establishing right action in your life. In this manner you will gain dominion and exercise authority.

To think is to create. A thinker is a creator. He lives in the world of his own creation. You are a thinker; therefore you are a creator. Consequently, you live in a world of your own creation. At first this doesn't seem to be true and you may deny it, but finally you will come to see that if this were not true, you could not be a free individual. If it is true, then your very bondage is a result of an ignorant use of your freedom.

To think is to create. This is really the key which opens the doorway to wisdom and power. That doorway is already within you. Somewhere within you the Mind of God reveals this truth, that you were born free, that the will of God for you is one of goodness, truth and beauty, that all the power there is, is for you, and all the will there is, wills life. You are the image and likeness of this Life; you are a personification of It; you are the personality of God. The Kingdom of Heaven is already within you and the Law of that Kingdom is harmony, peace and joy.

But if this Law of God within you is one with the All-Law, then there is no opposite to It, nothing can contradict Its final, absolute, supreme authority. You must know this. And in knowing it you will exercise that authority which the Eternal Principle has incarnated in you. But if to think is to create, thoughts are things and the law of things is a law of thought. Change your thinking, then.

This will not be easy at first because old thought habits are prone to reassert themselves, to claim they have a right to remain in your consciousness, to harass and torment you. But now you are wise and you know they have no such authority. You see them to be exactly what they are—false impressions claiming to be the truth. They are traitors to your True Self, false representations of the Divinity within you. They are a misuse of your law of freedom, but you will cast them out. You will say to them, "I no longer accept you. Begone!" And because they are only thoughts, they will evaporate.

What a wonderful thing to realize that this Mind within you is also the Law within you, and that the Spirit within you, which is God, acts through this Mind, upon this Law, at your direction. You should rejoice that at last you are awakening to this realization of truth, that there is no law for you but your own soul shall set it, in the one great Law of all Life, Truth, and Wisdom.

THE POWER THAT IS WITHIN YOU

The Power that is within you is the power of your word. This Power is not so much a will, as it is a willingness; that is, you will never have to WILL things to happen, you will merely have to KNOW that they are happening.

This Power as Law, which is within you, is neutral and impersonal. You are not to think of It as though it were God, for the Law of Mind within you is merely a mechanical force which you may use for definite purposes. Hence, it is no more God than electricity is God. It is the

III

reaction of the Law of Cause and Effect to your word. This Law of Cause and Effect is merely a way, a medium. It is an all-powerful medium and an all-perfect way.

You have been exercising an authority and a power over this Law through your word, but, you were not entirely conscious of this word because this word was just as much subjective as it was objective, it was more or less unconscious, rising out of race suggestion. You are not to think of the Power within you as a person. It is merely a principle, It is a principle of nature, a law of cause and effect, a medium.

You have the power to use this medium in any way you see fit. Therefore you have thought that the law of your being was one of bondage. Now you are going to discover that it is freedom. Just as it was discovered that the law which causes a piece of iron to sink will cause an iron boat to float, so you will discover that the very law which has produced discord in your life can as easily produce harmony.

Therefore you will not be using two powers, but one Power in two different ways, and experience has already taught you the better way to use this Power. In other words, you wish to use this Power to produce happiness and success, joy, love and friendship, rather than their opposites. You wish to make iron float by the very law which made it sink, that is, you are going to reverse your mental position, for this is your authority in the law. You are going to realize good instead of evil. You are going to use your authority in the Law to create beauty, peace and joy. They will respond just as quickly as the more ugly manifestations have responded, and you are going to have the greatest satisfaction which can ever come to you—the satisfaction of knowing that you are really a free mental agent in a spiritual universe which holds nothing against you but which always desires your good.

No greater good can come to you than to know that the Power already within you is the power to live, the power to create. Not only to create for yourself, but for others—the power to do good, the power to heal, the power to prosper. You are to realize that the Power within you is a Divine Authority. It is a dispenser of the Divine Gifts. It is a giver of life, of joy. It proclaims the Kingdom of Heaven, the harmony of the soul and the unity of all being.

This Power within you responds definitely to direct, conscious thought. It responds as a mathematical and mechanical law of cause and effect. No one can hinder your use of this Power since It is an immediate presence at the center of your own being. No one can reverse your use of It since nothing can contradict Its authority. Therefore you not only have some power at the center of your being; you have access to all the Power there is at the center of your being, to all the Presence that there is, and to the only God there is.

You must begin to contemplate this Power within you as answering your every need, supplying your every want, fulfilling your every wish; and you must believe that It does this immediately, right now—not tomorrow but today, because the Law of this Power within you knows no time. Therefore, when your word directs the Law within you, it must always direct It for today. You must give conscious direction to this Law and you must definitely expect It to respond. When you say to the Law within you, "Do this!" you must know It is going to do it; you must believe, there must be no doubt in your consciousness. For the Power, Presence and Law are one and the same thing, and the creative imagination of your own thought is the dictator of your destiny.

THE FRIEND THAT IS WITHIN YOU

You have a Friend within you who is closer than your shadow. This Friend anticipates your every desire, knows your every need and governs your every act. This Friend is the God within your own soul, the animating Presence projecting your personality which is a unique individualization of the Living Spirit.

This Friend within you is Infinite, since He is a personification of

God. He is not limited by previous experiences which you may have had, by present conditions nor passing situations.

He has no inherited tendencies of evil, lack or limitation. He has never been caught in the mesh of circumstance. He is at all times, radiant, free and happy.

To your intellect this invisible Friend may seem to be someone else, not your Real Self, but such is not the case. Some have believed that this Friend within you is a mediator between you and the Creative Spirit. Others have believed Him to be the reincarnation or the re-birth of your previous self, while still others have sincerely believed Him to be some discarnate soul. But you are not to accept such beliefs for the Real Person within you is a direct personification of the Universal Spirit. He is your inner, absolute and perfect Self.

The Friend within you is different from all other persons, yet He is united with all. There is some part of you which reaches into the nature of others, thus irresistibly drawing them to you and drawing you to them, binding all together in one complete unity. Right now you are one with all persons, all places, all events.

The Friend within you lives in a state of poise, He is above fear, He is beyond hurt, He is sufficient unto Himself.

The Friend within you is continuously looking after your well-being. He always wishes you to be happy, to be well, to be radiant. Being the very fountain of your life, this Friend is a luminous Presence, evermore emerging from pure Spirit, evermore expanding your consciousness. He is the High Counselor, the Eternal Guide. He is your intellect, the essence of its understanding, the nicety of its calculation, the appreciation of its temperament.

There can be no greater unity than exists between you and this inner Friend. He spreads a table before you in the wilderness of human thought. His cup of joy runneth over. He laughs at disaster, triumphs over human failure, and mocks the grave. When this present experience shall be rolled up like a scroll, He will pass on to new and greater experiences. But today He is here. Trust Him, then, today, and you may trust Him for all the tomorrows yet to come. Thus your "tomorrow and tomorrow and tomorrow" will be but an expansion of your endless today.

Your personality is an outpicturing of the impressions which you have received from this inner Friend, this Deep Personality, this Radiant and Divine Presence whose Life is light, whose Consciousness is peace and whose Presence is power. You are an incarnation of this Person, this Presence and this Power.

Possibly it will be difficult for you to believe that there is such a Friend, but He is there at the very center of your being, directing your thought and causing you to triumph over every defeat, for He is an unconquerable hero. He who keeps silent watch within you, lifts your consciousness to the realization that you are forever protected, forever safe, forever perfect.

THE HEALING PRESENCE WITHIN YOU

There is a Healing Presence within you. This Healing Presence you must recognize before It can operate for you because, like every other thing in nature, It works according to exact and mechanical law.

The God who is within you has already created this marvelous mechanism, which you call your human body. The Intelligence which designed and projected this body must have a perfect knowledge of all its parts; must have a perfect understanding of all its needs, and It must be able to rebuild those parts and supply their needs. The Creative Agency within you knows how to re-create. But this Healing Presence, being the very essence of your own nature, must flow out into action through your consciousness of who and what you are. Hence you must recognize the Great Healer, the Divine Emancipator from physical bondage and pain, as your true Spirit.

Since the only final creative agency in the universe must be Mind, and since you are Mind, it follows that this Healing Presence performs Its beneficent act through your consciousness. This is why it is that you have always been told to believe. Therefore if you wish this Healing Presence to manifest Itself, you must believe that It WILL do so, and having believed that It WILL do so, you must state that It is doing so for it naturally follows that It can do for you only what It does through you.

You must believe in the Healing Presence within you and within all people and then you must speak your word in such a way that this Healing Presence may, as It flows through that word, perform the miracle of life which is the giving of form to the invisible. Your word, then, must be definite, conscious and concrete. You must know that the God within you, as a healing presence, is now the law of perfect life in your physical body. This Healing Presence is reforming your physical body. Continuously It is re-creating all of its parts.

The only way this Healing Presence can create for you is through the images of your thought, through the beliefs which you entertain, whether these beliefs be hope, fear, doubt, faith or failure. Therefore you must correct all beliefs which deny this Healing Presence. In fact you must go so far as to deny that there are any negative agencies and to affirm that the Life Principle within you not only destroys all fear in your mind, but dissolves every object of fear in your physical body.

If you succeed in healing your thought, then this Healing Presence will heal your body as It flows through the new thought pattern. For every denial of physical wholeness, then, you must supply an affirmation of your faith and confidence that the Spirit within you, being perfect, acts as a law of wholeness to your body. Your body is a body of right ideas. The Healing Presence within you, flowing through all these ideas, lubricates them with the oil of gladness and makes perfect every organ, every function, every action and reaction. The Healing Presence within you already is perfect and it is your recognition of this Perfect Indwelling God, which makes possible the execution of the Law of wholeness.

The Healing Power within you, being the same Healing Presence within all people, may not only become the law unto your own individual physical experience, but you also may use this God Power within you to help and heal others. And since everyone exists in the same medium of Mind, when you desire to speak your word of healing for someone else, you should first recognize the Healing God who is within you, after which you should recognize the same Healing Presence within the one whom you wish to help. Then you should make your direct statements for him as though he were yourself. Your statements about him, then, will become the law unto him just as they have become the law unto yourself, establishing harmony in his physical being. State that your word is the law unto him; that it removes doubt and fear from his consciousness, and with the disappearance of doubt and fear there will be a corresponding disappearance of their manifestation.

The more you use the law of this Healing Presence within you the more completely aware you will become of Its effectiveness, and the more certain you will be that it is not I, "but the Father that dwelleth in me, he doeth the works."

THE PEACE THAT IS WITHIN YOU

God is Peace. This Peace which God is belongs to man and is some part of his spiritual nature. Whatever God is in the Universal, man is in the particular. The nature of God is incarnated in every living soul.

The Peace that is within you is not something separate from God. It is not something that bombards you from without. This Peace is something that expands from within. Always this Peace has been in you. Always this Peace has nestled at the center of your being, ready to reveal Its perfection and harmony.

Peace stands at the door of your consciousness and awaits your acceptance of It. However, It does not stand outside your door, waiting for entrance, so much as It stands inside waiting to be expressed in everything you do. If the possibility of your peace were dependent upon some external event, some outside circumstance, some objective fact, then you would not have a Principle of Peace within you. You would merely be hoping that one might either develop or be imposed externally.

"The Kingdom of Heaven is within you." Within you is the Kingdom of God and within the Kingdom of God is Peace. A conscious knowledge of this Peace, coupled with a definite use of the Law of Mind, gives to each the possibility of freedom from the bondage of doubt, fear and uncertainty.

Peace is within you now. The Peace that passeth all human comprehension is there. The Peace that is at the very heart of the Universe is there. The Peace that said to the waves, "Be still!" is there. The Peace that healed the lunatic of his obsessing thought is in you. Peace is within you now—the Peace that stilled the tempest and walked the turbulent waters of human discord.

Because God is Peace and because God is in you, the Peace of God must also be in you. You should no longer go in search of Peace, for this is confusion. Search Him not out, but seek Him at the center. He has always been there. Did not the Spirit of Truth, speaking through the understanding of one who realized the Divine Presence, say, "Before Abraham was I am"? And, "Destroy this body and I will raise it up again"?

Because Peace is within you, It is available. If It were somewhere else you would never find It. Act as though Peace already possessed your soul and It will possess it. Act as though Peace already emanated from your spirit and It will emanate from it. Speak Peace into confusion and your peace will heal that confusion. This healing power is to be used and not merely believed in. There is a vast difference between believing in a principle and using it. To believe in and understand a principle is essential to the use of it. But to believe in and understand a principle is merely preliminary to the use of such a principle.

Peace is at the center of your own soul, it is the very Being of your being. This Peace, which is at the center of your being, has never been disturbed. It has never been afraid. It never desired to harm anyone, therefore it never has been hurt. How, then, shall you use this great gift which nestles at the very center of your being? You are to use it consciously. You are to speak the Word of Peace wherever discord appears. And when you do speak the Word of Peace, let no doubt arise in your thought. You must know that Peace stills the tempest. You must know that your Peace has all Power because It is the Peace of God within you.

The Peace which is at the center of your being was not born from human struggle, evolution or accomplishment. It is something that always existed. It was not given by the world. The world cannot take it away. It remains perfect, exactly what it always has been. It awaits your recognition that you may enter into conscious partnership with It. And when you have joined the forces of your intellect with Its infinite calm, then your heart will no longer be disturbed, nor will it be afraid.

Above the wind and higher than the whirlwind, enshrined in the
Heart of God, there is a Voice within you which says:
"Peace! Be not afraid. It is I." This "I" is YOU.
This "YOU" IS GOD WITHIN
YOU. This God within you
IS Peace.

IV

GOD,
YOUR IMPERSONAL SELF

PART III

I AM THAT WHICH I AM

I Am that which I Am, I Am the Eternal Presence of your own Self. Thus there is no mediator between you and Myself but your own thought. This I Am has been revealed to you in innumerable ways through the inspired writings of the ages. Each inspiration has been a proclamation that I Am is in the midst of you. I Am the writer, the inspirer, and the thing written about. I Am the Creator of history, the One who experiences it. I Am its record and its interpretation. Everything which has ever transpired has but symbolized My Divine Presence at the center of all.

I Am within you is the only Presence there is. I create innumerable centers of My Consciousness, personified as people, yet I Am is the thread of unity running through all, binding all back to Myself. Because I Am a Perfect Oneness, all of Me exists everywhere. Therefore, wherever you recognize Me, there I Am. And whether or not you recognize Me, I Am still there. Hence it is written, "Behold, I stand at the door and knock." This Divine Visitor, which is your True Self, and which is That Which I Am, is both the one who stands at the door and knocks, and the one who opens the door.

It is the glory of this recognition which has given to the enlightened true mastership. Do not look, then, for masters outside Me, nor mediators between yourself and Myself. There is but One Self, who needs no mediator. This Self is immediate, present and available. Any thought or belief which would seek to separate That Which I Am from that which you are, would be an illusion, no matter how lofty its concept nor how sacred its purpose. For it would seek to deny the ever-present I Am, the completeness of My Perfection, the God within you, the inspired thought back of your act.

Your True Self constitutes the only mediator between the visible and the Invisible. I Am that Self. Be still, then, and know that you are one with Me and My Being in you is your personality. It is also your body, mind and spirit. Every cell of your body, every thought of your mind, every glory of your spirit. Hence that which you have so ardently sought after has never been separated from you for one moment. My desire within you to be expressed has been the motivating Power, impelling and compelling you evermore to reach out, on and up.

I Am the Christ dwelling at the center of every soul. Human yet Divine; Infinite yet flowing through that which is apparently finite; unmanifest yet forever manifesting Myself; birthless and deathless yet forever being born; timeless, I Am forever creating time. And you, the expression of Myself, appear to be separated from Me merely because you are a unique personification of Myself. For I Am that personality which you are and which all people are. I Am in all and I Am all. When the recognition comes, within you, of this I Am Which I Am, you will have discovered your true Savior, your true Sonship and you will know that this Sonship is a projection of Myself, forever different from any other projection, immortal yet forever expanding.

Here you find the True Ideal, the Cosmic Pattern, the Eternal Friendship of the soul to itself, the God who is personified, the Person who is God-in-man. And how great is this Divine riddle! How inscrutable is the Sphinx! Truly, men have sought through the countless ages to solve this mystery—how can unity and multiplicity exist together without division? But now you have solved this mystery. You have compelled the Sphinx to answer her own question and she no longer devours you, but, like circumstance, must bow to that Divinity within you; like all created things, must acknowledge the supremacy of That Which I Am within you. This mystery of unity and multiplicity without division I have already proclaimed through the enlightened of the ages. But only the enlightened have understood My meaning; the unenlightened have not even realized that those who did understand Me were even as they. They thought that they were different, they believed them to be great prophets, great mediators, governed by invisible masters, controlled by those whom they have called saints.

But since I create both saint and sinner, know neither big nor little, good nor bad, and being ageless, since I create all ages, I am that which reveals and that which is revealed. And the stone which the builder rejected has become the chief stone of the corner, for the vulgar did not know that, which even the high priests failed to recognize, that the Ark of My Covenant was in the sanctuary of their own soul, that the Scroll of Life concealed in this Ark had inscribed on it merely these words: "I AM."

I AM THE ABUNDANCE WITHIN YOU

I Am come that you might have a more abundant life. To those who know not their true nature, believing themselves separated from good, I Am come. To those weary with disappointment and struggle who have sought life outside themselves, I point the way to certain salvation.

I Am in the midst of you is mighty to heal, to comfort, and to prosper. I have come to arouse you from your long dream of separation, from your night of despair. The dawn has come. The sun of truth rises over the horizon of ignorance. The light dissipates the darkness. The morning dew is upon the petals. They glisten in the sun. I Am that sun of truth dwelling within the sanctuary of your heart. I Am the morning star, guiding you to the manger of your salvation, wherein lies the child born from your own consciousness. This inner life is your only savior, the creator of your destiny, the arbiter of your faith.

Therefore, awake, become aware of My presence, for I Am life. I Am not something apart from your being. I Am your being. Closer than breathing, nearer than hands and feet, I Am. You have thought you denied My existence by affirming lack, fear and failure, but in reality you have merely affirmed My power to be to you that which you believed. I Am the Reality of your being, but I have always appeared to you in the form of your belief. I Am more than your conscious mind. I Am that which projects this mind which you call "you." I Am that which creates your personality and projects it from the center of My own Divine Originality.

I Am the Power which has bound you to your false belief. I Am the Presence which alone can give you freedom. Bondage and freedom are one and the same. I Am, who is in the midst of your being, can project one as easily as the other. Bondage does not bind Me, it merely expresses Me. That which you call your bondage is really My freedom misused.

I have come to awaken you from the sense of limitation; to proclaim to you the eternal days of God-abundance. I have come to acquaint your mind with the truth, to convert your soul by reason, inspiration and illumination, to the realization that I Am is all there is, beside which there is none other. Within you is the secret place of the Most High, the Tabernacle of the Almighty, the Indwelling Good, the Ever-Present

Father and the Eternal Child. This Ever-Present Father and this Eternal Child are one and the same Being. I Am that Being. I Am the All-Being. I Am your being. You are My Being. "I am that which thou art, thou art that which I am." Therefore, you may know that the Universal "I Am" is also the individual "I." Hence the individual "I" merges into the Universal "I Am"; is omnipotent wherever good impels the activities of Its thought. For the human thought is as Divine as is its consciousness of Reality, and the Omnipotent Law forever obeys its will.

If you can put aside your fear, doubt, and hurt which is but an expression of your sense of isolation; if you can put aside all negation and turn to Me alone, then you shall be made free. Be still and know that I Am God, your True Self. Be still and know that I Am the Life Principle. Be still and know that I Am the Truth, dispelling all error. I Am Power, neutralizing all weakness. I Am Abundance, swallowing up all lack. I Am your Real Self.

Nothing that you have ever said or done, no law that you have ever set in motion, is as great as I Am, for I transcend all uses of the Law. I, the Creator, re-create. I, the Molder, re-mold. I, the Maker, re-make. Therefore, you may trust what I shall do, for I Am God, the Living Spirit in the midst of you—not some-mighty, but All-Mighty. There is no law opposed to My Will. There is no opposite to My Nature. There is no darkness which My Light does not dissipate. There is no knowledge which I do not possess, for I Am Wisdom, the source of all knowledge. I Am Light, the source of all illumination. I Am Power, the source of all strength.

Therefore, be still and know that I Am the Creator and the thing created. My Presence dissipates all apparent evil. Hence I have ever proclaimed. "Come unto me, all ye that labour and are heavy-laden, and I will give you rest."

V

I AM THE CREATIVENESS
WITHIN YOU

Because I Am the Creativeness of the universe, and because My imagination is My creativeness, then you may know that to think is to create.
Hence were the worlds formed by the power of My Word. Hence is
your world formed by the power of My Word in you, for your word is
My Word in you, your thought is My Thought in you, your power is My
Power in you. I, the Universal, and you, the individual, are one and the
same Being. I, the Universal, think in you, the individual, thus I the
Universal endow you, the individual, with life, with creativeness—I Am
that life and that creativeness within you.

"I Am the way, the truth and the life," means that the Infinite
I, within the apparently finite you, is God. Thus your thought is creative. Thus your imagination projects form upon the screen of your experience. This is because I, the Creative Principle, dwell within you,
projecting the law of My creativeness through your imagination. To
know how to think is to know how to create, and this power to create
through thought is the execution of My Will in you, the manifestation
of My Being through you. This is My Image and Likeness manifest at
the level of your consciousness. If you can consciously realize this, then
you may know that I am still creating through your thinking.

I, the Universal, am now individual. I, the Impersonal, am now
personal. And yet in My personality and individuality I still remain
Universal, but I, the Universal Creative Mind, now become at the
same time the individual and personal creative mind through your will,
through your desire. Because you are some part of Me, you have the
power to think and to create. This power is My Power, it is also your
power, and because this is so, that which you have believed has come
upon you, that which you have thought has transpired. Until now you
have not known that the very power which binds you can give you free-

dom, that the very power which has created physical infirmities may also heal. I, the Eternal within, do all these things.

Because you believe that which you experience to be necessary, you perpetuate such experience. This also is My Mind working at the center of your being. "I Am" in the midst of you is the sole and only creative agency in the universe, whether that creative agency calls itself your imagination or My Will. It is one and the same. "I Am" in the midst of you can easily dissolve one creation and project another. The Master resides within and is never external. The picture is never the artist, the creation is never the creator. The Thinker existed before any particular thought, and when your present universe shall be rolled up like a scroll and numbered with the things once experienced, "I Am" will still be in the midst of you. You will remain and project another universe and yet another and beyond that more.

Neither your body, your environment, nor your mind are masters. You are the master of body, environment, and mind. They are your servants. They are My servants. Therefore they are your true servants when your thought is in harmony with beauty and at peace with Reality. You may permit Me to create a new experience for you, patterned after your own thought. But first you must have the idea of this better experience. You must conceive it in the silence of your imagination. This conception will be My Imagination working at the center of your being; My Will dominating yours, not dissolving it, but more fully expressing Myself through it, for My Will and your will are one and the same because all ideas finally come from Me.

You can have no ideas separate from Mine because you are that which I Am and I Am that which you are. You are Myself individualized. Your personality does not restrict me nor do I hinder it from expanding.

Hence the joy of spontaneity and self-expression are real in you because they are real in Me. If you turn from fear to faith you will discover that fear has vanished and faith alone remains. If you turn from despair to certainty you will discover that weakness has fled and when you understand the subtle processes through which this transmutation has taken place, you will know that always you could have created one condition as easily as another. Always you have been the master of your fate.

I AM THE CHRIST WITHIN YOU

Be still and know that "I Am that which thou art and thou art that which I Am." Be still and know that I Am God within you. Be still and know that every atom of your body is in tune with Perfect Life. Be still and know that every organ of your body is in harmony with Me. Be still and know that every activity of your physical being moves in accord with my Divine Perfection. I Am the Principle of Perfection within you and I Am also the activity of that Principle, forever manifesting Myself in Perfect Form. I Am not caught in your body, but I Am your body. Never limited by its action, I produce its action.

By some divine intuition, by some inner whispering of your soul, by some light upon your path, you have progressed. I Am that light, that urge, that whisper, that voice.

I Am your real Self, the Christ within you proclaiming His Divine Presence to your human consciousness. This Christ within you is at the center of every person and every thing. Being the All Being, I Am the Being of all, from the smallest particle to the greatest, from the lowest form to the highest intelligence.

You must understand that this I Am, at the center of your being, is the I Am at the center of every man's being, of every animal's being, at the center of all being. When you do understand this, all nature will have a new meaning to you, for you will know that the odor of the rose is the radiation of My consciousness; you will know why the intelligence in the animal responds to you; you will understand the mystery of mysteries. You will possess the key which unlocks the storehouse of nature. You will be bound with an inseparable unity to all that exists. What you have called bondage is but a shadow, it is not a reality, for I Am your immortal self, your Divine being, unbound, unfettered and free.

The mind which you use is in reality your comprehension of Me at this present time. And yet I Am ever more than this comprehension, for your present experience is but a faint glimpse of My presence. Your limitation is My freedom expressed in a meager way. This Life Principle in you, which I Am, and this use of that which I Am by your intellect, seems to contradict and deny My Universal Being, and yet, it really affirms My Being, of which you are a part.

Since all parts of Me are forever one with the wholeness of My Being, then that part which you are is never separated from My Being, but is forevermore united with It. Even the cells of your body are some part of this Being, one in consciousness with Me, and if you would be made whole, know that each cell of your body is in union with Me, has never been separated from Me, is forever at one with My Life. They have the consciousness of My Being and this consciousness of My Being alone constitutes Life.

You are the execution of My Will as I Am the One within you which conceives the purpose of that will. I Am the love, you are the beloved. I Am the abstract, you are the concrete. I Am the impersonal, you are the personal. There could be no you without Me. You as an individual are but one unique manifestation of My Being. Because My Being is in all people, each may recognize the other. I Am that which they recognize and I Am the intelligence which responds in each and through all.

This is the mystery of life, the enigma of the universe—how is it that I can remain Universal and still be individual? It is an understanding of this which has come to the great, which has led them back to the unity of the Whole, which has given them the power they possess. It is the awakening of this lesser self to the greater Self which is the New Birth. It is the surrender of the limited to the limitless, of the finite to the Infinite, and of restriction and bondage to freedom.

I, the Universal Self, multiply my Self-expression countlessly through My individual Selves. The soul of you and of all, the imperishable part of all, is a different manifestation, a unique expression of Myself. The understanding of this is the key to the mystery of life which unlocks the hidden treasures of My Being—this consciousness of Oneness, this knowledge that the Universal I Am is also the individual I, this recognition that "the highest God and the innermost God is One God." To know this is to know the Truth which makes you free.

You must know that the infinite creativity of My Nature, the limitless creativeness of My Imagination, projecting My Substance within the void, giving form to the formless, that this inner imagination is the final, sole and only creative agency in the universe. You must realize that this Creative Power which I Am is also the Creative Power which you are, for you and I are One.

I AM THE SUSTAINER WITHIN YOU

Nothing is or can be unless it be some expression of My Life and Intelligence. In the heart of each I live; at the center of all creation I dwell. I fill all space. I Am All-in-All, over all and through all. Being the One Infinite Reality, I create and control. There is no personality, no individuality, separated from me, since I Am the Essence and the Life of each and all. Infinite and impersonal, I Am still personified.

The illusion which you suffer and the grief you bear are not because you are separated from Me, but because you do not realize that you are forever united with Me, for I am at the center of your being; and being that which you are, I Am forever personifying Myself in you. At the center of your comprehending mind, I, the All, the Infinite, the Impersonal, am individualized and personified. Therefore the "I Am" which speaks is the real you, your true Self. From the mightiest form to the smallest atom, in you and in all—in the animal, vegetable and mineral kingdoms—My Intelligence projects all. My Power envelops all. My Life animates all.

You are not merely a shadow of Myself; you are the Substance of Me. You are My Mind in action, the enforcement of My Law, the Law of your own Divinity. This Law of your Divinity is both freedom and bondage, even as you use It, for my Law reflects to you the images of your own thought. Bondage and limitation, joy and grief are one to Me. They are merely different manifestations of the eternal expressions of Myself, for I Am not a dualism, but a Unity.

I Am not little in one place and big in another. I Am not good in one place and evil in another. I Am above big and little, good and evil, just as I transcend time and space, yet I Am in you, creating what you call time and space, sickness and health, happiness and misery, good and evil. When you awake to the realization of that which I Am in the midst of you, from the very substance of impoverishment you will enrich yourself. Sitting in the presence of confusion you will be at peace, where the fires of hell burn not, for they are consumed by a greater passion. They are extinguished by the reversal of your own thought, for "Behold, I Am in the midst of you" creates heaven and hell, condemns and saves, gives birth to Adam and Christ, is the seeker and that which is sought after. Behold, I Am the See-er and the thing seen.

I Am within you, then, is the Creator and Sustainer. I Am the One who projects My imagination upon the screen of your experience and the images of My thought are manifest throughout all creation. Creation is nothing other than an image of My thought. But you are not an image of My thought. You are My thought, for you and I are One, not two. You are My thought personified; through you I, the Timeless, enter into time; I, the Formless, take form; I, the Impersonal, become personal.

Thus, all ideas, all desires, all thoughts, come from Me, for I Am all there is. If you listen deeply to yourself, you are listening to Me. Your mind becomes illumined because I Am light. Your mind knows, because I Am knowledge. Your thought is the enforcement of My Law, because My Law is your thought. This is why it is that your thought is creative. Even though you have misused this gift of Life, you have never changed its nature nor destroyed its purpose. All your desires are basically good, and the Divine Urge within you which impels you toward self-expression is My Nature, the irresistible desire within Me to become self-expressed through you.

Every event that has ever transpired, all human history, are but different imprints of my thought, creating as they do time, space, and circumstance. I Am both cause and effect. I Am all processes between cause and effect, therefore the "I Am" in you remains forever unconditioned by any existing form; is never bound to any outline or to any particular experience; has come through no processes of evolution whatsoever. That which you call evolution is but the manner of My Self-expression. That which you call unfoldment is but an ever-awakening consciousness within you of My Presence, for My Presence covers all, pervades all, and animates all.

"I Am that I Am," beside which there is no other Presence, no other animating Principle. I Am your omnipresent Self. Wherever you look you will see Me. Wherever you go you will find Me.

VI

GOD,
THE SELF-EVIDENT TRUTH
WITHIN YOU

Part IV

I t is self-evident that we live. As Descartes said. "I think, therefore I am." This might be called an axiom of reason whereby one perceives that he exists. An axiom of reason is a truth so self-evident, so universally experienced, so immediately known to the mind that reason cannot deny its existence. That there are such final truths no one doubts.

We wish to establish our identity in the universe, the limitless possibility of self-expression, and the certainty of eternal unfoldment. We wish to establish identity, individuality, unity, completion.

Out first self-evident proposition is, that the Truth is that which is. We are using Truth in the sense of Its absolute meaning—not some truth, or a truth, but the Truth, the ultimate Reality. The Truth, being that which is, must include all that was, is, or ever shall be. And being that which is, and being all that is, there can be nothing unlike It, different from It, nor opposed to It.

While it is true that our present finite comprehension does not grasp such an infinity, and while it is equally true that appearance seems to contradict this fundamental premise, we may be certain that even the judgment of the senses is no final criterion. The earth and the sky do not finally meet anywhere. We all have such apparent horizons attached to our experience. But we must postulate an absolute, unconditioned Truth somewhere. This is the Truth Jesus referred to when he said, "Ye shall know the truth and the truth shall make you free." What this Truth is, and how It operates through us, is the nature of our inquiry.

That which reason cannot doubt, that to which the essence of reason can find no opposite, but which clear thinking must have complete confidence in—by the very fact of its inability to conceive an opposite—that is Truth. The Bible tells us, "For by thy words thou shalt be justified, and by thy words thou shalt be condemned." The concept of Truth formulated in our thought becomes our word, becomes our affirmation of our relationship to the universe. For instance, we either believe that God is all there is or we do not believe that God is all there is.

If clear reasoning does deliver the perception of the allness of Truth, and if Truth is a synonym for God, then we may say: God is all there is. And we may add that it is impossible to conceive any opposite, otherness, difference, unlikeness, either in what we call the past (which is memory), in what we call the present (which is experience), or in what we call the future (which is anticipation). For past, present and future is but a continuity upon which is threaded the sequence of experience.

If God is all there is, then past, present and future; time, experience and form, if they exist at all, must exist as some part of Truth. If this Truth is all there is, then we also must be included in It, and we should identify ourselves with It. Thus the allness of Truth automatically includes the reality of our own being.

We arrive next at the conclusion that Truth, being all there is, must be universal. That is, Spirit plus nothing equals Spirit. Since there is no such thing as that which is not, a lie merely becomes a denial of Truth. A lie has no validity, no power, remaining merely a suppositional opposite to that which of itself is positive, absolute and eternal. Truth is universal. Cancelling what is not and leaving what is, we arrive at the conclusion that nothing has ever happened to the Truth. It was not born, It will not die. It did not come, It will not go. It has no degrees of being. It is universally present.

Thus we arrive at the conclusion that Truth is indivisible. Having nothing unlike It, with which to divide It, being all, It remains a complete unity. Therefore, every announcement of being is an announcement of Truth. The indivisible wholeness of Truth includes all that really is, and since I can say, "I am," Truth includes myself.

Emerson tells us that no power of genius has ever yet had the smallest success in explaining existence. The perfect enigma remains. Truth is not explained, nor is It explainable. Our unity with It is not something which we acquire. It is a reality which we discover. This is a conclusion at which we arrive, not by intellectual processes alone, because the genius of the intellect has never explained its own existence, it has merely experienced it. If the Truth is all there is, if It is universal and a unit, then nothing came before It and nothing came after It, but Itself was, is, and remains, all. The indivisibility of Truth guarantees Its unity and Its unity guarantees not only our oneness with It and Its oneness with us, but the inseparable allness of this one-ness. Transcendent, even while it is immanent. The Truth unifies transcendence and immanence. The perceiver and the thing perceived are united in one common Mind and Existence.

Something cannot be divided by nothing. If the Truth is all there is, and if there is nothing unlike It, then there is no dividing line between God and man. Hence the self-evident perception of Jesus when he said, "The Father and I are one." Such all-ness announces independence. That which we call the attributes of Truth are not attributes of something which projects such alleged attributes, but are activities of that which constitutes such attributes. Essence and performance are identical. Truth and attribute are one. This must have been what Jesus had in mind when he said, "The words I speak unto you, they are spirit and they are life." He was not thinking of his word reflecting or transmitting some overdwelling power, but that Power Itself was undivorced from the word. His word was that Power, not merely an expression or an extension of It. The attribute was the essence. Hence Power is never separated from Itself and the Mind which conceived the cosmos, giving birth to its infinite forms, is identified with the plot in the latest play—the same Mind, because all Mind is One.

Within all people and within everything that lives there is an impulsion toward self-expression. This impulse is dynamic and irresistible. The very fact that there is an insistent urge for self-expression in all individuals proves that this urge is cosmic because the apparent parts substantiate the characteristics of the universal wholeness, if our axiom of Unity is correct. Therefore, the desire for self-expression is not only legitimate, it is irresistible. To seek escape from this desire would be an unconscious attempt toward self-annihilation. Each individual must interpret the universe for himself, since he has to interpret it to himself. The universe can interpret itself for him only by interpreting itself to him, through him. God can give us—only what we take, and the taking is the self-expression of God in us—not something else, something other, or different from God, not something which has succeeded in passing a dividing line, but itself is God.

The urge, then, which causes us to say "I am," is more than an urge causing us to express a Power which extends Itself through us or an Intelligence which uses us as an instrument for Its activity. This urge in us which causes us to say "I am" is God. Hence our self-awareness is Its self-awareness. This perception of unity has been basic to the spiritual genius of the ages and is but another way of saying that God is all there is. The enigma of unity is solved in such degree as one perceives unity in multiplicity and multiplicity in unity.

We are using this illustration of axioms, not to confuse nor to mystify, but to show that through all of the attempts which ever have been made to teach the Truth, this one central theme has run—the indivisible unity of God and man. Every sacred literature of the ages contains it. The ancient Jewish faith proclaimed it when, in the Sixth Chapter of Deuteronomy, Moses said, "Hear, O Israel, the Lord our God is one Lord," and Jesus when he said, "The Father that dwelleth in me, he doeth the works."

To realize that this Indivisible Wholeness is at the center of our own being is to understand that the power of our individual word is an activity of the Infinite and Eternal I Am, the Everlasting and Perfect Spirit. That Spirit in us, is us. No greater unity could be delivered than that which, by the very nature of being, cannot be withheld. This deliverance is not partial, but complete.

Next we arrive at another self-evident proposition, which is that the Truth is unchangeable. This is self-evident since there is nothing for the Truth to change into. It cannot change into nothing because there is no such thing as nothing. It cannot change into Itself because It already is Itself. It remains, persistent, permanent. It was this perception that caused Emerson to say that no moment in eternity is any better than the present one, and the New Testament Prophet to exclaim, "Beloved, now are we the sons of God." Jesus stood in the midst of passing human events, and proclaimed that the Kingdom of Heaven is at hand, or within man.

If the Truth cannot change, if It is permanent, if It is ever-present, then It is always reliable. There is nothing but stability and nothing but security. The Truth is faithful. Truth has neither birth, evolution nor decay. Because the Truth is eternal and changeless, and because I exist, and because that which I am is It in me, it is self-evident that I am eternal. Such is the perception of immortality, deathlessness and everlasting being. This is but another way of saying that God cannot die, that God is all there is, that God is the essence of my life and is my life; that I am an immortal and an eternal being now.

We next arrive at a conclusion which tends to liberate the mind from the thralldom of circumstances. The Truth, being all there is, is both cause and effect. It is self-evident that Truth has no cause and that there is no effect external to It. Therefore, cause and effect are one and the same thing. There is neither cause nor effect external to Truth. Hence, any belief in the cause and effect of bondage has no substantiality, for if it did bondage would be permanent, changeless and inescapable. If Truth were bondage, freedom would be unthinkable. The Truth which sets us free is not the introduction of some higher power on a lower plane. It is the knowledge that there are no higher and no lower planes in Truth, no higher and no lower laws in Truth. There is merely what is and the self-action of what is proclaiming Itself to be that which It is. If Truth were bondage instead of freedom, then the very knowledge of Truth would create more bondage. But since the Truth is freedom then a knowledge of Truth is freedom. Hence, to know the Truth is to be free. Truth and freedom are identical.

Cause and Effect, therefore, becomes a plaything, a something to be used. Karma and Kismet become bubbles to be blown about. Such is the perception of power. Such is the realization that the knowledge of Truth is power. Power is that which compels, necessitates, authorizes, commands. "He (Jesus) taught them as one having authority and not as the scribes." This was because he understood the nature of the spontaneous Spirit within him and realized that the Law of Cause and Effect is merely the mechanical method through which the Word of Power proves Its authority.

We arrive next at the perception of person, individuality, personality, and humanity, for again we may say, "I think, therefore I am." Also our fellowman may say, "I think, therefore I am." The allness of Truth delivers this message, that in a certain sense each is all, because of the indivisibility of Truth, and all is in each. Such is the mystery of individuality, which the mask of personality but dimly reveals. The Truth, being all, means that each individual is forced to be Truth and nothing but Truth. Truth does not deny individuality, personality, nor humanity. It affirms that each exists in his apparently separate star, maintaining an eternal, changeless and perfect identity in the allness of good. Each is an individualized expression of the One.

There is nothing which separates one individual from another, even while there is nothing which can annihilate, subtract from or add to the individuality of each. Such totality in individuality and such individuality in totality is perceived, not so much by an intellectual process as by the very axiom itself which delivers the necessity of accepting the Principle of Omnipresence.

This Principle of Omnipresence also declares the Principle of Omniscience. Truth is not only all-presence, It is all-knowledge. It is because this is so that an inventor may say, "I know the answer to my problem"; the author can say, "My plot is worked out"; the organizer can say, "My organization is complete." By consciously practicing Omnipotence, Omniscience and Omnipresence, we prove in some measure that these self-evident abstractions are real necessities, reliable, substantial and available. We need, then, labor under no illusion that it is necessary to deny individuality, personality or humanity in order to affirm the allness of God; for such is the perception of unity.

But if Truth is all there is, then Truth is Intelligence, Truth is what we call Mind, Truth is Idea. Idea becomes absolute. Idea reflects experience. The allness of Idea destroys the belief in any physical, mental or material universe external to concept. Creation becomes the contemplation of Truth. Such is the perception of creativeness. Forms are real but not self-sustained, they are nothing in themselves. There is nothing in such a reflected idea to have control even over itself.

Having established unity, indivisibility, permanence, power, Omniscience, Omnipresence and Omnipotence, we arrive at the conclusion of eternal dominion. It is self-evident that if the objective world were a thing in itself and we were in no way connected with it, other than by experiencing it as an external fact, then we could not possibly exercise dominion. The Truth would be in fragments, which we should never be able to put together; hence we never could attain wholeness. The greatest teachings of the ages contradict the fragmentary theory and insist on resolving all apparent multiplicity into a final unity. This unity is not some far-off event, but a present fact. Modern science tends in the same direction.

This allness of Truth, stated in the simplest manner, affirms that God is all there is. God never changes. God is in me. God is that which I am. God is in the universe. God is the universe.

At first man is ignorant of his true nature. The Word has become flesh, but self-conscious life has not yet emerged. The fusion of will, desire and volition, without which there can be no personality, has not taken place. Finally the Word not only becomes flesh, it also becomes person. Man awakes to life, turns toward the light and triumphs over limitation.

Therefore, our final self-evident proposition delivers the perception of bliss, wholeness and perfection. The universal I Am and the individual I are One in peace, joy, love, wisdom, beauty and power.

In the beginning was the Word, and the Word was Life, and the Word was Law, and the Word was Light; and the Light through Law produced form; and the created form turned to the Light; and the Light of consciousness dawned; and man beheld the Light and walked in It; and the Light was All.

VII

WHAT RELIGIOUS SCIENCE TEACHES

INTRODUCTION

Religious science is not a personal opinion, nor is it a special revelation. It is a result of the best thought of the ages. It borrows much of its light from others but, in so doing, robs no one, for Truth is universal.

The Christian Bible, perhaps the greatest book ever written, truly points a way to eternal values. But there are many other bibles, all of which, taken together, weave the story of spiritual Truth into a unified pattern.

All races have had their bibles as all have had their religions; all have pointed a way to ultimate values but can we say that any of them has really pointed The Way? It is unreasonable to suppose that any one person, or race, encompasses all truth, and alone can reveal the way of life to others.

Taking the best from all sources, Religious Science has access to the highest enlightenment of the ages. Religious Science reads everyman's Bible and gleans the truths therein contained. It studies all peoples' thought and draws from each that which is true. Without criticism, without judgment, but by true discrimination, that which is true and provable may be discovered and put to practical use.

What is the Truth? Where may it be found? And how used? These are the questions that an intelligent person asks. He finds his answer in the study of Religious Science. Shorn of dogmatism, freed from superstition, and always ready for greater illumination, Religious Science offers the student of life the best that the world has so far discovered.

It has been well said that "religions are many; but Religion is one." The varying faiths of mankind are unnumbered, but the primal faith of the race is today, as of old, the One Faith; an instinctive reliance upon the Unseen, which we have learned to call God. Religion is One. Faith is One. Truth is One. There is One Reality at the heart of all religions, whether their name be Hindu, Mohammedan, Christian or Jewish. Each of these faiths, limited by its outlook upon life and the universe, evolved its own specific statements of faith called creeds and beliefs, and henceforth was governed by the same.

Spiritual experience is always a new thing; it ever seeks to express itself in a new way. The history of religion is a history of a periodic breaking away from the older body and the formulation of a new body of disciples to whom had come new light and a more satisfying experience.

While the Universal Mind contains all knowledge and is the potential of all things, only as much truth comes to us as we are able to receive. Should all the wisdom of the universe be poured over us we should yet receive only that which we are ready to understand. Each draws from the source of all knowledge that to which he inwardly listens. The scientist discovers the principle of his science, the artist taps the essence of beauty, the saint draws Christ into his being, because to each is given according to his ability to receive.

Emerson taught the immanence of God; the spiritual impulse underlying all life; the divinity of the universe including mankind, and his message gradually permeated the sodden mass of the accepted theological concepts of the day. He wrought a revolution in religious thinking, the full effects of which we are only beginning to realize in our own time. "Yourself," he said, "a new born bard of the Holy Ghost, cast behind you all conformity, and acquaint men at first hand with Deity. Look to it first and only that tradition, custom, Authority, are not bandages over your eyes, so that you cannot see. . . . Let me admonish you first of all to go alone, to refuse good models, even those sacred in the imagination of men; dare to love God without mediator and without veil." . . . "O my brothers, God exists: There is a soul at the center of Nature, and over the will of every man, so that none of us can wrong the universe. . . . things do not happen, they are pushed from behind."

The central principle of the teaching of Religious Science is this immanence of God. "God is an eternal and everlasting essence." All phenomena appearing in the natural world are manifestations of the spiritual world, the world of causes. "Our thought is an instrument of Divine Mind." "Christ is the reality of every man, his true inner self. Christ is the unseen principle in Man. God is in Man." The whole universe is the manifestation of a Unity which men call God.

Religious Science believes sincerely in what is known as "the silence," that is, it accepts the teachings of Jesus that "the Kingdom of God is within." The new sayings of Jesus from Oxyrhyncus quotes the statement as follows: "The Kingdom of Heaven is within you and whoever knows himself shall find it. Strive therefore to know yourselves, and ye shall be aware that ye are the Sons of the Almighty Father, and ye shall know that ye are in the City of God, and ye are the City."

Believing that the Universal Spirit comes to fullest consciousness in man, as his innermost Self, we strive to cultivate the inner life, knowing that religious certainty is the result of an impact of God upon the soul. Like the Methodism of old, we seek the witness of the Inner Spirit. We call this becoming Christ conscious or God conscious, meaning by that, Soul certainty.

THE PURPOSE OF
RELIGIOUS SCIENCE

In its practice and teachings, Religious Science endeavors to include the whole life. It is not a dreamy, mystical cult, but the exponent of a vigorous gospel, applicable to the everyday needs of our common life. Indeed, this is the one distinctive tenet of its teaching that accounts for its rapid growth. Men and women find in it a message that fits in with their daily needs.

The conventional idea of the future life, with its teachings of rewards and punishment, is not stressed; the gospel is the good news for the here and now. Religion, it says, if it means anything, means right living, and right living and right thinking wait upon no future, but bestow their rewards in this life—in better health, happier homes, and all that makes for a well-balanced, normal life.

The following is a brief Statement of Belief of the Institute of Religious Science:

The Universe is fundamentally good.

Man is a manifestation of Spirit, and for It to desire evil for him would be for It to desire evil for Itself. This is unthinkable and impossible, for it would cause Spirit to be self-destructive; therefore, we may be certain that the Spirit of Life is for, and not against, man.

All apparent evil is the result of ignorance, and will disappear to the degree that it is no longer thought about, believed in, or indulged in. Evil is not a thing in itself. It has no entity and no real law to support it.

God is Love, and Love can have no desire other than to bless all alike, and to express Itself through all.

Many that had lost faith in God have, in this new manner of thinking, found what their souls had sought. The emphasis is insistently on God, ever present, ever available; and on man's ability to make himself receptive to the inflow of the Divine Spirit. In essence, this was the primal message of the enlightened prophets of all the ages, and this is the message of Religious Science.

The thought of the ages has looked to the day when science and religion shall walk hand in hand through the visible to the invisible. A movement which endeavors to unify the great conclusions of human experience must be kept free from petty ideas, from personal ambitions and from any attempt to promote one man's opinion. Science knows nothing of opinion but recognizes a government of law whose principles are universal. These laws, when complied with, respond alike to all. Religion becomes dogmatic and often superstitious when based on the lengthened shadow of any one personality. Philosophy intrigues us only to the extent that it sounds a universal note.

The ethics of Buddha, the morals of Confucius, the beatitudes of Jesus, together with the spiritual experiences of other great minds, constitute view points of life which must not be overlooked. The mystical concepts of the ancient sage of China keep faith with the sayings of Emerson, and wherever deep cries unto deep, deep answers deep.

All men seek some relationship to the Universal Mind, the Over-Soul, or the Eternal Spirit which we call God. That we are living in a spiritual universe which includes the material or physical universe has been the conclusion of most of the deepest thinkers of the ages. That this spiritual universe must be one of pure intelligence and perfect life, dominated by love, by reason and by the power to create, is an inevitable conclusion.

Science, philosophy, intuition and revelation, all must unite in an impersonal effort if Truth is to be gained and held. Ultimately that which is true will be accepted by all. The Institute of Religious Science is an educational as well as a religious movement and endeavors to co-ordinate the findings of science, religion, and philosophy, to find a common ground upon which true philosophic conclusions, spiritual intuitions and mystic revelations may agree with the cold facts of science, thus producing fundamental conclusions, the denial of which is not conceivable to a rational mind.

It goes without saying that such conclusions cannot contradict each other. No system of thought can stand which denies human experiences; no religion can remain vital which separates humanity from Divinity, nor can any science which denies the spontaneous appearance of volition and will in the universe maintain its position.

Old forms, old creeds are passing, but the eternal realities abide. Religion has not been destroyed; it is being discovered. God, the great innovator, is in His world and that means that progress is by divine authority. Through all the ages one increasing purpose runs, and that purpose can be no less than the evolution of the highest spiritual attributes of mankind. It is the unessential only that is vanishing, that the abiding may be made more clearly manifest.

What wonder that religious faith in our day is breaking from the narrow bounds of past teaching, and expanding both in breadth and depth. It is not because men believe less in God and the true essentials of spiritual life, but because they must believe more; they are literally forced by the inevitable logic of facts to build for themselves concepts of the Infinite commensurate with the greatness and glory of the world in which they live.

As Emerson so truly said—when the half gods go the great God arrives. Religious Science is reaching out to a truer concept of a God, immanent in the universe as the very substance, law and life of all that is. The difference between the older way of thinking and the new is that we have come to see that the One Supreme Cause and Source of all that is, is not a separate Being outside His world, but is in fact the actual Spirit of Life shining through all creation as its very Life Principle, infinite in Its working, and eternal in Its essence. The universe is none other than the Living God made manifest, so that Paul voiced a literal truth when he said: "In him we live, and move, and have our being." Such is the reverent conclusion of Religious Science, a faith that is winning its way in this our new day.

The religious implications of this new viewpoint of life are revolutionary. It means that there is a moral and spiritual order in the cosmos to which mankind is intimately related. Faith in God is not, as many would have us believe, a retreat from reality, a projecting of the personal wish into a cosmic postulate. Faith in God is a reasonable expanding of the facts of life to their wisest and inevitable vision and logical end; it is the logical complement of a world order, every fibre of which has a teleological meaning. Religious faith, in fact, is rooted in the facts and realities of the natural order, inwrought into the very texture of life. Since supreme wisdom and life are in reality all that exist, including Man, religious faith is but deep calling unto deep; God recognizing His own existence and presence.

THE TEACHING OF RELIGIOUS SCIENCE

The future religion will be free from fear, superstition and doubt and will ask no man where God may be found. For the "secret place of the most High" will be revealed in the inner sanctuary of man's own heart, and the eternal God will sit enthroned in his own mind. We can know no God external to that power of perception by which alone we are conscious of anything. God must be interpreted to man through man's own nature.

Who would know God, must be as God, for He who inhabits eternity also finds a dwelling place in His own creation. Standing before the altar of life in the temple of faith one learns that he is an integral part of the universe and that it would not be complete without him.

That native faith within, which we call intuition, is the direct impartation of Divine Wisdom through us. Who can doubt its gentle urges, or misunderstand its meaning?

This inner life may be developed through meditation and prayer. Meditation is quiet, contemplative thought, with a definite purpose always in mind. Prayer is a receptive mental and spiritual attitude through which one expects to receive inspiration.

There is a Presence pervading all. There is an Intelligence running through all. There is a Power sustaining all, binding all into one perfect whole. The realization of this Presence, Intelligence, Power and Unity constitutes the nature of the mystic Christ, the indwelling Spirit, the image of God, the Sonship of the Father.

Christ means the universal idea of Sonship; the entire creation, both visible and invisible. There is One Father of all. This One Father, conceiving within Himself, gives birth to all the Divine Ideas. The sumtotal of all these ideas constitutes the mystic Christ.

Jesus was a man, a human being, who understood his own nature. He knew that as the human embodies the Divine it manifests the Christ nature. Jesus never thought of himself as different from others; his whole teaching was that what he did others could do. His divine nature was aroused; he had plunged beneath the material surface of creation and found its spiritual cause. This cause he called God or the Father. To this indwelling God he constantly turned for help, daily guidance and counsel. To Jesus, God was an indwelling Reality, the Infinite Person in every personality. It was by the power of this Spirit that Jesus lived. He clearly understood the unity of God and man.

Every man is a potential Christ. From the least to the greatest the same life runs through all, threading itself into the patterns of our individuality. He is "over all, in all and through all." As Jesus, the man, gave way to the Divine Idea, the human took on the Christ Spirit and became the voice of God to humanity.

Conscious of his divinity, yet humble as he contemplated the infinite life around him, Jesus spoke from the height of spiritual perception, proclaiming the deathless reality of the individual life, the continuity of the individual soul, the unity of the Universal Spirit with all men.

Religious Science, following the example of Jesus, teaches that all men may aspire to divinity, since all men are incarnations of God. It also teaches a direct relationship between God and man. The indwelling Spirit is God. It could be nothing less, since we have Spirit plus nothing, out of which all things are made. Behind each is the Infinite, within each is the Christ. There is no boundary line between the mind of man and the Mind which is God.

Religious Science teaches that human personality should be, and may become, the highest manifestation of God. There is a reservoir of life and power as we approach the center, loosed and flowing through to the circumference as we realize the unity of the whole and our relationship to it. God is incarnated in all men and individualized through all creation without loss to Himself.

To be an individual means to exist as an entity. As God is the Infinite Person, rightly understood, so the Spirit is the Infinite Essence of all individuality. Within the One Supreme Mind, since It is infinite, exists the possibility of projecting limitless expressions of Itself; but since the Infinite is infinite, each expression of Itself is unique and different from any other expression. Thus the Infinite is not divided, but multiplied.

While all people have the same origin, no two are alike except in ultimate essence—"One God and Father of us all," but numberless sonships, each sonship a unique institution in the universe of wholeness. Man is an individualized center of God-consciousness and spiritual power, as complete as he knows himself to be, and he knows himself only as he comprehends his relationship to the whole.

This overbrooding Presence, this inner sense of a greater Reality, bears witness to Itself through our highest acts and in our deepest emotions. Who is there who has not at times felt this inner Presence? It is impossible to escape our true nature. The voice of Truth is insistent. The urge to unfold is constant. In the long run each will fully express his divinity, for "good will come at last alike to all."

We stand in the shadow of a mighty Presence while love forever points the way to heaven. Mingled with the voice of humanity is the word of God, for Truth is a synonym for God, and whoever speaks any truth speaks the word of God. Science reveals eternal principles; mathematics, immutable laws, and illumined minds reveal the Eternal Spirit. Behind all is a unity, through all is a diversity, saturating all is a divinity.

We can no more do without religion than we can do without food, shelter or clothing. According to our belief about God will be our estimate of life here and hereafter. To believe in a God of vengeance is one thing, and to believe in a God of love and a just law of cause and effect is another.

To believe in a special dispensation of Providence robs us of our own immediate accessibility to goodness and creates the necessity of mediums, others than our own souls, through which we must gain entrance to Reality. We cannot reach beyond the vision of our own souls. We must have direct access to the Truth.

To believe in a specialized Providence is both scientific and sensible. We are always specializing some law of nature; this is the manner in which all science advances. Unless we can thus specialize the great Law of Life Itself—the Law of Mind and Spirit—we have no possibility of further advancement in the scale of being.

The unique power that Jesus expressed was a result of his conscious union with the creative Principle which is God. Jesus realized that we are living in a spiritual universe now, and like Buddha, Plato and Socrates, Swedenborg, Emerson and Whitman, he clearly understood and taught a law of parallels or spiritual correspondences. The parables of Jesus were mostly illustrations of the concept that the laws of nature and the laws of thought are identical. This has been one of the highest perceptions of the enlightened of all ages.

The universe in which we live is a spiritual system governed by laws of Mind. There are not two minds, there is but One Mind, which is God. The out-push of the Mind of God through the mind of man is the self-realization of Spirit seeking a new outlet for Its own expression. Ideas come from the Great Mind and operate through the human mind. The two are one. In this way the Infinite Mind is personal to each individual.

It is from the infinite self-knowingness of God that our power to know arises, because our mind springs from the Universal Mind. In this way the Infinite multiplies Itself through the finite.

Religious Science teaches that God is personal, and personal in a unique sense, to everyone. It teaches that conscious communion with the indwelling Spirit opens the avenues of intuition and provides a new starting point for the creative power of the Almighty.

No man ever lived who valued the individual life more than Jesus. He proclaimed his divinity through his humanity, and taught that all men are brothers. Every man comes from the bosom of the unseen Father. As the divinity of Christ is awakened through the humanity of man, the divine spark shot from the central fires of the Universal Flame warms other souls in the glow of its own self-realization.

We can give only what we have. The only shadow that we cast is the shadow of the self. This shadow lengthens as we realize the great Presence in which we live, move and have our being.

Religious Science not only emphasizes this unity of God and man, it teaches us that in such degree as our thought becomes spiritualized, it actually manifests the Power of God. In doing this, it literally follows the teaching of Jesus when he proclaimed that all things are possible to him who believes.

It is written that "the prayer of faith shall save the sick, and the Lord shall raise him up." It is self-evident that the prayer of faith is a positive acceptance of the good we desire. Faith is a movement within the mind. It is a certain way of thinking. It is an affirmative mental attitude. Throughout the ages, and practiced by every religion, wonderful results have been obtained through the prayer of faith. There is a law governing this possibility, else it never could have been. It is the business of Religious Science to view these facts, estimate their cause, and in so doing, to provide a definite knowledge of the law governing the facts.

Religious Science teaches that right thinking can demonstrate success and abundance; can offer help to those who are in physical distress, and bring peace to those who are lost in the maze of confusion, doubt and fear.

Religious Science teaches that the Kingdom of God is at hand; that there is a perfection at the center of all things, and that true salvation comes only through true enlightenment, through a more conscious and a more complete union of our lives with the Invisible.

Religious Science does not place an undue importance either on mental healing or the law of abundance. Its main emphasis is placed not on visible things but on the Invisible. It teaches that there is an invisible law governing every man's life. This law is a law of faith or belief; it is a law of mind and consciousness. This will make a great appeal to the practical person, for when the Law of our being is understood it may be consciously used, thus providing every individual with a certain way to freedom, to happiness and to success.

Religious Science is a religion of joy; it is a religion free from fear and uncertainty; it is a religion of faith, a faith justified by results. All men are instinctively religious, and everyone has an intuition within him which, should he follow it, would lead him inevitably to a place not only of an inner sense of certainty, but to a place of the outer condition of security.

The Divine Spirit is not limited, nor does It wish to limit us. Its whole intent is to give us a more abundant life. The time has come when religion must be made practical, and when faith in the invisible must be consciously developed free from dogma, superstition and fear.

Religious Science today offers the world what the ages have been waiting for. It is the culmination of the hope, the aspiration and the faith of the enlightened of all time. The Truth it teaches is old; it has run through spiritual philosophies of the ages, but it has always been more or less handicapped by the dogmas and superstitions imposed upon it by the theology of its times.

The new age demands that the fear and superstition surrounding religious conviction be removed, and that the Truth, plain, simple and direct, be presented that men may learn to live now, in the present, with the assurance that the "eternal God is thy refuge . . ."

OUR DECLARATION OF PRINCIPLES

We believe in God, the Living Spirit Almighty; one indestructible, absolute and self-existent Cause. This One manifests Itself in and through all creation. The manifest universe is the body of God; it is the logical and necessary outcome of the infinite self-knowingness of God. *** We believe in the incarnation of the Spirit in man and that all men are incarnations of the One Spirit. *** We believe in the eternality, the immortality and the continuity of the individual soul, forever and ever expanding. *** We believe that the Kingdom of Heaven is within man and that we experience this Kingdom in the degree that we become conscious of it. *** We believe the ultimate goal of life to be a complete emancipation from all discord of every nature, and that this goal is sure to be attained by all. *** We believe in the unity of all life, and that the highest God and the innermost God is one God. *** We believe that God is personal to all who feel this Indwelling Presence. *** We believe in the direct revelation of Truth through the intuitive and spiritual nature of man, and that any man may become a revealer of Truth who lives in close contact with the Indwelling God. *** We believe that the Universal Spirit, which is God, *operates through a Universal Mind, which is the Law of God; and that we are surrounded by this Creative Mind which receives the direct impress of our thought and acts upon it. *** We believe in the healing of the sick through the power of this Mind. *** We believe in the control of conditions through the power of this Mind. *** We believe in the eternal Goodness, the eternal Loving-kindness and the eternal Givingness of Life to all. *** We believe in our own soul, our own spirit and our own destiny; for we understand that the life of man is God.*

>+<

The following explanation, which is an analysis of our belief, illustrates how Religious Science keeps faith with the spiritual thought of the ages.

We believe in God, the Living Spirit Almighty:

God is defined as: the Deity; the Supreme Being; the Divine Presence in the universe permeating everything; the Animating Principle in everything, as Love, and the Source of all inspiration and power, the Source of guidance and of divine protection.

God has been called by a thousand different names throughout the ages. The time has now come to cast aside any points of disagreement and to realize that we are all worshiping one and the same God.

The Sacred Books of all peoples declare that God is One; a unity from which nothing can be excluded and to which nothing can be added. God is omnipotent, omnipresent and omniscient. God is our Heavenly Father and our Spiritual Mother; the Breath of our life. God is the Changeless Reality in which we live, move and have our being.

The Bible says: "I am the Lord, I change not." "Forever, O Lord, thy word is settled in heaven." "One God and Father of all, who is above all, and through all, and in you all." "Know that the Lord he is God; there is none else beside him." "I am Alpha and Omega, the beginning and the ending . . . which is, and which was, and which is to come, the Almighty." "In whom are hid all the treasures of wisdom and knowledge." "God is Spirit: and they that worship him must worship him in spirit and in truth." "All things were made by him; and without him was not anything made that was made." ". . . there is but one God, the Father, of whom are all things, and we in him." ". . . the Lord he is God in heaven above, and upon the earth beneath: there is none else." "For with thee is the fountain of life; in thy light shall we see light." "God is light, and in him is no darkness at all." "Thy righteousness is an everlasting righteousness, and thy law is the truth."

From the Text of Taoism: "The Tao considered as unchanging, has no name." "There is no end or beginning to the Tao." "The great Tao has no name, but It effects the growth and maintenance of all things." "The Tao does not exhaust itself in what is greatest, nor is it ever absent from what is least; and therefore it is to be found complete and diffused in all things." "Thus it is that the Tao produces (all things), nourishes them . . . nurses them, completes them, matures them, maintains them, and overspreads them."

The Hermetic Teaching defines God as a " . . . Power that naught can e'er surpass, a Power with which no one can make comparison of any human thing at all . . ." This teaching defines God as a Oneness which is the ". . . Source and Root of all, is in all things . . ." "His being is conceiving of all things. . . . He ever makes all things, in heaven, in air, in earth, in deep, in all of cosmos (that is in the entire universe). . . . For there is naught in all the world that is not He." "God is united to all men as light to the sun."

From the Sacred Books of the East: "There is but one Brahma which is Truth's self. It is from our ignorance of that One that god-heads have been conceived to be diverse." "As the sun, manifesting all parts of space, above, between, and below, shines resplendent, so over-rules the all-glorious adorable God . . ." "The One God, who is concealed in all beings, who pervades all, who is the inner soul of all beings, the ruler of all actions, who dwells in all beings . . ." "God is permanent, eternal and therefore existence itself." "All is the effect of all, One Universal Essence." "The Supreme Soul hath another name, that is, Pure Knowledge."

The Zend-Avesta defines God as "Perfect Holiness, Understanding, Knowledge, The most Beneficent, The uncomparable One, The All-seeing One, The healing One, The Creator."

The Koran says that "He is the Living One. No God is there but He."

In Buddhism we find these thoughts: ". . . the Supreme Being, the Unsurpassed, the Perceiver of All Things, the Controller, the Lord of All, the Maker, the Fashioner . . . the Father of All Beings . . ."

In the Apocrypha we read that God is ". . . the Most High who knows . . . who nourishes all. The Creator who has planted his sweet Spirit in all . . . There is One God . . . Worship him . . . who alone exists from age to age . . ."

From the Talmud: "Our God is a living God." "His power fills the universe . . . He formed thee; with His Spirit thou breathest."

We believe in God, the Living Spirit Almighty; one, indestructible, absolute, and self-existent Cause.

In Religious Science self-existent is defined as "living by virtue of its own being." An absolute and self-existent Cause, then, means that Principle, that Power and that Presence which makes everything out of Itself, which contains and sustains everything within Itself. God is absolute and self-existent Cause. Therefore, the Divine Spirit contains within Itself infinite imagination, complete volition and absolute power.

We are to think of God not as some power, but as All Power; not as some presence, but as the Only Presence; not merely as a god, but as The God. Spirit is the supreme and the only Causation.

Emerson said, "There is, at the surface, infinite variety of things; at the center there is simplicity of cause." "We are escorted on every hand through life by spiritual agents, and a beneficent purpose lies in wait for us." It was Emerson's belief that we are all sleeping giants: "Sleep lingers all our life time about our eyes, as night hovers all day in the boughs of the fir tree." "Into every intelligence there is a door which is never closed, through which the creator passes."

This One manifests Itself in and through all creation but is not absorbed by Its creation.

Our textbook defines creation as "the giving of form to the substance of Mind. . . . The whole action of Spirit must be within Itself upon Itself." Creation is the play of Life upon Itself; the action of a limitless Imagination upon an infinite Law.

What God thinks He energizes. The universe is God's thought made manifest. The ideas of God take innumerable forms. The manifest universe springs from the Mind of God.

The Bible says that "the Lord by wisdom hath founded the earth: by understanding hath he established the heavens." "In the beginning God created the heaven and the earth." "By his spirit he hath garnished the heavens." "For he spake, and it was done; he commanded, and it stood fast." ". . . the worlds were framed by the word of God . . ." "The heavens declare the glory of God; and the firmament sheweth his handiwork."

The Hermetic Philosophy states that "with Reason, not with hands, did the World-maker make the universal World . . ."

From a Hindu Scripture: "From the unmanifest springs the manifest." "Mind, being impelled by a desire to create, performs the work of creation by giving form to Itself."

Everything that exists is a manifestation of the Divine Mind; but the Divine Mind being inexhaustible and limitless, is never caught in any form; It is merely expressed by that form. The manifest universe, then, is the Body of God. As our Declaration of Principles reads: "It is the logical and necessary outcome of the infinite self-knowingness of God." God's self-knowingness energizes that which is known, and that which God knows takes form. The form itself has a Divine Pattern within it.

In the Hermetic Teaching we find this remarkable statement:

"All things, accordingly, that are on earth . . . are not the Truth; they're copies (only) of the True. Whenever the appearance doth receive the influx from above, it turns into a copy of the Truth; without its energizing from above, it is left false. Just as the portrait also indicates the body in the picture, but in itself is not the body, in spite of the appearance of the thing that's seen. 'Tis seen as having eyes; but it sees naught, hears naught at all.

"The picture, too, has all the other things, but they are false, tricking the sight of the beholders,—these thinking that they see what's true, while what they see is really false. All, then, who do not see what's false see truth. If, then, we thus do comprehend, or see, each one of these just as it really is, we really comprehend and see. But if (we comprehend, or see, things) contrary to that which is, we shall not comprehend, nor shall we know aught true."

One of the problems of Religious Science is to distinguish between that which is temporal and that which is eternal. God or Spirit is the only Reality, the One Substance or Essence. The material universe is real as a manifestation of life, but it is an effect. This is why Jesus told us to judge not according to appearances.

The Talmud says that "unhappy is he who mistakes the branch for the tree, the shadow for the substance."

In Hebrews we find: "For Christ is not entered into the holy places made with hands, which are the figures of the true; but into heaven itself, now to appear in the presence of God for us."

And from Colossians: "Let no man therefore judge you in meat, or in drink, or in respect of an holyday, or of the new moon, or of the sabbath days: Which are a shadow of things to come; but the body is of Christ."

Back of all form there is a Divine Substance. Hid within every appearance there is an adequate cause. If we judge by the appearance alone, as though it were self-created, we are mistaking the shadow for the Substance.

In Fragments of a Faith Forgotten it says: "Gain for yourselves, ye sons of Adam, by means of these transitory things . . . that which is your own, and passeth not away."

We are to translate all creation into spiritual Causation. Then we shall be viewing it rightly. The created form has no being of itself, it is an effect. In Ramacharaka we read: "That which is unreal hath no shadow of Real Being, notwithstanding the illusion of appearance and false knowledge. And that which hath Real Being hath never ceased to be—can never cease to be, in spite of all appearances to the contrary."

There is a Divine Pattern, a spiritual prototype, in the Mind of God which gives rise to all form. Jesus saw through the form to the Pattern, for he was quickened by the Spirit. "It is the spirit that quickeneth: the flesh profiteth nothing . . ." "For (now) we know in part, and we prophesy in part. But when that which is perfect is come, then that which is in part shall be done away." "Now we see as through a glass darkly." That is, our spiritual vision is not quickened to a complete perception of the Divine Reality, the spiritual prototype back of the image.

All scriptures warn us to beware of false judgments; to judge not according to appearances but to plunge beneath or through the objective form to its spiritual cause. This does not mean that the physical universe is an illusion; it does mean that it is a logical and necessary expression of the Divine Mind. If we were to think of the physical universe as the shadow of its spiritual Reality we should be rightly interpreting it.

Religious Science translates physical form into mental and spiritual causation. It does not do this by denying the form, but through a right of the invisible. The invisible is the cause, the interpretation of it. The visible is an evidence visible is the effect.

We believe in the incarnation of the Spirit in man and that all men are incarnations of the One Spirit.

All scriptures declare that man is the spiritual image and likeness of God. This is emphatically revealed in the inspiration of our own scripture which says: "God created man in his own image." "The spirit of God hath made me, and the breath of the Almighty hath given me life." "Hereby know we that we dwell in him, and he in us, because he hath given us of his Spirit." "Thou hast made him a little lower than the angels, and hast crowned him with glory and honour. Thou madest him to have dominion over the works of thy hands; thou hast put all things under his feet." "Be ye therefore perfect, even as your Father which is in heaven is perfect."

"Now there are diversities of gifts, but the same Spirit." "There is one body, and one Spirit . . . one Lord, one faith, one baptism, one God and Father of all, who is above all, and through all, and in you all." "One faith, and one baptism" means that through faith and intuition we realize that we are living in one Spirit, or, as Emerson said, "There is one Mind common to all individual men."

"Have we not all one Father? Hath not one God created us?" "To us there is but one God, the Father, of whom are all things." "Beloved, now are we the sons of God." "Ye are the sons of the living God." "And because ye are sons. God has sent forth the Spirit of his Son into your hearts." In other words, there is but one son of God which includes the whole human family, and the Spirit of this son, which is the Spirit of Christ, is incarnated in everyone. Therefore, the Bible says that "he (man) is the image and glory of God."

"Know ye not that your body is the temple of the Holy Ghost which is in you . . . therefore glorify God in your body, and in your spirit, which are God's." "That which is born of the Spirit is spirit." We could have no more definite statement of the Divine Incarnation than this. Every man is an incarnation of God. Since God is the Universal Spirit, the one and only Mind, Substance, Power and Presence that exists, and since all men are individuals, it follows that each man is an individualized center of the Consciousness of the One God.

When Jesus said, "I and my Father are one," but "my Father is greater than I," he was stating a mathematical proposition. Every man is an incarnation of God, but no single incarnation of God can exhaust the Divine Nature. Everyone can use the figure 7 to infinity without ever exhausting its possibility. The more Divine Power we use the more Divine Power is placed at our disposal, for "there is that which scattereth, and yet increaseth."

Not only is every individual a incarnation of God, and, therefore, a manifestation of Christ, but since each individual is unique, every person has access to God in a personal sense. The Spirit is most certainly personal to each one of us—individually and uniquely personal. We could not ask for a more complete union than this, for the union is absolute, immediate and dynamic.

According to the revelation of the ages, man has a spiritual birthright which gives him dominion over all evil. But the old man must be put off; that is, transmuted into the new man, which is Christ. The real spiritual man is here now could we see him. It is ignorance of this fact which produces all evil, all limitation, all fear. It is a sense of separation from our Source which begets all our troubles. In the midst of the possibility of freedom we are bound. Thus, the Hermetic philosophy states that though we are born of harmony we have become slaves because we are overcome by sleep. And our own scripture says that we must awake from this sleep; that we must arise from the dead in order that Christ may give us life.

The Koran says: "We created man: and we know what his soul whispereth to him, and we are closer to him than his neck-vein."

In the Talmud we read: "First no atom of matter, in the whole vastness of the universe, is lost; how then can man's soul, which is the whole world in one idea be lost?"

The following quotations are drawn from various Hindu Scriptures: "The ego is beyond all disease . . . free from all imagination, and all-pervading." "As from a . . . fire, in thousand ways, similar sparks proceed, so beloved are produced living cells of various kinds from the

Indestructible." "If ye knew God as he ought to be known, ye would walk under seas, and the mountains would move at your call." (This is similar to the teaching of Jesus when he said that if we had faith the size of a grain of mustard seed, we could say unto the mountain, "Remove hence to yonder place.") "There is that within every soul which conquers hunger, thirst, grief, delusion, old age and death."

Perhaps one of the most remarkable sayings in the Scriptures of India, relative to the self, is the following: "Let him raise the self by the Self and not let the self become depressed; for verily is the Self the friend of the self, and also the Self the self's enemy; The Self is the friend of the self of him in whom the self by the Self is vanquished; but to the unsubdued self the Self verily becometh hostile as an enemy." This, of course, refers to the deathless Self, the incarnation of God in us.

"He who knows himself has come to know his Lord . . ." This refers to the complete unity of the Spirit, or, as Jesus said, "I and the Father are one." "And he who thus hath learned to know himself, hath reached that Good which doth transcend abundance . . ."

From the Text of Taoism are gathered the following inspiring thoughts: "Man has a real existence, but it has nothing to do with place; he has continuance, but it has nothing to do with beginning or end." "He whose whole mind is thus fixed emits a Heavenly light. In him who emits this heavenly light men see the (True) man."

Referring to the one whose mind is fixed on Reality, "His sleep is untroubled by dreams; his waking is followed by no sorrows. His spirit is guileless and pure; his soul is not subject to weariness." In spiritual revelation a calm contemplation of spiritual Truth is held important. The mind must be like a mirror if it is to reflect or image forth the Divine Prototype, the incarnation of God in man. "Men do not look unto running water as a mirror, but into still water:—it is only the still water that can arrest them all, and keep them in the contemplation of their real selves."

The Hermetic Philosophy tells us that if we would know God we must be like Him, for "like is knowable to like alone." "Make thyself to grow to the same stature as the Greatness which transcends all measure . . ." "Conceiving nothing is impossible unto thyself, think thyself deathless and able to know all, —all arts, all sciences, the way of every life." It tells us to awake from our deep sleep, as though our spiritual eyes were dulled by too much looking on effect and too little contemplation of cause.

We believe in the eternality, the immortality and the continuity of the individual soul, forever and ever expanding.

If man is an incarnation of God, then his spirit is God individualized, and as such it must be eternal. Since it is impossible to exhaust the limitless nature of the Divine, our expansion must be an eternal process of unfolding from a limitless Center.

Immortality is not something we purchase. It is not a bargain we make with the Almighty. It is the gift of heaven. It is inherent in the divine nature of man. When the disciples of Jesus asked him what is God's relationship to the dead, he answered as we should expect one to answer who had already plunged beneath the material surface of things and discovered their spiritual cause. He said, "He is not a God of the dead, but of the living: for all live unto him."

God is Life, and that which is Life cannot produce death. What we call death is but a transition from one plane or one mode of expression into another. "In my Father's house are many mansions."

Jesus said to one who passed with him, "Today shalt thou be with me in paradise." In the philosophy of this spiritual genius, this God-saturated man, death was but a transition.

The Gita tells us, "He is not born, nor doth he die; nor having been, ceaseth he any more to be; unborn, perpetual, eternal and ancient, he is not slain when the body is slaughtered."

From the Bible: "He asked life of thee, and thou gavest it him, even length of days for ever and ever." "And this is the promise that he hath promised us, even eternal life." "To an inheritance incorruptible, and undefiled, and that fadeth not away, reserved in heaven for you."

We believe that the Kingdom of Heaven is within man and that we experience this Kingdom to the degree that we become conscious of it.

The Kingdom of Heaven means the kingdom of harmony, of peace, of joy and of wholeness. It is an inward kingdom. This is why Jesus said that we should not lay up treasures on earth, but "lay up for yourselves treasures in heaven."

Heaven is not a place but an inward state of consciousness. It is an inward awareness of Divine Harmony and Truth. It is the "house not made with hands, eternal in the heavens." Ezekiel said, "The spirit took me up, and brought me into the inner court; and, behold, the glory of the Lord filled the house." The glory of God fills every man's consciousness who is aware of that glory.

Jesus likened the Kingdom of Heaven to a child: "Except ye be converted, and become as little children, ye shall not enter into the kingdom of heaven." This refers to the childlike consciousness, to a simple trust in the goodness of God.

The Spirit has placed divine intuition within everyone. This divine intuition is the gateway through which the inspiration of the Almighty enters the mind. This is why the Psalms tell us to "lift up our gates." That is, lift up the intuition and permit the Divine Light to enter.

When Jesus said that we are to be perfect even as God within us is perfect, he certainly implied that there is such a Divine Kingdom already established within man. "When the without shall become as the within" then the Kingdom of God shall be established here and now. Jesus said that we should assume a childlike attitude toward this Kingdom. "Whosoever therefore shall humble himself as this little child, the same is greatest in the kingdom of heaven." "And when he was demanded of the Pharisees, when the kingdom of God should come, he answered them and said, The kingdom of God cometh not with observation: Neither shall they say, Lo here! or, lo there! for, behold, the kingdom of God is within you." This certainly refers to a state of inner awareness.

The kingdom to which Jesus referred is not external but within. It is not to be placed outside the self, "Neither Lo here! or, lo there!" but it is to be perceived as an everlasting dominion within. The Kingdom of Heaven is something we possess but have not been conscious of. It is not some far off divine event, "for the kingdom of heaven is at hand." It is neither in the mountain nor at Jerusalem, but within the mind.

Jesus likened the Kingdom of Heaven ". . . unto treasure hid in a field; the which when a man hath found, he hideth, and for joy thereof goeth and selleth all that he hath, and buyeth that field." The treasure of the inner kingdom is already hid at the center of our being and when we discover it great joy follows. Our whole desire is to possess this inner kingdom; to drill deep into the well-spring of our being and bring up the pure oil of Spirit; to tunnel the granite rock of our unbelief and at the center of our being discover "the pearl of great price."

"And the disciples came, and said unto him. Why speakest thou unto them in parables? He answered and said unto them, Because it is given unto you to know the mysteries of the kingdom of heaven, but to them it is not given." On first reading, this sounds as though Jesus were withholding his teaching from the common multitude, but such was not the case. He spoke in parables realizing that those who comprehended their meaning would understand his teaching, for he had already instructed his disciples in the mysteries of the kingdom. That is, he had directly taught them the inner meaning of life.

In Corinthians it says: "But we speak the wisdom of God in a mystery, even the hidden wisdom, which God ordained before the world unto our glory." This is a direct reference to the inseparable unity between God and man. God has ordained that forever man shall be one with His own being, that the kingdom of good shall forever be at hand. Since we are individuals, God has also ordained that our good shall make its appearance when we recognize it.

Emerson said that "Nature forevermore screens herself from the profane, but when the fruit is ripe it will fall." The inner mysteries of the Kingdom of God are hid from the vulgar, not because the Divine withholds Itself, but because only to the pure in heart, to the child-like in mind, can the Kingdom be revealed.

One of the greatest of the Greek philosophers said that this kingdom is something which every man possesses but which few men use. Encased in materiality, filled with the din of objective confusion, we do not hear the still small voice which evermore proclaims, "Look unto me, and be ye saved, all the ends of the earth."

Again Jesus likened the Kingdom unto ". . . a grain of mustard seed, which a man took, and sowed in his field . . ." He then goes on to say that very soon this small seed becomes a tree which puts forth branches. Here Jesus is referring to the Tree of Life, which means the unity of God with man. The little seed is the consciousness of the little child which becomes aware of its relationship to the Divine Parentage. Out of this inner awareness grows and blossoms a concept of harmony. The Tree of Life expands and puts forth branches; its shade provides shelter.

No matter how small our concept of heaven may be to begin with, it has the possibility of eternal unfoldment. The power to live is within the self, implanted by the Divine. Ultimately every man will realize his inner kingdom which will become to him as the Tree of Life providing food and shelter, perfection and joy.

Again Jesus said, "The kingdom of heaven is like unto leaven, which a woman took, and hid in three measures of meal, till the whole was leavened." He is referring to the action of consciousness of the Kingdom of God in the mind as yeast spreading through the whole lump of mortal thought, lifting the weight of the burdens of life into lightness.

Jesus is referring to the Kingdom of God as the Bread of Life; the eternal Substance upon which the soul feeds; the everlasting Presence upon which the inner eye feasts; the house not made with hands in which the Spirit dwells forever.

"Again, the kingdom of heaven is like unto a merchant man, seeking goodly pearls: Who, when he had found one pearl of great price, went and sold all that he had, and bought it." Since the greater includes the lesser, Jesus told us that we are first to seek the Kingdom because everything is included in it. "Pearl" stands for purity and perfection. When we discover the purity and perfection at the center of our own being, we shall naturally sell the dross, the fear and the doubt that infest our thought world, in order that we may possess this inner purity, that we may become conscious of this inner perfection.

Jesus did not wish us to feel that, in seeking this inner kingdom, we are losing anything worth while in the outer life, for he said that everyone who has sought the inner kingdom shall "receive manifold more in this present time, and in the world to come life everlasting." This is in line with all the other teachings of Jesus, that the reward for right living is immediate. The Kingdom is not something reserved only for future states; it is something which we experience here and now through the manifold blessings which the Spirit automatically bestows on us when we seek first things first.

In his parable likening the Kingdom of Heaven unto the wise virgins, Jesus clearly teaches that every man possesses the Oil of Spirit and that no man need borrow from another.

The Kingdom of God is not something we create, not something we purchase, but something that we must realize—it is something we become inwardly aware of. There is a perfection at the center of man's being. Browning tells us that we must loose this imprisoned splendor, while Plato and his followers taught that "over yonder" there is a prototype of perfection. With them "over yonder" had a meaning identical with the teaching of Jesus that the Kingdom of Heaven is within. The

Greek philosophers taught that when the image, that is, the external, turns to its prototype, it is instantly made whole because it is instantly unified with its inner perfection.

Let us see what other bibles of the world have taught about this inner kingdom.

In the Text of Taoism we find this: "Without going outside his door . . . without looking out from his window, one sees the Tao of Heaven. The farther one goes from himself the less he knows." "What is heavenly is internal; what is human is external. If you know the operation of what is heavenly . . . you will have your root in what is heavenly . . ." "Take the days away and there will be no year; without what is internal there will be nothing external." "He who knows . . . completion . . . turns in on himself and finds there an inexhaustible store."

The Gita tells us: "He who is happy within him, rejoiceth within him, is illumined within, becomes eternal." And in Fragments of a Faith Forgotten it says: ". . . the Kingdom of Heaven is within you; and whosoever shall know himself shall find it." "Seek for the great and the little shall be added unto you. Seek for the heavenly and the earthly shall be added unto you."

In the Upanishad we read: "As far as mind extends, so far extends heaven." "In heaven there is no fear . . . it is without hunger or thirst and beyond all grief."

The Pistis Sophia says: "Be ye diligent that ye may receive the mysteries of Light and enter into the height of the Kingdom of Light."

We believe the ultimate goal of life to be a complete emancipation from all discord of every nature, and that this goal is sure to be attained by all.

The ultimate goal of life does not mean that we shall ever arrive at a spiritual destination where everything remains static and inactive. That which to our present understanding seems an ultimate goal, will, when attained, be but the starting point for a new and further evolution. We believe in an eternal upward spiral of existence. This is what Jesus meant when he said, "In my Father's house are many mansions."

The Koran tell us that God has made many heavens, one on top of another, which means that evolution is eternal. The Hermetic philosophy taught an infinite variation of the manifestation of life on an ever-ascending scale. All evolution proves the transition of the lesser into the greater.

The original sources of spiritual thought, from which the great religious conceptions of the ages have been drawn, have taught that evolution is an eternal manifestation of life on an ascending scale. As we ascend from a lower to a higher level, the limitations of the previous experience must drop away from us. Since the Kingdom of God or the Kingdom of Reality is already established in Spirit, our transition from one plane to another is a matter of consciousness, and since all persons are incarnations of the Divine Spirit, every soul will ultimately find complete emancipation, not through losing itself in God, but, rather, through finding God in itself.

Tagore tells us that Nirvana is not absorption but immersion. Browning said that we are all Gods though in the germ. Jesus proclaimed that the Kingdom of Heaven is within, and that we shall attain this kingdom in such degree as we become consciously aware of, and unified with, it. This does not mean that there is any finality to evolution, for every apparent ultimate is but the beginning of a new experience.

We believe in the unity of all life, and that the highest God and the innermost God is one God.

The enlightened in every age have taught that back of all things there is One Unseen Cause. This teaching of Unity . . . "The Lord our God is one God . . ." is the chief cornerstone of the sacred scriptures of the East, as well as our own sacred writings. It is the mainspring of the teachings of modern spiritual philosophies, such as Unity Teachings, the New Thought Movement, the Occult Teachings, the Esoteric or

Inner Teachings, our own Religious Science, and even much that is taught under the name of Psychology. Science has found nothing to contradict this unity, for it is self-evident. An entire chapter in our textbook is available for further elucidation of this subject.

There is One Life of which we are a part; One Intelligence, which we use; One Substance, which takes manifold forms. "That they all may be one; as thou, Father, art in me, and I in thee, that they also may be one in us."

In the Bible we find these passages: "Now there are diversities of gifts, but the same Spirit." "Whither shall I go from thy spirit? or whither shall I flee from thy presence? If I ascend up into heaven, thou art there: if I make my bed in hell, behold, thou art there . . . If I say, Surely the darkness shall cover me; even the night shall be light about me." "We all, with open face beholding as in a glass the glory of the Lord, are changed into the same image . . . by the Spirit of the Lord." "I shall be satisfied when I awake with thy likeness."

"Know ye not that your body is the temple of the Holy Ghost which is in you?" "That which is born of the Spirit is spirit." "The Lord our God is one God . . . He is God in heaven above and upon the earth beneath. There is none else." ". . . His word is in mine heart as a burning fire shut up in my bones." "And the Word was made flesh, and dwelt among us . . ." ". . . I will put my words in his mouth . . . the word is very nigh unto thee, in thy mouth, and in thy heart, that thou mayest do it."

All sacred scriptures have proclaimed the unity of life; that every man is a center of God Consciousness. This is the meaning of the mystical marriage, or the union of the soul with its Source. Jesus boldly proclaimed that he was one with the Father. This is the basis for all New Thought teaching, the spiritual union of all life.

The Qabbalah states that "every existence tends toward the higher, the first unity . . . the whole universe is one, complex. The lower emanates from the Higher and is Its image. The Divine is active in each."

Unity is a symbol of the soul's oneness with the Higher Nature, implying complete freedom from bondage to anything less than itself. All positive religions have taught that the supreme end of humanity is a union of the soul with God.

"The Atman, which is the substratum of the ego in man, is One." The Hermetic Teaching tells us that "this Oneness, being source and root of all, is in all." And the Gita explains that "when he (man) perceiveth the diversified existence of beings as rooted in One, and spreading forth from It, then he reacheth the eternal."

Again the Bible tells us: "Thus saith the Lord . . . I am the first and I am the last . . ." "I am Alpha and Omega, the beginning and the ending . . . which was and which is to come . . ."

From The Awakening of Faith: "In the essense (of Reality) there is neither anything which has to be included, nor anything which has to be added."

In one of the Upanishads we find this quotation: "The One God who is concealed in all beings, who is the inner soul of all beings, the ruler of all actions . . ." "All is the effect of all, One Universal Essence." And again in Ephesians, "One God and Father of all, who is above all, and through all, and in you all."

In Echoes from the Gnosis we find: "Oh Primal Origin of my origination; Thou Primal Substance of my substance; Breath of my breath, the breath that is in me."

From the Bible: "To us there is but one God, the Father, of whom are all things, and we in him . . ." And from another Bible, "All this universe has the Deity for its life. That Deity is Truth, who is the Universal Soul."

From the Apocrypha: "He is Lord of Heaven, sovereign of earth, the One existence." And the Upanishads tell us. "He who is the Ear of the ear, the Mind of the mind, the Speech of the speech, is verily the Life of life, the Eye of the eye."

Religious Science teaches an absolute union of man with his Source. So complete is this union that the slightest act of human consciousness manifests some degree of man's divinity. Man is not God, but he has no life separate from the Divine; he has no existence apart from his Source. He thinks God's thoughts after Him. He is divine neither by will nor through choice, but by necessity. The whole process of evolution is a continual process of awakening. It is an understanding of this indwelling union which constitutes the Spirit of Christ.

Our textbook defines Christ as "the Word of God manifest in and through man. In a liberal sense, the Christ means the Entire Manifestation of God and is, therefore, the Second Person of the Trinity. Christ is Universal Idea, and each one 'puts on the Christ' to the degree that he surrenders a limited sense of Life to the Divine Realization of wholeness and unity with Good, Spirit, God."

Christ is the Higher Self, the Divine Life proceeding from the Father. This Christ enters the world of manifestation and animates all things. Christ is in everything; we are rooted and centered in Him who is "the way, the truth, and the life."

Christ is the supreme ideal which Jesus made manifest through the power of his word. Christ is the Divine Nature of all being and the Supreme Goal of Union toward which all individual and collective evolution moves.

The realization of this union gives birth to the consciousness of Christ in the individual, and has been called "the light of the world." When Peter said to Jesus, "Thou art the Christ, the son of the living God," Jesus answered by telling Peter that no man had revealed this to him but that it was a direct revelation of the Spirit. This is in accord with our statement that:

We believe that God is personal to all who feel this Indwelling Presence. . . . We believe in the direct revelation of Truth through the intuitive and spiritual nature of man, and that any man may become a revealer of Truth who lives in close contact with the Indwelling God.

"Know ye not that ye are the temple of God, and that the Spirit of God dwelleth in you?" "God is in his holy temple." Augustine said that the pure mind is a holy temple for God, and Emerson that God builds His temple in the heart. Seneca said that "temples are not to be built for God with stones . . . He is to be consecrated in the breast of each."

Every man is an incarnation of God, and since each person is an individual, everyone is a unique incarnation. We believe in the Divine Presence as Infinite Person, and personal to each. God is not a person, but the Person. This Person is an Infinite Presence filled with warmth, color and responsiveness, immediately and intimately personal to each individual.

The Spirit is both an over-dwelling and an indwelling Presence. We are immersed in It and It flows through us as our very life. Through intuition man perceives and directly reveals God. We do not have to borrow our light from another. Nothing could be more intimate than the personal relationship between the individual and that Divine Presence which is both the Center and the Source of man's being.

Not some men, but all men, are divine. But all men have not yet recognized their divinity. Our spiritual evolution is a gradual awakening to the realization that the Spirit is center, source and circumference of all being. It is in everything, around everything and through everything, and It is everything.[1]

The main body of the Christian religion is built upon three grand concepts: first, that God is an Over-dwelling Presence; next, that God is also an Indwelling Presence; and third, that the conscious union of the Indwelling and the Over-dwelling, through the mind of man, gives birth to the divine child, the Christ, the Son of God. It was this revela-

---

[1] *See Your Invisible Power*, an Institute publication. Also read carefully section on *The Perfect Whole in The Science of Mind*, textbook of the Institute.

tion which enabled Jesus to perform his wonderful works. He became so conscious of his union with God that the very words he spoke were the Words of God spoken through him.

The only way that the Power of God can be manifest through man is by man's realization that it is the Father who dwelleth in him who doeth the works. Everyone should practice this close and intimate relationship between the individual and the Universal. Everyone should practice the Presence of God. This Presence is a reality, the one, great and supreme reality of life. There is a "light which lighteth every man." Man is spoken of in the Bible as "the candle of the Lord," and Jesus said, "Let your light so shine before men, that they may see your good works, and glorify your Father which is in heaven."

Through spiritual intuition Jesus perceived his union with God. What suffering, what unuttered anguish, what persistence, effort and discipline this man may have gone through to arrive at this exalted state, we know not, but we may be gratefully aware that he passed through every gamut of human suffering and emerged triumphant, supreme. Christ is the divine and universal Emanation of the Infinite Spirit incarnated in everything, individualized in man and universalized in God.

Whatever God is in the universal, man is in the individual. This is why all spiritual leaders have told us that if we would uncover the hidden possibility within, we should not only discover the true Self, the Christ, we should also uncover the true God, the One and Only Cause, the Supreme Being, the Infinite Person.

Jesus taught a complete union of man with God. He proclaimed that all men are divine; that all are one with the Father; that the Kingdom of Heaven is within; that the Father has delivered all power unto the son; and that the son thinks the thoughts of God after Him, and imbibes spiritual power through realization of his union with his Source.

We believe that the Universal Spirit, which is God, operates through a Universal Mind, which is the Law of God; and that we are surrounded by this

Creative Mind which receives the direct impress of our thought and acts upon it.

This deals with the practical use of spiritual Power.[2]

In Religious Science we differentiate between Spirit, Mind and Body, just as all the great major religious have done. Spirit is the conscious and active aspect of God, as distinguished from the passive, receptive and form-taking aspect. Spirit imparts motion and manifests Itself through form. Thus, the ancients said that Spirit uses matter as a sheath.

Philo, often called Philo Judaeus, born about 10 B.C., one of the greatest of the Jewish philosophers of the Alexandrian school, said that the Active Principle, which is Spirit, is absolutely free and that the passive principle is set in motion by the Spirit, giving birth to form. Plotinus, considered the greatest of the Neo-Platonists, taught that Spirit, as Active Intelligence, operates upon an unformed substance, which is passive to It, and that through the power of the Word of Spirit this substance takes form and becomes the physical world.

The spiritual teachings of antiquity all taught a trinity or three-fold unity.[3] In order that anything may exist there must be an active principle of self-assertion, acting as law upon a passive principle, which Plotinus called an indeterminate substance whose business it is to receive the forms which the contemplation (the word or the thought) of Spirit gives to it. In Religious Science, following the example of the Christian scriptures, we have named this trinity "The Father, Son and Holy Ghost." The Father, the supreme creative Principle; the Son (the Christ) the universal manifestation of the Father; and the supreme Law of Cause and Effect, the servant of the Spirit throughout the ages.

---

[2] Read carefully the definition of Universal Power, Universal Soul, Universal Spirit, and Universal Subjective Mind on pages 641 and 642 in *The Science of Mind* textbook.

[3] See pamphlet published by the Institute of Religious Science, *Religious Science: The Thing Itself, the Way It Works, What It Does, and How to Use It.*

The Father means Absolute Being, the Unconditioned First Cause, the Source of all that is. Jesus called this Life Force "The Father." He referred to himself, and to all other men, as "The Son." "He is the image of the invisible God . . ." The ancient Hindus referred to The Son as Atman, the innermost spiritual self. Atman is the manifestation of Brahma as individuality. Man is an individualized center of the Consciousness of God. The Christian scripture refers to the same self when it speaks of Christ in us, for the Christ Principle has a meaning identical with Atma-Buddhi, which means divine illumination, "the Light of the world."

The Bible says that "the first man (Adam) is of the earth . . . the second man is the Lord from heaven." This refers first to the physical being, formed after the manner of all creation, and next to the Christ Principle animating this being. The birth of Christ, through Jesus, was the awakening of his consciousness to a realization of his union with God—"I and my Father are one." Jesus clearly taught that all men must come to this realization if they would enter into the kingdom of harmony, into conscious union with God, and thus gain wholeness.

"The first Adam is of the earth, earthy, and liable to death. The second is 'from heaven,' and triumphant over death. For 'sin has no more dominion over him.' He, therefore, is the product of a soul purified from defilement by matter, and released from subjection to the body. Such a soul is called virgin. And she has for spouse, not matter—for that she has renounced,—but the Divine Spirit which is God. And the man born of this union is in the image of God, and is God made man; that is, he is Christ, and it is the Christ thus born in every man, who redeems him and endows him with eternal life."[4]

From *Ibid:* "For, as cannot be too clearly and forcibly stated, between the man who becomes a Christ, and other men, there is no difference whatever of kind. The difference is alone of condition and degree, and

---

[4] From *The Perfect Way.*

consists in difference of unfoldment of the spiritual nature possessed by all in virtue of their common derivation. 'All things,' as has repeatedly been said, 'are made of the divine Substance.' And Humanity represents a stream which, taking its rise in the outermost and lowest mode of differentiation of that Substance, flows inwards and upwards to the highest, which is God. And the point at which it reaches the celestial, and empties itself into Deity, is 'Christ.' Any doctrine other than this,—any doctrine which makes the Christ of a different and non-human nature,—is anti-Christian and subhuman. And, of such doctrine, the direct effect is to cut off man altogether from access to God, and God from access to man."

And from Basil Wilberforce, *Problems*: "In the evolution of God's life in man there are no short cuts, but a gradual unfolding of a principle of interior vitality. And the motto from this thought is, 'Rest in the Lord and wait patiently for Him,' while the child-Christ nature within you 'increases in wisdom and stature, and in favour with God and man.'"

J. Brierley, in his book *Studies of the Soul*, says: "God as the Absolute can, in the nature of things, only come into contact with man by a self limitation . . . In Christ, to begin with, we have a revelation of the Absolute in the limited. In Him, as the Church all along has joyfully confessed, we see God."

"The second coming of Christ is a symbol of the completion of the process of purification and development of the souls of humanity, when the lower consciousness rises to union with the higher." From Mystical Religions, and quoting from Luke, "And then shall they see the Son of man coming in a cloud with power and great glory. But when these things begin to come to pass, look up, and lift up your heads; because your redemption draweth nigh."

R. M. Jones goes on to say: "This refers to the consummation of the physical at the end of the cycle. Then as perfection of the soul-state approaches, the indwelling Christ appears in glory within the souls of the saints, or is raised above the condition wherefrom at first his descent was made. The 'cloud' signifies a temporary veil which obscures the splendour of the Highest. The 'lifting up of heads' refers to the aspiration of the minds, needful so that liberation from the lower nature may be effected." And quoting from Luke again, "Verily I say unto you, this generation shall not pass away, till all things be accomplished," he explains: "Christ here points out that each grade of evolution of qualities now existent, shall not be extinguished until the complete process of soul-growth on the lower planes has been carried out."

To return to our analysis of the Trinity, the Father is the Absolute, Unconditioned, First Cause; the Infinite Person; the Divine in Whom we live and move and have our being. The entire manifestation of the Infinite in any and all planes, levels, states of consciousness, or manifestations, constitutes the Son.

So far as we know from teachings handed down to us from antiquity, the Holy Ghost signifies the feminine aspect of the Divine Trinity. It represents the divine activity of the higher mental plane; the Breath of God, or the Law of Being. It is difficult for us to transpose the meaning of ancient symbols into modern language, but it seems to be the consensus among the scholars who have studied this subject that the Holy Ghost means the relationship between the Father and the Son, or the divine, creative fertility of the universal soul when impregnated by the Divine Ideas. If creation is to take place, there must be a Divine Imagination which is spontaneous and a creative medium through which It acts. This creative medium is the Law of Mind.

When any individual recognizes his true union with the Infinite, he automatically becomes the Christ. He is born from the lower to a higher plane and awakes to a greater consciousness of his union with the Father—"I shall be satisfied when I awake in thy likeness."

In Religious Science it is made clear that there is a universal Law of Mind which receives the impress of our thought and acts upon it. This Law is not God, but the servant of God.

The ancients called this Law the "Feminine." Realizing that there must be an active, energizing principle which is God, the Masculine, they also recognized that there must be a creative principle in nature, which they spoke of as Feminine, whose business it is to receive God's thought and bring it into creation.

This creative Law is, of course, the Law of Mind. It is what we mean when we say there is a Universal Mind through which the Universal Spirit operates. In other words, when we think of God as pure, self-knowing Spirit, as "our Father which art in heaven," as the Absolute, the Unconditioned, as Infinite Person and Limitless Being, we are thinking of Divine Intelligence. But when we think of the universe as law, we are thinking of the Principle of Mind which receives the impress of our thought and acts upon it, always creatively, always mathematically, and without any respect to persons.

All great spiritual teachings have proclaimed such a creative Principle. It has been called by a thousand names, but careful analysis will show that every scripture has differentiated between God the Spirit and God the Law.

The ancients said that Spirit is the Power that knows Itself. They also taught the karmic law, which is the medium for all thought and action. Karma means the fruit of action.

When Jesus said, "The words that I speak unto you, they are spirit, and they are life," he was speaking from the consciousness of Christ which dominates the mental plane. His mind was such a perfect transmitter that it reflected, imaged, emanated, or automatically became an instrument through which the Divine worked.

Knowing that his word was in absolute accord with Divine Harmony he found no difference between it and the Word of God. It was his implicit confidence in his divine inspiration, arrived at through a lifetime of contemplation and of conscious union with the Infinite, which gave him the confidence to say, ". . . till all these things be fulfilled.

Heaven and earth shall pass away, but my words shall not pass away." Jesus was relying upon the Law of Mind to execute his word.

In the Science of Mind we are very careful to draw a distinction between Universal Spirit and Universal Mind. The Science of Mind is the tool which the Religious Scientist uses, starting with the realization that the manifest universe is, as every scripture has declared, a logical result of the Thought of God, and realizing that man is a center of God Consciousness.

The Religious Scientist knows that in such degree as he inwardly realizes the Truth, this Truth which he realizes, operating through a universal Law of Mind, will find outward or physical manifestation in the world of form. This is what we mean when we say that the Spirit operates through a Law of Mind; that we are surrounded by this Mind which receives the impress of our thought and acts upon it.

Let us see what different scriptures have had to say on this subject, starting with our own Bible. "In the beginning was the Word, and the Word was with God, and the Word was God." "Forever, O Lord, thy word is seated in heaven." "And, Thou, Lord . . . hast laid the foundation of the earth; and the heavens are the works of thine hands." "Our God is a living God. His power fills the universe . . . with his spirit thou breathest."

In referring to the Law of Mind the Bible says: "Every idle word that men shall speak, they shall give account thereof . . . for by thy words thou shalt be justified, and by thy words thou shalt be condemned." "And they were astonished at his doctrine: for his word was with power." "Be ye doers of the word and not hearers only . . ." "For there are three that bear witness in heaven, the Father, the Word, and the Holy Ghost: and these three are one."

Our Bible is based on the premise that God is pure Spirit; that He creates through the power of His word, and that the universe is a manifestation of His imagination (His imaging within Himself through knowing Himself to be what He is). God is Spirit. The Spirit speaks, the Law is invoked, and a manifestation necessarily takes form. This is the first principle.

The next principle advanced is that man is the spiritual image and likeness of God, and is of like nature with God; that he is made of the essence of God, and is an individualized center in the Consciousness of God.

Then, having stated man's divine pedigree, and having carefully pointed out what happens to man through his misuse of the Law of Freedom, commonly called "the fall of man," the conclusion is devoted to man's redemption. The old prophets intuitively perceived this; the New Testament demonstrates it, for in the person of Jesus there arose a man who became so conscious of his union with good that all evil disappeared from his imagination.

Through trial, temptation, suffering, through success and failure, this glorified soul, in a sense, fought the battle of life for all men and thus automatically become the savior of mankind. But when they mistook the man Jesus for the Christ Principle, the wisdom of Jesus caused him to withdraw himself that the Spirit of Truth might awaken in them a corresponding realization of their own union with the Divine.

The whole teaching of the Bible may be simmered down to this simple statement, presented to each one of us individually as though a Divine Hand delivered it unto our individual keeping: You are one with the creative Spirit of the universe. There is a universal, divine Spirit which will inspire, guide, direct and companion you, but there is also a universal Law of Cause and Effect which sees to it that every act, every thought, every motive, must be accounted for. Finally, through suffering, you will learn to distinguish right from wrong; you will live in conscious union and in conscious communion with the Divine Spirit.

From then on your words, thoughts and acts will be constructive and you will come into complete salvation. God has done all He can for you because He has delivered His entire nature into your keeping. But, since this nature is truth, goodness, beauty, wisdom, love and power, you can never enter completely into the kingdom of harmony until you consciously unify with harmony.

This is the balance between truth and justice, between love and reason, between true divine freedom and the misuse of the Law, which is not liberty but license. This is why Moses said. "I set before you this day a blessing and a curse; a blessing, if ye obey the commandments . . . a curse, if ye will not obey the commandments."

The whole problem of evil, as stated by the different scriptures of the world, is not a problem of dealing with an entity of evil, but with the misuse of a dynamic power which, rightly used, alone guarantees freedom.

The Koran says that "whatsoever good betideth thee is from God and whatsoever betideth thee of evil is from thyself." And our Bible says of the Spirit. "Thou art of purer eyes than to behold evil, and canst not look on iniquity."

From the Teachings of Buddha we learn: "For the cause of the karma (cause and effect) which conducts to unhappy states of existence, is ignorance." "Therefore it is clear that ignorance can only be removed by wisdom." The Zend-Avesta says, "The word of falsehood smites but the word of truth shall smite it." And from The Book of the Dead: "It shall come to pass that the evil one shall fall when he raiseth a snare to destroy thee . . ."

From the Text of Taoism we learn: "Whatever is contrary to the Tao soon ends." "He who injures others is sure to be injured by them in return."

We believe in the healing of the sick through the power of this Mind.

Spiritual mind healing has long since passed the experimental stage, and we now know why it is that faith has performed miracles. We live in a universe of pure, unadulterated Spirit, of perfect Being. We are, as Emerson said, in the lap of an infinite Intelligence. There is a spiritual prototype of perfection at the center of everything. There is a cosmic or divine pattern at the center of every organ of the physical body. Our body is some part of the Body of God; it is a manifestation of the Supreme Spirit.

In the practice of spiritual mind healing we start with this simple proposition: God is perfect. God is all there is. God includes man. Spiritual man is a divine being, as complete and perfect in essence as is God. When in thought, in contemplation, in imagination, in inward feeling, we consciously return to the Source of our being, the divine pattern which already exists, springs forth into newness of manifestation. When we clear the consciousness, that is, the whole mental life, both conscious and subjective, of discord, we are automatically healed.

The Science of Mind, which is the tool of the Religious Scientist, gives us a definite technique for doing this. It teaches us exactly how to proceed on a simple, understandable basis. It is a science because it is built upon the exact laws of Mind, for the laws of Mind are as exact as any other laws in nature. They are natural laws. From a practical viewpoint, this is done by making certain definite statements with the realization that they have power to remove any obstacle, to dissolve any false condition, and to reveal man's spiritual nature.

True mind healing cannot be divorced from spiritual realization, therefore the practitioner of this science must have a deep and an abiding sense of calm, of peace, and of his union with the Spirit. He must have an unshakable conviction that spiritual man is perfect, that he is one with God, and he must know that in such degree as he realizes, senses, feels, this inner perfection, it will appear. The physical healing itself is a result, an effect, of this inward consciousness.

The laws of this science are so simple, direct and usable that anyone may demonstrate them who cares to make the effort. Read carefully the entire section on mind healing in our textbook, *The Science of Mind*, and you will discover that there is no mystery about this. The reason that throughout the ages people have been healed through a prayer of faith, is that faith complies with the Law of Mind in producing an affirmative result. Faith is an unquestioned acceptance.

Faith also is a certain definite mental attitude. When Jesus said, "It is done unto you as you believe," he implied that there is a law, a force, or an intelligent energy in the universe which acts upon the images of our belief. Faith is an affirmative way of using this Law, this Energy, this Force. Therefore, all scriptures have announced the necessity of having faith.

"Be ye transformed by the renewing of your mind." "Be renewed in the spirit of your mind." "Let this mind be in you which was also in Christ." "I will put my laws into your mind." "Hear, O earth, behold I will bring evil upon these people, even the fruits of their thoughts." "And he sent his word and healed them." "He forgetteth all thine iniquities; he healeth all thy diseases." "O Lord, my God, I cry unto thee and thou hast healed me." "Then shall thy light break forth as morning, and thine health shall speed forth speedily." "And it shall come to pass, that before they call, I will answer; and while they are yet speaking, I will hear." "I will take sickness away from the midst of thee." "The tongue of the wise is health." "Behold I will bring health . . . I will cure them . . ."

"Jesus turned him about, and when he saw her, he said, Daughter, be of good comfort; thy faith hath made thee whole. And the woman was made whole from that hour." "Then touched he their eyes, saying. According to your faith be it unto you. And their eyes were opened." "Heal the sick, cleanse the lepers, raise the dead, cast out devils: freely ye have received, freely give." "And great multitudes followed him, and he healed them all." "And the blind and the lame came to him in the temple, and he healed them."

In spiritual mind healing thought becomes a transmitter for Divine Power, therefore, the thought must always be kept free from confusion.

It is interesting to note that, while all the great scriptures of the ages concur about the nature of God and of man, and the relationship between the spiritual and the physical, outside the Christian scriptures very little is mentioned about healing or the control of conditions through the use of Divine Power, although they all agree that when the mind reflects the Divine Perfection, healing and prosperity follow.

In the Text of Taoism we find: "The still mind . . . is the mirror of heaven and earth . . ." "Maintain a perfect unity in every movement of your will. You will not wait for the hearing of your ears, but for the hearing of your mind. You will not wait even for the hearing of your mind, but for the hearing of the Spirit." "Purity and stillness give the correct law to all under heaven." And from the Koran: "The Lord of the worlds He hath created me and guideth me; He giveth me food and drink and when I am sick He healeth me." "And never Lord have I prayed to thee with ill success."

Jesus, the last of his particular line of prophets, was the first to introduce spiritual mind healing, and definitely to instruct his followers to practice it. People have been healed through all faiths, but the great healing shrines of the Christian belief have undoubtedly emphasized this more than most others, although we do find many instances of healing through all the various beliefs.

It is more particularly since the advent of what has been called "The New Thought," which started in America and has since spread throughout the world, that we find great emphasis placed upon spiritual healing.

This has been a sincere, earnest and effective attempt to get back to some of the first principles which Jesus taught. He sent out his disciples, telling them to heal the sick as a proof, not only of their Divine Power, but their Divine Authority, and he said, "Lo, I am with you alway." Since it is self-evident that Jesus, as a human being, could not be with them always, common sense compels us to accept that when he said, "I am with you alway," he was referring to the Divine Power, the Christ Principle, which he used.

To speak of the science of Jesus is no misnomer, for he certainly knew what he was doing, and repeatedly stated that his words acted as spiritual law. It might be said of Jesus that he was a practical idealist. He did not believe that the Kingdom of God is some far-off event; to him it was an ever-present reality; it was always at hand waiting merely to be perceived by the inner spiritual intuition, which is the voice of God operating through man.

"Faith without works is dead." Therefore, faith should be justified through manifestation, and if we have faith we can scientifically prove this. For, after all, science is the knowledge of universal principles and laws consciously applied for definite purposes.

There is a science of Mind and Spirit because there is a principle of Mind and Spirit. There is a possibility of using this science because we now understand how the laws of Mind and Spirit work in human affairs. The Principle of Mind operates through our thought, through our faith and conviction, and, most effectively, through an attitude of love, of compassion and of sympathy constructively used. It is impossible to make the highest use of the laws of Mind without basing such use of these laws upon inward spiritual perception, upon a conscious realization of the union of man with God.

When the physician and the metaphysician come better to understand each other they will more closely co-operate. It is self-evident that each is seeking to alleviate human suffering. No intelligent person would deny the need of physicians, surgeons and hospitals. On the other hand, it is generally agreed that a large percentage of our physical troubles are mental in their origin, and that all have some relationship to mental processes. It is most important, then, that the work of the sincere metaphysician should be both understood and appreciated.

It is not at all probable that the psychologist can take the place of the metaphysician, for just as the mere healing of the body, without an adjustment of the mental and emotional states, is insufficient, so the adjusting of mental and emotional states without introducing spiritual values will be ineffectual. Hence, there is an important place for the metaphysician, and his assistance should be sought.

Physician, metaphysician and psychologist should co-operate. There should be no sense of mistrust or criticism among them. The metaphysician should appreciate both the psychologist and the physician.

In the early days of spiritual therapeutics it was believed that one could not treat people mentally with success if they were being attended by a physician, or if they were using material methods for relief. Now we know that this idea was based on superstition. We no longer give it any serious thought. The metaphysician feels it a privilege to be called into consultation with a physician or with a psychologist. He has learned to appreciate the field of medicine and surgery.

The day is certain to come when the field of medicine will recognize, appreciate and co-operate with the metaphysical field. Even today this practice is far more common than the average person realizes. When the metaphysician stops making foolish statements or denying that his patient is ill, he will find a greater inclination toward recognition from the medical world.

Today most physicians recognize the power of thought in relation to the body. All realize the dynamic energy of the emotions. Psychiatric hospitals are being built and psychiatric wards are being added to hospitals already in existence. Just as psychology and psychiatry are being introduced into the medical world, so the metaphysical gradually will be understood, accepted and appreciated. Already many psychologists are affirming the necessity of introducing spiritual values into their practice. Who is going to meet this need unless it be the metaphysician?

Progress is inevitable and co-operation between all right-minded workers in the healing art is certain. Let us do all that we can to remove superstition, intolerance and bigotry which, after all, merely result in stupidity. We should unite in one common cause, not only to alleviate physical suffering but, in so far as possible, to remove its cause. If much of this cause lies hidden in the realm of mind, then surely those who are equipped to work in this realm are contributing their share to the meeting of a human need.

We believe in the control of conditions through the power of this Mind.

While all sacred writings affirm that when we are in harmony with the Infinite we are automatically prospered, the Christian scriptures lay greater stress on prosperity through spiritualizing the mind than any other of the bibles of the world. Our Bible, truly understood, is a book for the emancipation of man from the thralldom of every evil, every lack and limitation.

From the teaching of Moses, running through the thought of the major prophets and culminating in the brilliant manifestation of the Mind of Christ through the thought of Jesus, over and over this idea is reiterated—that if we live in harmony with the Spirit everything we do shall prosper.

Religious Science teaches that through right knowledge of the Science of Mind we may definitely and consciously demonstrate, that is, prove or show forth, practical results of spiritual thought.[5] Countless thousands have proved this principle and there is no longer any question about its effectiveness. The greatest guide we have for this is found in the inspired writings of the Christian scriptures.

"Prove me now herewith, saith the Lord of hosts, if I will not open to you the windows of heaven, and pour out a blessing, that there shall not be room enough to receive it." "And he shall pray unto God and he will be favorable unto him." "For every one that asketh receiveth; and he that seeketh findeth; and to him that knocketh it shall be opened."

---

[5] Read carefully the entire section on the control of conditions in *The Science of Mind* textbook.

"Ask, and it shall be given you." "And all things, whatsoever ye shall ask in prayer, believing, ye shall receive."

Whether we choose to call this faith or understanding makes no difference. It really is faith based upon understanding; it is belief elevated to the mental position of unconditioned certainty. For Jesus said that whoever could believe ". . . and shall not doubt in his heart, but shall believe that those things which he saith shall come to pass; he shall have whatsoever he saith. Therefore I say unto you, What things soever ye desire, when ye pray, believe that ye receive them, and ye shall have them."

Nothing could be more definite or concise than this statement. We must actually believe that there is a power, an intelligence, a law, which will make this desire manifest in our experience.

There is a Law of Mind which follows the patterns of our thought. This Law works automatically. It will always respond by corresponding. Thus Jesus said that it is done unto us as we believe. The word as is important since it implies that the creative Intelligence, in working for us, must work through us at the level of our acknowledgment of It as working. This is working in spirit and in truth, and according to law. And there must be law even in prayer, if there is to be cosmic order.

Man's mind has been likened to the "Workshop of God" for it is here that the tools of thought consciously may fashion destiny, may carve out a new future. We have been told to do this according to the pattern shown us on the Mount.

This means that we are to formulate our ideas on the premise that there is an all-sustaining Power and an all-pervading Presence around us, and an immutable Law ever serving us when our lives are in harmony with the Divine Nature. Through an exact law, demonstration follows the word of faith. This calls for a surrender of the intellect to a spiritual conviction which dares to believe, disregarding any evidence to the contrary.

We must continue in faith until our whole mental life, both conscious and subjective, responds. If we would pray and prosper we must believe that the Spirit is both willing and able to make the gift. But since the Spirit can only give us what we take, and since the taking is a mental act, we must train the mind to believe and to accept. This is the secret of the power of prayer.

One need not have great intellectual attainment to understand these simple things. Jesus said that the Kingdom of Heaven is reached through childlike faith. Again he said, "I thank thee, O Father . . . because thou hast hid these things from the wise and the prudent, and hast revealed them unto babes."

Just as the teachings of Jesus announce the Divine Presence, so his works prove the presence of a Law which received the impress of his word and brought it forth into form. He asked no authority other than that which was demonstrated through his act. Since Jesus taught the most definite system of spiritual thought ever given to the world, as well as the most simple and direct, and since he was able to prove his teaching by his works, we could do no better than to follow his example. There are two ways in which we may do this. One is blind faith, and we cannot doubt its effectiveness; the other is through coming to understand what the teachings of Jesus really meant. Thus knowledge passes into a faith so complete that it is unshakable.

Jesus left very implicit instructions relative to prayer. He said, "Judge not according to appearances." That is, do not be confused by the conditions around you. This is the first great instruction of Jesus—to have such faith and confidence in the Invisible that appearances no longer disturb you.

Next we come to the preparation for prayer. Having shut out all appearances to the contrary, enter the closet. To enter the closet means to withdraw into one's own thought, to shut out all confusion and discord. Here in the silence of the soul, look to the all-creative Wisdom and Power, to the ever-present Substance. When we have entered the closet and shut the door to outward appearances, we are to make known our requests—"what things soever ye desire."

Next Jesus tells us that we are to believe that we actually possess the objects of our desire, disregarding all appearances to the contrary. We are to enter into this invisible inheritance acting as though it were true. Our faith in the substance of the Invisible is to take actual form. The Divine Giver Himself is to make the gift but first we must believe that we have received it, and then we shall receive it—". . . believe that ye receive them, and ye shall have them."

This is a veiled statement of the Law of Cause and Effect operating in human affairs. When we have believed that we have, we have actually given birth to the form that is to be presented. Having made known our request with thanksgiving and received the answer with gratitude, we must rest assured that the Law will bring about the desired result.

"Thy Father which seeth in secret himself shall reward thee openly." Everything passes from the Invisible into the visible to be temporarily experienced and again to be withdrawn. This is the eternal play of Life upon Itself; the eternal act of creation. "Thy Father which seeth in secret himself shall reward thee openly." Rest in peace knowing that it is done. This profound principle which Jesus announced (and the simple technique of its use in which he counselled his followers) exists today in all of its fullness. It is the very cornerstone upon which our philosophy is built.

Even in divine communion we are dealing with the Law of Cause and Effect. Our prayer invokes this Divine Law and causes It to manifest in our external world at the level of our inner perception of Its working. Because this is true, prayer should always be definite, conscious and active.

Prayer ties us to a Power that is able, ready and willing to fulfill every legitimate desire; to bring every good thing to us; to do for us even more abundantly than we have expected. "Before they call, I will answer; and while they are yet speaking, I will hear." This shifting of the burden is important, for when we feel isolated, alone and struggling against tremendous odds, we are not equal to the task before us. Life becomes a drudgery rather than a jubilant beholding. But if we know the burden is lifted and set upon the shoulders of the Law, then power and speed come to hands and feet; joy floods the imagination with anticipation.

The reflection of an image in a mirror is an exact likeness of the image which is held before the mirror. So the Law of Cause and Effect reflects back to us a likeness of the images of our thought. Thus we are told that we reflect the glory of God. But too often we reflect the fear and limitation of man rather than the glory of God.

We must find new meanings to life if we hope to create new images which, in their turn, will supply new reflections. Jesus told us to judge not according to appearances but to judge righteously. If we judge only according to what is now transpiring, our reflection of these images will merely perpetuate the old limitation, but if we judge righteously, that is, if we look to the omnipotence of Good, we shall create new images of thought which will reflect greater abundance.

Prayer, then, is a mirror reflecting the images of our thought through the Law of Good into our outward experiences. What are we reflecting, the glory of God or the confusion of man? However, Jesus carefully pointed out that before we can reach this position of absolute power, we must first have complied with the Law of Love. For the whole impulsion of the universe is an impulsion of love, the manifestation of Divine Givingness.

The Apostle Paul said, "I will pray with the spirit and I will pray with the understanding also . . ." This is an instruction for us to combine spiritual intuition with definite mental acceptance. He is telling us that the gift of God is to be consciously used.

We are also told to pray without ceasing, to maintain a steadfast conviction, disregarding every apparent contradiction, obstruction or appearance that would deny the good we affirm. "But let him ask in faith, nothing wavering. For he that wavereth is like a wave of the sea driven with the wind and tossed." "To the righteous good shall be repaid." "The minds of the righteous shall stand." "Behold the righteous shall be recompensed in the earth." "The righteous is delivered of all trouble." A righteous man means one who is right with the universe; one who lives in accord with the Divine Will and the Divine Nature; one who lives in harmony with good.

We have the right then to expect, and we should expect, in so far as our inner thought is in tune with the Infinite, that everything we do shall prosper.

We believe in the eternal Goodness, the eternal Loving-kindness and the eternal Givingness of Life to all.

The Spirit gives Itself to everyone, the Power of God is delivered to all. "Whosoever will may come." No matter what the mistakes of our yesterdays may have been, we may transcend both the mistake and its consequence through imbibing the Spirit of Truth, which is the Power of God.

This does not mean that we may continue living in the mistake without suffering from it. We must transcend it. That is, we must transmute hate into love, fear into faith and a sense of separation into conscious union with good. When we have done this, the entire record of the past is blotted out and we are again free—freed with that freedom which the Almighty has ordained, and which man may claim as his own.

But liberty is not license and the Law of Life cannot be fooled. It is exact and exacting. "Therefore," Jesus said, "all things whatsoever ye would that men should do unto you, do ye even so to them." "Give, and it shall be given."

This is a statement of the Law of Cause and Effect which is invariable, immutable, but which is also the plaything both of God and man, for while the Law Itself cannot be broken, any particular sequence of cause and effect in It can be transcended. The same law which brought poverty, sickness and death, rightly used, will bring peace, wholeness, prosperity and life.

This is the great challenge of spiritual faith. The Christian philosophy bids us not to look with doleful introspection on previous errors, but coming daily to the Fountain of Life, to be renewed in mind, thought and spirit, we shall find that we also are renewed in bodily conditions and in physical affairs.

The Scripture boldly declares the triumph of the Spirit of Christ over all evil: Be ye transformed by the renewing of your mind; by the putting off of the old man and the putting on of the new man, which is Christ. "Lo, I am with you alway, even unto the end of the world."

We believe in our own soul, our own spirit and our own destiny; for we understand that the life of man is God.

Man is not only a center of God Consciousness; he is an immortal being, forever expanding, forever spiraling upward, forever growing in spiritual stature. Not some men, but all men are immortal, for everyone will finally overcome or transcend any misuse of the Law which he has made in his ignorance. Complete redemption at last must come, alike, to all.

What transformations must ensue, what change of consciousness must take place before this is finally brought about, the finite has not yet grasped, but through the whisperings of divine intuition we know that even though we now see as through a glass darkly, we shall some day behold Reality face to face. We shall be satisfied when we consciously awake in the likeness of that Divinity which shapes our ends.

"Beloved, now are we the sons of God, and it doth not yet appear what we shall be: but we know that, when he shall appear, we shall be like him; for we shall see him as he is." We are all in the process of spiritual evolution, but there is certainty behind us, certainty before us and certainty with us at every moment. The Eternal Light will break through wherever we permit It to.

Potentially, everything that is to be exists now, but our spiritual vision has not yet become completely in tune with the Infinite. This is the high task set before us as Religious Scientists, this is the deathless hope implanted in our mind by the Divine.

The trials and troubles of human experience; the blind groping of the finite toward the Infinite; the sickness, poverty, death, uncertainty, fear and doubt that accompany us, constitute the cross upon which we must offer, as a sacrifice to our ignorance, that which does not belong to the Kingdom of Good. But from this cross something triumphant will emerge, for, as Emerson said, "The finite alone has wrought and suffered; the infinite lies stretched in smiling repose."

Shall we not, then, with joy, go forth to meet the new day, endeavoring so to embody the Spirit of Christ that the Divine in us shall rise triumphant, resurrected, to live forever in the City of God? More could not be asked than that which the Divine has already delivered; less should not be expected.

APPENDIX

Professor Max Muller, one of the greatest European Orientalists and author of *The Sacred Books of the East,* has well said that "the true religion of the future will be the fulfillment of all the religions of the past. . . . All religions, so far as I know them, had the same purpose; all were links in a chain which connects heaven and earth; and which is held, and always was held, by one and the same hand. All here on earth tends toward right and truth, and perfection; nothing here on earth can ever be quite right, quite true, quite perfect, not even Christianity—or what is called Christianity—so long as it excludes all other religions, instead of loving and embracing what is good in each."

Like many other religions of antiquity, the origin of Taoism is more or less obscure. According to some authorities it is said to have begun around 600 B.C. which antedates Confucius, who was born in 551 B.C. The world generally associates Taoism with Lao-Tze, a Chinese metaphysical philosopher who was fifty-three years older than Confucius. It was this philosopher who must have gathered together these teachings. Archdeacon Hardwick tells us that the Chinese word "Tao" ". . . was adopted to denominate an abstract cause, or the initial principle of life and order, to which worshippers were able to assign the attribute of immateriality, eternity, immensity, invisibility."

The Upanishads, the Vedas, the Mahabharata, the Raja Yoga philosophy, as well as the Bhagavad-Gita, are all drawn from the ancient wisdom of India.

The philosophy of Buddha, who was born in the sixth century B.C., is too well known to need any comment.

The Sacred Book of the Parsis is called the Zend-Avesta, which is a collection of fragments of ideas that prevailed in ancient Persia, five years before the Christian era and for several centuries afterwards.

The Book of the Dead is a series of translations of the ancient Egyptian hymns and religious texts. They were found on the walls of tombs, in coffins and in papyri. Like many other sacred traditions, there probably were no written copies in the earlier days; they were committed to memory and handed down from generation to generation.

Some students believe that the books of Hermes Trismegistus, which means "the thrice greatest," originally derived from ancient Egyptian doctrine. Hermes was a Greek god, son of Zeus and Maia, daughter of Atlas. To Hermes was attributed the authorship of all the strictly sacred books generally called by Greek authors, Hermetic. (*Encyclopaedia Britannica*) According to some scholars, the Egyptian Hermes "was a symbol of the Divine Mind; he was the incarnated Thought, the living Word—the primitive type of the Logos of Plato and the Word of the Christians . . ."

Fragments of a Faith Forgotten are taken from the Gnostics, those "who used the Gnosis as the means to set their feet upon the Way of God." Gnosticism was pre-Christian and originated in the ancient religion and philosophy of Greece, Egypt, and Jewry.

According to H. Polano, the Talmud contains ". . . the thoughts . . . of a thousand years of the national life of the Jewish people."

The Koran is the sacred book of the Mohammedans, consisting of revelations orally delivered at intervals by Mohammed and collected in writing after his death. (*Oxford English Dictionary*) The Koran is considered one of the most important of the world's sacred books.

The Apocrypha refers to a collection of ancient writings. The Greek word "Apocryphos" was originally used of books the contents of which were kept hidden, or secret, because they embodied the special teaching of religious or philosophical sects; it was only the members of these sects who were initiated into the secrets of this teaching. (*Encyclopaedia Britannica*)

PRAY AND PROSPER

PRAY AND PROSPER

What is prayer? We pray either to an Infinite Mind or an Omnipotent Power. Prayer is always some form of communion with the Universal.

It reaches its highest possibility when it rises above the limitations of any existing circumstance. This is why Jesus told his followers not to judge by appearances. Jesus did not deny the appearance, he merely said do not accept it as the only criterion. How could anyone arrive at such a faith unless he knew that he was dealing with a Power which can rearrange facts and create new ones?

A belief in the Invisible is the very essence of faith. Prayer, or spiritual communion, demands a complete surrender to the Invisible. It knows that because the Creative Power of God is at hand, all things are possible. Man is powerful because he deals with Power. He may become wise because he is immersed in Wisdom. Thus he has an inexhaustable Source from which to draw.

Whatever our idea of God may be, the perception of Reality is always an inner perception. As Moses tells us, the word is not afar off but in our own mouths, and Jesus, that the Kingdom of Heaven is within. The prayer of power is not so much a petition as it is an inner recognition.

We cannot doubt that the Spirit has already made the gift of Life—since we live. Ours is the privilege of acceptance. Thus we are to assume the attitude of a greatful beneficiary of the Divine gifts. This should be done simply and directly. The Spirit is not something that was, or that is going to be or become. The Truth is that which is; it exists at the very center of our being. To pray in spirit and in truth means to recognize this indwelling Spirit and to declare the truth about Its activity through us.

God is not popr, weak, sick or unhappy. God is not impoverished, limited or in bondage. It is this Spirit to which we pray, the Reality which we approach at the center of our own being. It is the Silent Partner in every man's life—a wise and loving Presence ever ready to respond to us. Since we neither created this Presence nor incarnated It within us, there is nothing we can do but accept It. Jesus said, "Ye must be born again." The second birth is a birth from appearances to Reality. Robert Browning said. "There is an inmost center in all of us where Truth abides in fullness."

The purpose of prayer, or spiritual communion, is to seek conscious union with this indwelling Presence. Jesus claimed that the words he spoke were not his but were the activity of the Spirit within him. Since there is but One Mind this must be true. It is impossible to lose this "imprisoned splendor" unless we comply with Its nature, which must be Truth, Harmony, and Wholeness.

Hate, disunion, fear and uncertainty may knock at the door of Reality; only peace can enter. This is the peace to which Jesus referred when he said, ". . . not as the world giveth, give I unto you. Let not your heart be troubled, neither let it be afraid." Peace is at the very center of our being. Sometimes we arrive merely at a partial unity with Spirit. At other times we more completely enter into the contemplation of Reality. Always our prayer will be as effective as is the realization generated in the act of communion. Thus our words become "clothed upon" with the living Presence of an invisible Power ever projecting Itself into form through our meditation.

There is a Law of Mind which follows the pattern of our thought. This Law works automatically. It is a mechanical law and a mathematical one. It is the Law of Cause and Effect. We should not have any anxious thought concerning the operation of this Law; It will always respond by corresponding. Thus Jesus said that it is done unto us as we believe. The word as is important since it implies that the Creative Intelligence, in working for us, must work through us at the level of our acknowledgment of It as working. This is praying in spirit and in truth, and according to law. And there must be law even in prayer, if there is to be Cosmic order.

Spiritual communion is deeper than intellectual perception. The prayer of the intellect may be perfect in form; but this form must be warmed and colored by feeling and conviction. The Bible refers both to the "letter" and the "spirit" of the Law. It implies that both are necessary. That is, we should not only state our word definitely, but we must believe it sincerely, deeply. Paul tells us to be transformed by the renewing of the mind. We must cast off the intellectual doubt which affirms that things must continue as they always have been. We must enter into a deep, spiritual communion with Reality, realizing that a new creation is taking place through our consciousness. This judgment may be contrary to appearances, but it is nevertheless a true judgment.

Man's mind has been likened to the "Workshop of God" for it is here that the tools of thought consciously may fashion destiny, may carve out a new future. We have been told to do this according to the pattern shown us in the Mount. This means that we are to formulate our ideas on the proposition that there is an all-sustaining Power and an all-pervading Presence around us, and an immutable Law ever serving us when our lives are in harmony with the Divine Nature. Through an exact law, demonstration follows the word of faith. This law is a law of polarity, of reflection, of cause and effect. It is written that "I will be to them as they have spoken." Again, "Be firm and ye shall be made firm." "Act as though I am, and I will be." This calls for a surrender of the intellect to a spiritual conviction which dares to believe, disregarding any evidence to the contrary.

We must continue in faith until our whole mental life, both conscious and subjective, responds. If we would pray and prosper we must believe that the Spirit is both willing and able to make the gift. But since the Spirit can only give us what we take, and since the taking is a mental act, we must train the mind to believe and accept. This is the secret of the power of prayer.

One need not have great intellectual attainment to understand these simple things. Jesus said that the Kingdom of Heaven is reached through childlike faith. Again he said, "I thank thee, Father . . . because thou hast hid these things from the wise and the prudent, and hast revealed them unto babes." Everything that Jesus said and did was said and done to provide an example for our benefit. His whole life and teaching was to describe the nature of Reality. All of his works, which have been miscalled miracles, were to prove that his teaching was correct. He asked those around him whether it was easier to announce a philosophy or to prove it. They had been arguing about his spiritual authority and he asked them ". . . whether it is easier to say, Thy sins be forgiven thee; or to say, Arise and walk." And that they might know that "the Son of man hath power on earth to forgive sins," he said to the man with palsy, "Arise, take up thy bed, and go unto thine house."

Just as the teachings of Jesus announce the Divine Presence, so his works prove the presence of a Law which received the impress of his word and brought it forth into form. He asked no authority other than that which was demonstrated through his act. Since Jesus taught the most definite system of spiritual thought ever given to the world, as well as the most simple and direct, and since he was able to prove his teaching by his works, we could do no better than to follow his example.

There are two ways in which we may do this. One is blind faith, and we cannot doubt its effectiveness; the other is through coming to understand what the teachings of Jesus really meant. Thus knowledge passes into a faith so complete that it is unshakable.

Jesus gave specific instructions for prayer. He likened the Divine Spirit to a Heavenly Father, and he placed the Kingdom of this Spirit at the center of Man's being.

Our Father which art in heaven. The God Principle within us; the eternal Truth within us; the everlasting Presence within us.

Hallowed be thy name. Thy name is perfect; It is the all-inclusive name of the "I am" beside which there is none other. It is the One, Only and All which includes everything that was, is, or is to be. The same yesterday, today and forever.

Thy kingdom come. Thy will be done in earth, as it is in heaven. When the Kingdom of God is perceived and the Will and Nature of God understood, then shall the Power within us recreate and control our environment after the pattern of Wholeness and Abundance. When that which is without shall be controlled by that which is within; when the Kingdom of God comes on earth among men, It will heal all nations of sickness, war and poverty, for the Kingdom of God is Wholeness, Unity and Peace.

Give us this day our daily bread. This is an acknowledgment that Substance forever takes form in our affairs as "manna from heaven." "Give us this day our daily bread." This is meant to include everything we shall ever need, whether it be a house to live in, an automobile to ride in (in our day), a suit of clothes to wear, bread to eat and butter to put on the bread. It includes, according to the words of Jesus, "what things soever ye desire." We must, however, be certain that the desire is consistent with the nature of Reality; and we may be certain that if our desire is toward a greater degree of livingness for ourselves and others, and harms no one, then it is the Divine Will. "Give us this day our daily bread," includes everything we can ever need—friendship, love, beauty, peace, poise and power—for God in not only All, He is All-in-all and through all.

And forgive us our debts, as we forgive our debtors. We might say with Shakespeare, "There's the rub," for it is a bold statement that mere protestations do not suffice. We must actually partake of the Divine Nature if we are to portray It. We must forgive if we are to be forgiven, we must love if we would be loved. "Give, and it shall be given unto you; good measure, pressed down, and shaken together, and running over, shall men give into your bosom." And we must not overlook another statement of Jesus, "Judge not, that ye be not judged. For with what judgment ye judge, ye shall be judged; and with what measure ye mete, it shall be measured to you again." Once more, there's the rub: do we forsake all animosity in our desire to surrender our entire being to love? Jesus plainly tells us that it is useless to lay our gifts upon the altar while our own mind is diseased with animosity and with strife. "Forgive us our debts, as we forgive our debtors." This is the Law of Cause and Effect. There is no escape from it.

And lead us not into temptation, but deliver us from evil. The All-Creative Truth can never lead us into temptation, but an acknowledgment of Its presence and a desire to embody Its essence delivers us from every form of evil. "He shall give his angels charge over thee to keep thee in all thy ways."

For thine is the kingdom, and the power, and the glory, for ever. The Kingdom, the Power and the Glory of Reality never change. They are always the same, ever available, unwavering, consistent. The glory of Truth, the kingdom of Reality and the power of Law are ever with us. It is also written that "as many as received him, to them gave he the power." That is, to those who embody and acknowledge the nature of Reality, is given the power to portray It. Not only to drink from the well-springs of life but to pass the refreshing draught to others. Jesus very definitely taught that when we have complied with the Divine Nature, then we shall have a power at our command which will be irresistible. His teaching was so simple and yet so profound; so quiet and yet so dynamic, it will yet revolutionize human conduct.

Jesus left very implicit instructions relative to prayer. It was one of the customs at that time for people to stand at the street corners and pray, using a loud voice, petitioning God with vehemence, screaming their affirmations, proclaiming their denunciations; sometimes in wrath, sometimes in fear, and sometimes with reverence. This rather boisterous and noisy approach to the Spirit did not disturb Jesus. With a calm sense that every man is rewarded according to his own consciousness, disregarding what his particular method may be, Jesus said, "Verily I say unto you, They have their reward." What magnificent understanding! What depth of reason! What profound insight into Reality! Jesus did not condemn, but in teaching his more intimate followers, those to whom he said it was given "to know the mysteries of the kingdom," Jesus counselled another approach, calm, simple, direct, and childlike.

First of all he said, "Judge not according to appearances." That is, do not be confused by the conditions around you. The waves may be turbulent and the boat storm tossed. This appearance is real enough, but do not be confused over it. "Be still, and know that I am God." This is the supreme test. "Judge not according to appearances." They may appear dismal and forlorn, or as hideous monsters rising out of the deep, but I shall command them to be still, "It is I who speak unto you." The inner Spirit is proclaiming Its own nature; It is announcing Its own program.

This is the first great instruction of Jesus—to have such faith and confidence in the Invisible that appearances no longer disturb you. Are there five thousand people waiting to be fed and only a basketful of loaves and fishes, brought by a small boy for his own lunch, as he sat listening in wonder to the words this man spoke as man never spake before? Jesus did not say: Send the multitude home! But with confidence and faith he calmly said, in substance, "Let them be seated; make them comfortable; remove their fear; break down the barriers; let us bless the bread and the fish; and let the Lord of the Harvest increase the supply and feed the famished." Jesus was not afraid when they brought the insane boy to him. Calmly he spoke to his troubled thought and stilled the strife that was raging in the mind of the demented. This, then, is the first great lesson—"Judge not according to appearances."

Next we come to the preparation for prayer. Having shut out all appearances to the contrary, enter the closet. Jesus was not referring to any physical room or hiding place. To enter the closet means to withdraw into one's own thought, to shut out all confusion and discord. Here is the silence of the soul look to the All-Creative Wisdom and Power, to the ever-present Substance. When we have entered the closet and shut the door to outward appearances, we are to make known our requests—"what things soever ye desire."

Next Jesus tells us that we are to believe that we actually possess the objects of our desire, disregarding all appearances to the contrary. We are to enter into this invisible inheritance acting as though it were true. Our faith in the substance of the Invisible is to take actual form. The Divine Giver Himself is to make the gift, but first we must believe that we have received it, and then we shall receive it—". . . believe that ye receive them, and ye shall have them." This is a veiled statement of the Law of Cause and Effect operating in human affairs. When we have believed that we have, we have actually given birth to the form that is to be presented. Having made known our request with thanksgiving and received the answer with gratitude, we must rest assured that the Law will bring about the desired result.

"Thy Father which seeth in secret himself shall reward thee openly." Everything passes from the Invisible into the visible to be temporarily experienced and again to be withdrawn. This is the eternal play of Life upon Itself; the eternal act of creation. "Thy Father which seeth in secret himself shall reward thee openly." Rest in peace knowing that it is done. This profound principle which Jesus announced (and the simple technique of its use in which he counselled his followers) exists today in all of its fullness. It is the very cornerstone upon which our philosophy is built.

Suppose we call this prayer a treatment, and its answer a demonstration. Would it not logically follow that, since the law which Jesus announced when he said, "what things soever ye desire," is a law of reflection, each treatment or prayer should be definite? In every case, one would have to convince himself that whatever is specified in his treatment or prayer will be brought about. Thus each one becomes inspired by the Divine Presence and specializes the Creative Principle for his individual use or for the use of others.

The following examples of the possibility of prayer, merely suggest certain ways in which this may be accomplished.

PRAYER IS MIND IN ACTION

Prayer is a thing of thought and feeling, therefore, it is Mind in action. God is Infinite Knowingness. We cannot explain creation on any basis other than that this Infinite Knowingness, moving as Law, produces form. The mathematics of this Mind must be exact.

Prayer is a movement through our consciousness upon the universe itself. It is the Law of Mind in action. Whenever our acceptance makes it possible, there will be an answer to our prayer which will mathematically correspond to the use we have been making of this Law of Mind. Jesus tells us that when we comply with the Law it is done unto us as we believe. We cannot doubt that Jesus was teaching the Law of Mind in action; the exercise of the God Power within us as a mathematical sequence of cause and effect.

Since prayer is Mind in action, we must be certain that the thoughts running through our prayers are those of exalted acceptance; of complete fulfillment, here and now.

PRAYER INVOKES THE MENTAL LAW

Even in divine communion we are dealing with the Law of Cause and Effect. Our prayer invokes this Divine Law and causes It to manifest in our external world at the level of our inner perception of Its working. Because this is true, prayer should always be definite, conscious and active.

When we plant a garden we invoke the creative fertility of the soil for definite purposes; we specialize its creative action that it may fulfill specific desires. And in the greater garden of the soul, the garden of the Life Principle Itself, where we deal with thoughts and ideas as seeds, we should follow the same pattern.

We should never forget that all physical nature is merely an out-picturing of the Invisible Cause which gives rise to it. Thus we are told to make known our requests with thanksgiving. But this is also a definite state. Not only should we assume the position of a thankful receiver, we should also assume the intelligent position of one who makes known his concrete requests. "What things soever ye desire" should consciously be accepted. In this way we invoke the Law of Cause and Effect for specific purposes. In this way the Law, which is the servant of the Lord, serves us. This is Its nature. This is the will of the Divine Being.

PRAYER AS COMMUNION

Communion is not petition; it is an inward sense of Reality; it is something we sense, feel and respond to. We have a good illustration of this in Moses at the burning bush. All nature, as Browning tells us, is alive, awake and aware with the potent Presence.

Communion is entering into conscious union with the essence of things. When we commune with nature she speaks to us, as the poet has suggested, in various ways. The burning bush spoke to Moses and proclaimed the presence of God. He realized he was on holy ground—all nature became animated with the Divine. Everywhere he looked he saw God. This is communion.

We must learn to commune with the indwelling Spirit; to feel Its presence; to sense Its power and to respond to Its influence. This is entirely a thing of feeling.

SPIRITUAL IDENTIFICATION THROUGH COMMUNION

We all know that it is impossible for one to become successful unless he first identifies himself with success. The great identification is with the "I Am" in the midst of our being. "The Lord thy God in the midst of thee, is mighty" to heal and to prosper.

If we wish love and friendship we must identify ourselves with them; we must embody them in our thinking. Spirit is the great actor, the final Cause of everything. It is with this inner Spirit that we commune. This is the meaning of prayer; to commune with the Spirit which is already within us; to identify ourselves with It, following which we automatically project this identification into our experience. The effect of the old mistakes is wiped out; old memory images are loosened until their content no longer harms. We are identified with the stream of accomplishment, the certainty that spiritual laws guide and protect us; and no evil can befall this identification. This act of spiritual identification, through conscious communion, is one of the supreme accomplishments of the soul.

SHIFTING THE BURDEN

Bunyan tells us in *The Pilgrim's Progress* that burdens drop from our shoulders as we scale the heights. The burden falls back into the slough of despond from which we have so recently emerged in our upward climb. Spiritual communion has this effect upon us. As consciousness ascends in realization, burdens gradually loosen themselves and roll backward, disappearing into the oblivion of their native nothingness. Thus prayer shifts the burden by entering into partnership with the Divine.

Prayer ties us to a Power that is able, ready and willing to fulfill every legitimate desire; to bring every good thing to us; to do for us even more abundantly than we have expected. ". . . before they call, I will answer; and while they are yet speaking, I will hear." This shifting of the burden is important for when we feel isolated, alone and struggling against tremendous odds, we are not equal to the task before us. Life becomes a drudgery rather than a jubilant beholding. But if we know the burden is lifted and set upon the shoulders of the Law, then power and speed come to hands and feet; joy floods the imagination with anticipation. We must learn to shift the burden to the perfect Law.

THE SECRET PLACE OF
THE MOST HIGH

Where is the Secret Place of the Most High other than in our own consciousness? It is written that "he that dwelleth in the secret place of the most High shall abide under the shadow of the Almighty." The word "shadow" is used because it suggests protection: the refreshing coolness of the shadow of a rock in a desert place. The shadow of the Almighty means a place of protection, a place of peace. But before we reach this place of protection we must dwell in the Secret Place of the Most High.

Since Spirit is everywhere present, It must be where we are. Therefore the Secret Place of the Most High is not a place at all but a state of consciousness, a contemplation of Reality.

The Secret Place of the Most High is at the center of our own being, where in silence we wait on Spirit and permit the Perfect Law to fulfill our desire. This is waiting upon the Lord. We permit the Divine images of perfection to flow through our consciousness, reflecting themselves through the Law of Cause and Effect into our objective conditions.

There is no confusion in this Secret Place; none can enter It for us; none can prohibit Its entrance to us. The door is always open, the gate ever ajar. The Secret Place of the Most High is a place of light, of illumination, of poise and assurance. It is a place of rest.

PRAYER AS A TRANSFORMING POWER

Silent contemplation of the Divine Presence transmutes lower energies into higher ones. This transmutation of the lower into the higher, a quest of the alchemists of old, is now recognized in the science of psychology. It is called "sublimation" which means transforming chaotic energies of the psyche into constructive outlets of self-expression. If this can be done on a psychological basis, how much more certain it is that the transforming power of spiritual vision will transmute every negation into a positive affirmation.

Prayer can convert disease into health, poverty into wealth, misery into happiness. It can transmute our beliefs in the devil, or evil, into a picture of an Angel of Light, a guardian angel ever protecting us, forever going before and preparing the way; forever making perfect, plain and immediate the way; forever announcing, "I am the way, the truth and the life." This transforming power of silent communion is manifest as our spiritual vision looks up and not down.

THE WORD OF POWER

"He taught them as one having authority, and not as the scribes." In silent communion with the Infinite, we create a consciousness of power through the recognition of the Divine Presence. Jesus said all Power is delivered unto the Son. Prayer is a conscious acceptance of this Power; a joyful recognition of the Divine Presence; a grateful acknowledgment of protection and guidance, of wholeness and of peace. All Power is given unto the Son. Prayer enables us to contact this Power and to make definite use of It for beneficent purposes, to heal to prosper, to make happy, to reveal the wholeness in everything.

Every man has this Power. Plotinus spoke of it as a power which all men possess, but which few use. The Bible tells us to stir up the gift that is within us. We must enter into the consciousness of power. This is done through silent recognition, acknowledgment, acceptance and definite projection. Prayer not only receives the Divine Power, it projects it into manifestation. Prayer directs the Invisible Power for definite purposes. It does this by acknowledging the Power and by accepting that It has no opposites. Nothing hinders Spirit; nothing limits the Infinite; there are no obstructions to It. We are told that this Power breaks down the iron doors, and the gates of brass. It penetrates every apparently solid object; It dissolves every obstruction; It creates every desired form. Such is the dynamic power of this silent communion with Reality.

PRAYER REFLECTS

The reflection of an image in a mirror is an exact likeness of the image which is held before the mirror. So the Law of Cause and Effect reflects back to us a likeness of the images of our thought. Thus we are told that we reflect the glory of God. But too often we reflect the fear and limitation of man rather than the glory of God.

We must find new meanings to life if we hope to create new images which, in their turn, will supply new reflections. Jesus told us to judge not according to appearances but to judge righteously. If we judge only according to what is now transpiring, our reflection of these images will merely perpetuate the old limitation, but if we judge righteously, that is, if we look into the omnipotence of Good, we shall create new images of thought which will reflect greater abundance.

Prayer, then, is a mirror reflecting the images of our thought through the Law of good into our outward experiences. What are we reflecting, the glory of God or the confusion of man?

CONCENTRATION AND VISUALIZATION IN PRAYER

Prayer does not concentrate Substance, it merely focalizes our attention upon It. The Spirit is already omnipresent. We do not gather the principle of mathematics together and pile it up or concentrate it for our use; we merely draw upon it. So it is in the act of prayer. It is attention and not concentration; willingness and not will.

The very idea that we must concentrate something suggests coercion. It suggests a reluctance on the part of the Law or the Spirit in its response to us. It suggests laborious effort. The Spirit never exerts effort, It merely remolds Itself in the form of Its own desire, and immediately experiences the form, because It reflects Its own glory in the law of Its own Being. There is nothing to concentrate, nothing to force, nothing to argue with, nothing to oppose.

If we wish to demonstrate that prayer or spiritual communion is a potent force, we must believe that both Energy and Divine Action are at our disposal; that the Creative Genius of the universe is already wherever we focus our attention. We must permit rather than petition.

PRAYER REMOVES TENSION

Spiritual communion is relaxing. There is neither stress nor strain in it. All the yesterdays of fear and failure are dropped from consciousness; today everything is filled with peace and joy. Jesus said, "My yoke is easy, and my burden is light." The Spirit has no burden, creates none and enters into none. As Emerson said, "It is the finite alone that has wrought and suffered, the Infinite lies stretched in smiling repose."

Spiritual communion is letting go of all negation; a reaching out and up toward freedom, wholeness and happiness. It is a calm, inward sense of Reality. There is no struggle, no tension, only peace. Since we are dealing with a power which can easily accomplish our desired good and give to us more abundantly even than we are able to receive, there should be no sense of compulsion, but rather a relaxed, yet an attentive and active, acceptance. All anxiety is dropped by the wayside.

Over-anxiety is one of the most negative states of mind we can experience. It is a complete denial of the Divine Beneficence, a feeling that the entire burden of life rests upon our shoulders. Spiritual communion relieves this tension, automatically straightens out the consciousness. Through recognition, acknowledgment and receptivity it readjusts the psychic stream of life. It frees the pent-up emotions and causes them to become sublimated or transformed into the energy of light, of power and of self-expression. Jesus tells us to take no anxious thought for the morrow. All of our tomorrows are still unborn; every day should view a new creation, a world more blessed than yesterday.

Anxiousness and anxiety arise from a sense of uncertainty of the future, not from frustrations of the past. We are to take no anxious thought for tomorrow. This does not mean that we are to act in an irresponsible or chaotic manner. It merely means that we are to live this day in calm confidence of the future. All of our memories of the past will be healed and all the pent-up energies of unexpressed desires will flow out from us in joyful expression, if our communion with nature and with the Spirit becomes complete. This is why quiet and secluded spots tend to rest us. But the only quiet and secluded spot in all the universe is at the center of our own being where pure Spirit reigns supreme.

PRAYER CONVERTS SUBSTANCE INTO ACTION AND SUPPLY

If we would pray and prosper we should realize that we are surrounded by a spiritual Substance which is forever taking the form of supply. Wherever we look we should see right action. Spiritual communion enables us to do this. It lifts our thought above the solid fact of a situation or circumstance. It resolves the fact into a fluid and remolds it into a new form; straightens out the lines of our energy, into harmonious currents of self-expression.

There is but one final Essence, which is pure Spirit. The act of prayer in spiritual communion lifts the consciousness into a perception of this Essence flowing out into action. At the center of everything there is Something which never moves, and yet all movement takes place within It. There is Something which Itself is not caused but from which all effect flows. Therefore Essence is both cause and effect. It is the actor, act and action.

Everything moves in circles, and when we silently contemplate the invisible Essence moving in our affairs, we shall discover that our thought comes back to us laden with the fruits of our expectation.

Some of the ancients spoke of the Karmic Law, or what today we call the Law of Cause and Effect, as the result of the fruits of our action. If we would have these fruits abundant, we must think of the Essence as forever passing into form; forever flowing around us, pressing against us, flowing out into everything we do; flowing into health, happiness and prosperity.

PRAYER IN ACTION

Evelyn Underhill tells us that our lives should swing between prayer, meditation and action. We used to pray, "Now I lay me down to sleep, I pray the Lord my soul to keep; if I should die before I wake, I pray the Lord my soul to take." Someone has suggested that we add to this beautiful evening prayer one for the new day: "Now I get me up to work, I pray the Lord I shall not shirk; if I should die before the night, I pray the Lord my work's done right."

It is not intended that we should spend all of our time in inaction, for the very law of our being is Mind acting. An active thought will always find itself surrounded with intelligent, objective activities. The passing of human events is no mere illusion, it is a logical and legitimate activity of Mind finding fulfillment. It is the action of a "jubilant and beholding soul" proclaiming God's works to be good. Every act should become a prayer, as Brother Lawrence so beautifully expressed in his life, which was the conscious practicing of the Divine Presence.

If God is in all events, then we should go forth gladly to meet them. Not only in the stillness of the evening, or the quiet of midnight, but also in the rising tide of human endeavor when the spiritual sun climbs high, flooding the earth with its effulgent glory, is the presence of God revealed.

JOY AND ENTHUSIASM

It has been said that joy infuses the commonplace with a creative activity. Emerson said the only thing he learned about grief was its emptiness. Jesus spoke of the joy which he had and which he desired his disciples to have, that their joy might be full. There is a song at the center of everything. The music of the spheres is no illusion. We must uncover the song and permit it to saturate our souls with joy.

Enthusiasm is the most creative of all the imaginative faculties. There is something light, unobstructed, weightless about it. We cannot associate the Spirit with sadness or depression. The very thought of the "Fountain of Life" suggests something gushing forth, bubbling up from a subterranean passage, whose flow is irresistible. It is no wonder that the ancients said that the wind whispers, the leaves clap their hands and the morning stars sing together. We are told that the shepherds heard this celestial music, the angelic chorus singing "Peace on earth, good will toward men."

Spiritual communion will cause the angels of our better self to sing, making our consciousness happy. Spiritual communion is not a droll affair, it is not a wailing wall, it is the triumphant procession of the soul into the Secret Place of the Most High, where the scroll of life is taken from the Ark of the Covenant, on which are inscribed the joyous words, "I am the Lord thy God in the midst of thee."

THE PRAYER OF THANKSGIVING

"Enter into his gates with thanksgiving"; "Make a joyfull noise unto the Lord"; "Bless the Lord, O my soul: and all that is within me, bless his holy name."

We are told to make known our requests with thanksgiving, and why shouldn't we be greatfull when we realize that the Divine gift is forever made? Why shouldn't our spirits rise in joyful praise to the Life Principle which has delivered Its entire nature to us, witholding nothing?

We know that when we praise animals they respond to us. We know that when we praise children they co-operate with us. Since the intelligence operating through animal and child responds to praise and thanksgiving, why shouldn't everything respond in like manner? There is but one Spirit in all things.

When we condemn any physical organ, we retard the circulation of the life forces through it. Therefore, Jesus tells us to judge not that we be not judged. We should praise every organ of the body—"Bless the Lord, O my soul; and all that is within me, bless his holy name." We should bless the action and the reaction of the life forces that flow through the body. We should bless everything that we do; everyone we meet, every letter we write, every person we think of, every incident that comes into our imagination. The desert is made to bloom and blossom as the rose, by blessing it with the presence of seed, water, personal attention and cultivation. The music of the spheres is heard only by those who listen—not with an ear dulled by condemnation and censure, but with praise and thanksgiving.

THE SELF-CREATIVE ENERGY OF PRAYER

Dr. Carrel, in an article on prayer, has suggested that faith is a luminous and self-creative energy. Faith lays hold of a Power which is not only creative, but which creates out of Its own being. It is self-energizing.

The creative energy of Spirit must be limitless. Therefore we can set no limit to the possibility of what it can do for us. Undoubtedly It is able to give us infinitely more than we have expected, understood or accepted. We must believe that It will not only make the gift, It will also, out of Its own energy, out of Its own power, out of Its own Being, create the way, the method and the means through which the gift is to come to us.

This is the Reality with which prayer deals. Infinite in Its possibility, ever ready to respond, the Creative Spirit awaits our recognition. We must learn to have faith, to walk in the light.

THE FIELD OF FAITH

Wherever people meet together for prayer and spiritual communion, a field of faith is created which reacts upon everyone who enters it. An atmosphere of Reality has been recognized; a new vibratory law has been set in motion. It is easy to break one twig, but if we bind many twigs together they become unbreakable. In group consciousness, the individual faith of each member is strengthened through union with all the others. "In union there is strength," is just as true in our mental life as it is in the body of our affairs.

Always we should seek the companionship of those whose faith may be added to ours. Thought atmospheres are real enough. We sense them in the quiet of the cathedral or at shrines where countless thousands have gathered with uplifted faith, seeking communion with the Eternal Reality. Thus the power of one is multiplied through combining it with the power of others. This is not because the Spirit listens to many more than to just one, but because often many create a larger hope and a greater expectancy. They develop a real dynamic field of faith.

PRAYER AND RECOGNITION

The art of prayer arrives at a point of certainty when it recognizes the gift even before it is made. In the creative order everything passes from the invisible into the visible through the act of idea manifesting itself as form. Therefore Jesus told his followers to pray, believing that they had and they would receive.

Recognition is an image of acceptance held in mind until the condition accepted appears either in the body or in the affairs. We are either accepting or rejecting at all times. We are either recognizing the Divine Principle as goodness or as evil. We cannot be too careful in studying to attain recognition. This really means that we must look into what appears to be empty space, into a void, and see a solid rock upon which the feet of faith may be planted. Always the rock appears out of the void through recognition.

The reason for this is plain. Everything Jesus said and did was descriptive of the Divine Nature and of the Law of Cause and Effect. He knew how things work from the invisible to the visible, and when he told us to recognize and accept, he knew what he was talking about. We must learn to recognize the gift even before it is made.

PRAYER AS PETITION

". . . nevertheless not my will, but thine, be done." This petition is not to a far-away God who may or may not respond. It is the recognition of the Divine Presence which is always ready and willing to respond. True prayer always says, "Thy will be done." An intelligent perspective of Truth recognizes that the Will of God and the Nature of the Divine Being are identical. God cannot will anything other than perfection; God cannot will anything other than abundance; God cannot will anything other than goodness, truth and beauty.

Submission to a superior Intelligence, not to an opposing power. Our request is made as to a friend who we know is both able and willing to respond. Therefore, the petition becomes a joyful recognition of the fact that "before they call I will answer." "Father, I thank thee that thou hast heard me. And I knew that thou hearest me always"—these words of Jesus give us an example of petition and acceptance.

It is the recognition of the Spirit as a Friend, and the acceptance that this Friend acts in our behalf immediately, and with power, that brings the answer. Do we not pray for a harvest when we plant the seed? Are not seed time and harvest two ends of one law of cause and effect? Petition and acceptance are two ways of recognizing the Divine Giving which says, "Son, thou art ever with me, and all that I have is thine."

PRAYER AS A SCIENCE

We should not think it strange to speak of prayer as scientific. Science is a knowledge of laws and causes. The principle of any science has always existed. The discovery of such a principle and the gradual accumulation of facts relative to it, prepare the way for a technique for its use.

This is also true of prayer. We know that throughout the ages, at all times and under all situations, prayers have been answered by some invisible Agency which apparently is no respecter of persons, times, races, creeds or cultures, but which forevermore proclaims, "Whosoever will, may come."

The Agency which answers prayer is not concerned over particular religious convictions; never does it ask if we are intellectual, cultured or ignorant; it responds alike to all. It is impersonal. But since some prayers have not been answered, it is self-evident that the Power which answers, must do so only under certain conditions. It is reasonable to assume that the one praying, either consciously or unconsciously has supplied the necessary conditions which make possible the granting of his request; that there is a science of prayer; that prayer deals not only with a Divine Beneficence but also with a law of Cause and Effect.

THE ART OF PRAYER

Prayer is more than an intellectual petition; it is a thing of feeling; a creative act. Just as an artist feels beauty, rather than sees it, so we feel the Divine Presence as warmth, color and life, ever responding to us. There is an artistry in spiritual communion: a combination of mental attitudes, of states of consciousness, of thoughts, words and feelings, which, combined, produce a subjective pattern of unity, harmony and beauty.

Prayer is both an art and a science. Scientifically, it has form; artistically, it has color, feeling, conviction. Perhaps it is the finest of all arts. The approach to Spirit is entirely a thing of feeling. This feeling rises out of conviction, an intuitional sense, an inner witness. There is something within us which knew Reality long before the conscious intelligence was born. We feel our way back to the original Creative Genius of the universe, the infinite Artist whose creations are spread throughout all time and space.

THE PRAYER OF ACCEPTANCE

Jesus plainly taught his followers that prayers would be answered when the one praying accepted the answer. This is why it is written that "the prayer of faith shall save the sick, and the Lord shall raise him up." This gives us an interesting side light on the Divine Law. First we have a prayer of faith, one of complete acceptance. We have an affirmation which completely embodies an idea. We believe. This is the prayer of faith which heals the sick. Next we have this thought, "and the Lord shall raise him up." There could be no clearer statement of the Law of Cause and Effect, the Law of Mind in action, than this. First our acceptance, then the healing of the sick through the action of Law, relieving us of any obligation or responsibility other than that of acceptance and belief.

The Law operates upon acceptance through our belief, at the level of our faith, according to our recognition. ". . . as thou hast believed, so be it done unto thee." This is the magic key to the storehouse of abundance. Our acceptance must be spontaneous as well as conscious. That is, the whole mind must accept, the whole being must respond. We must accept inwardly, outwardly, and completely.

CONSCIOUS UNION WITH GOD

". . . that they may be one, even as we are one." Jesus was praying that he might awaken the consciousness of his followers to a sense of their Divine union. The Oneness of all life is the pivotal point around which all spiritual meditation should revolve. "I am the vine, ye are the branches."

This "I Am" which is within us, is God, the living Spirit Almighty, branching out through us into self-expression. The Tree of Life flourishes in our experience when watered at its roots with the quiet contemplation of the union of the soul with its Source. Our consciousness is rooted in this Divine Presence, and should branch out into all our actions. Our actions are the fruit of this Tree of Life.

We are One with all the Power there is, all the Presence there is, and with the perfect Law of Liberty. We have always been unconsciously unified with good, but now that which was unconscious must become conscious. We must recognize this union and loose its power into action. Realizing that we are thinking the thoughts of God, we must know that nothing opposes the Truth which utters Itself through us.

Truth is One—"that they may be one, even as we are one." Truth is never divided against Itself. It is always available. If we would pray and prosper, we must so live that all our thoughts and acts are constructive, helpful and life-giving. Thus the Eternal Goodness Itself, flowing from the foundation of Its own indivisible Oneness, passes through us into creation.

DOMINION OVER EVIL

Whatever apparent evil besets us can be neutralized through conscious communion with the indwelling Spirit. This is done by resolutely turning from thinking about evil, to the contemplation of its opposite, which is good. All evil becomes suppositional; good alone is real.

One of the ancient scriptures tells us that whatever is of evil is of ourselves, but whatever is of good is of God. No matter what the negative experience appears to be, the real truth about it is its exact opposite. If apparent evil says that we are sick, then the Truth declares that we are perfect; if the apparent evil says that we are unhappy, then the Truth declares that joy belongs to us; if the apparent evil says that we are alone and friendless, then the Truth declares that we are never alone. We are always one with the great Reality in which is included everything that is.

Evil is not overcome by fighting it, or by recognizing it, but by non-resistance to it; by looking through the evil into the good. Thus evil becomes transmuted. Spiritual communion dissolves evil, as light dissipates the darkness. "For he shall give his angels charge over thee, to keep thee in all thy ways. They shall bear thee up in their hands, lest thou dash thy foot against a stone." Angels represent the higher activities of Mind; spiritual communion with the Infinite; the transcendent power of light penetrating every apparent obstruction, breaking down not only the walls of unbelief but the experiences which these walls have encompassed.

NOT MUCH SPEAKING
BUT DEEP FEELING

"Not everyone that saith unto me Lord, Lord . . . but he that doeth the will of my Father which is in heaven." "Our Father which art in heaven" is the Divine Presence incarnated in us. The will of this Divine Presence is peace, joy, goodness, truth and beauty. We know that this is the will of God because it is the Nature of God.

It is not because of much speaking that we are heard, but rather because of deep, earnest and prayerful acceptance. In this divine communion we should not try to think out beforehand what words we are going to use. Instead of listening to what we are saying, we should say what we are listening to; there is a vast difference between these two mental attitudes. Our words should be the outcome of a deep inner conviction which goes beyond words, but which, at the same time, gives birth to them.

There might be few words used in a certain prayer or meditation, but the words would be very meaningful. When we address the Divine Presence within and around us, we should not do so with empty phrases but with thoughts filled with the deepest sense of Reality. When we use the words "all power" there should be a reaction in our consciousness that All Power is actually loosed through these words. Thoughts, words, spoken in silence with this deep conviction, have more power than volumes merely repeated.

ANTICIPATION AND REALIZATION

How can we anticipate unless we realize? How can we realize unless we recognize? And how can we recognize unless we believe? Spiritual communion anticipates the answer to its prayer, recognizes the presence of the answer and rejoices in a complete acceptance that the request is granted. It sees the invisible take shape and form.

Spiritual communion enters into the joy of recognition, of acceptance, and anticipates that the Divine Abundance will provide a more lavish supply than we have ever conceived or dreamed of. Spiritual communion places its bowl of acceptance under the ever-outpouring horn of plenty, and it places its bowl right side up, rather than upside down. The Spirit can only give us what we take; and since the taking is an act of consciousness, we must be actively aware of the presence of our desire. We must know that the gift is made even before we see it. Consciousness must receive the gift.

RECOGNITION, UNITY AND COMMAND

When Jesus stood before the tomb of Lazarus, he first said, "Father, I thank thee that thou hast heard me." He recognized that the Divine would hear. He foreknew and accepted that what he was going to do would be received and acted upon. He recognized a principle of Creativity at work for him, in him, through him and around him; and in the direction which he indicated.

The next step in his prayer was, "And I knew that thou hearest me always." This was a recognition of complete unity and oneness. No doubts, no fears, no uncertainties, no lacks, limitations or restrictions; no forlorn hope, no idle daydreaming, no wistful wishing. He said, "I knew." How brief but how satisfying. How simple but how absolute. There is no subtlety nor subterfuge. No denial. "I know that thou hearest me always." This is neither a wail of despair nor a form of hope. It is free from both these illusions. It is complete unification.

Now a strange thing takes place in this remarkable prayer, this communication with the Infinite, that raised the dead and caused Lazarus to come out of his tomb. Jesus turned and in a loud voice cried, "Lazarus, come forth!" And he that was bound came forth. This is not a petition of supplication. It is not a sacrifice. It is a command. "Lazarus, come forth!" "Loose him, and let him go." Jesus spoke as one having authority. He had complied with the Law. He had recognized It; he had become unified with It; he had acknowledged the Divine Presence and infused Its Essence in his own soul. It breathed through his spirit and now It flowed forth through his word as a command—"Lazarus, come forth!" This is dominion.

THE CONTEMPLATION OF REALITY

Prayer touches the very well-springs of our being, and through faith projects the invisible into the visible—". . . things which are seen were not made of things which do appear." This means that what we see comes out of what we don't see.

We should contemplate the presence of this Divine Kingdom to which Jesus referred when he said, "The Kingdom of God is at hand," and when he said, "Seek ye first the kingdom" because all other things are included within it.

The prayer for wholeness is a contemplation of Wholeness. The prayer for beauty enters into the Essence of Beauty from which flows the beautiful. The soul is wed to the Source of its being. At the center of our thought God goes forth into creation. This creative act is eternal, tireless and without effort.

As we contemplate the Essence of Being, our oneness with all life, that which we dwell upon springs into our experience, projected from an invisible Source which is self-energizing and self-sustaining. To contemplate the nature of Reality is to embody the Essence of Spirit with all Its power, all Its beauty and all Its harmony. The highest prayer and the most powerful, is this type of communion through contemplation.

THE PRAYER OF LOVE
AND FRIENDSHIP

"That they may be one, even as we are one. I perceive the Spirit of Wholeness, the Union of all Life. Deep within my being I know that I am One with all people, all ages, all events. I am One with the Infinite and the Eternal. I am One with all the Goodness there is; One with all Power and One with the only Presence; the Presence of God in me. In everyone I meet, I perceive this union. I meet It with joy; I am accepted by It even as I accept It. I cannot reject myself nor can I be rejected by myself. There is only One Self, which is God the Eternal Self. I am One with this Self; one with Love; one with Joy; one with Friendship.

This Oneness peoples my world with the loving attention of innumerable friends, with every human manifestation of the Divine Reality. I appreciate this Friend of mine Whom I meet in innumerable forms. Everywhere I go I shall meet Him, everywhere I look I shall see Him. I am held in the embrace of the Eternal Presence. Every thought of disunion, separation or unhappiness is forever gone from my mind. Love, Joy and Companionship are permanently established in my experience."

THE PRAYER OF THE
PERFECT HEART

"I am a center of Divine Perfection within me. I am free from every sense of burden, strain or tension. My pulsation is in harmony with the Infinite Rhythm of the universe. There is no burden, no strain. I am not troubled nor concerned over the future, nor worried over the past, nor afraid of the present. Perfect Love casts out all fear. The rhythm of my action is in perfect relaxation; its vitality is complete. The walls of my being are whole.

Joyfully the Spirit circulates through me reaching every atom of my being with the message of perfect life and happiness. All tension, fear, strain, is removed. I rest in calm assurance that Eternal Goodness is forever around me. I am free from all condemnation, judgment or bondage. My whole life is joy, fulfillment, the happiness of expression and complete freedom. There is One Heart, that is the heart of pure Spirit, that is my heart, that is at the center of my being. I sing the song of the perfect heart."

PRAYER OF CIRCULATION, ASSIMILATION AND ELIMINATION

This prayer is a recognition of the Divine Indwelling Spirit: "The Spirit within me is circulating through every atom of my being; flowing in joy; carrying the life giving Essence of Love and Wisdom, Truth and Beauty; surging through every atom of my being with Divine Power, Energy and Perfection. Infinite Spirit of Wholeness and Happiness within me—joyful is Its flow; complete is Its surge; perfect is Its circulation. Every idea that enters my consciousness; everything that enters my physical being, is assimilated in the flow of this Divine Life; harmonized through Its unity and directed by Its intelligence. Everything is assimilated and digested.

"Therefore the activity and thought of my being are balanced and perfect; every function and organ is in harmony with the rhythmic flow of the universe. Nothing remains in me but the Truth. Truth eliminates everything unlike Itself. There is nothing unlike Truth. There is no stagnation, no inaction and no wrong action. There is One Actor, acting in and through me; One Wholeness manifest in every part of my being. I rejoice in this circulation and flow of Spirit. The peace and calm of eternal well-being (the joyful recognition of my union with good; the glad opening up of the gates of my whole being that I may become saturated with the Essence of Perfection) is now complete."

PRAYER FOR A SUCCESSFUL BUSINESS

Let us assume that our business has become sluggish or inactive. We then turn to the all-pervading Presence for Its inspiration and guidance in the same manner that we prayed for a physical healing, knowing that our success in business, the activity which we generate through the operation of the Law, depends upon our ability to conceive. We therefore eliminate from our thinking thoughts of failure, limitation or poverty, and we pray after this fashion:

"No matter what others may say, think or do, I know that I am a success now. I radiate joy and am filled with faith, hope and expectancy. I refuse to think of failure or to doubt my own power because I am depending on the Principle of Life Itself for all that I shall ever need.

"I know that there comes to my attention everything that I need in order to project my business in every direction with the certainty of success. I see this expansion and pray that it may bless everyone who contacts it; that I may serve all who come near me; that all who know me shall feel my love and friendship and shall sense a warmth and color within me. I pray that everyone that touches my business in any way shall be uplifted and satisfied. I bless and praise everyone who is in any way connected with my business. I draw them to me with the irresistible charm of Divine Union. I serve them and am served by them. The reciprocal action of Love prospers those I serve as well as me. I am success, happiness and fulfillment."

GROUP PRAYER

"The One Supreme Spirit is within, around and through every member of this group. Each is a center of God-conscious Life, Truth and Action.

"Infinite Intelligence governs, sustains and animates every member of this body. Good alone goes from them and good alone returns to them. Infinite Mind establishes harmony and right adjustment of all personal, family, business and social affairs or conditions in the life of each member. Each is supplied with every good thing. Each is happy, radiant and complete. The Spirit of God manifests in each one as Peace, Harmony and Wholeness.

"Everything that any one of this group does, says or thinks is governed by Infinite Intelligence and inspired by Divine Wisdom. Each is guided by Divine Intelligence into right action. Each is surrounded by friendship, love and beauty.

"Each person is the manifestation of the Divine Spirit which never tires, which is birthless, deathless and limitless. Each is receptive to the inexhaustible energy of the Universe and to Divine Guidance. Each person in this group is conscious of complete happiness, abundant health and increasing prosperity. Each is aware of his partnership with the Infinite. Each knows that everything he does shall prosper. Each is conscious of inner peace and poise. Each immediately becomes conscious of a more abundant life."

DISCOVER A RICHER LIFE

FOREWORD

Ernest Holmes was one of the great spiritual leaders of our day. He always wrote and spoke with a simplicity and directness that conveyed the essence and meaning of the philosophy of Science of Mind, which he formulated and by means of which countless thousands have been able to experience a better way of life.

At the time he passed on in 1960, he left a great wealth of unpublished material, most of which will eventually appear as articles in *Science of Mind* magazine.

For over thirty years he had regular monthly features in the magazine, and this material has never been available in any other way. This volume is the first of a series that will assemble these magazine articles, bringing them together in a related manner and in a permanent form.

It is felt that each additional volume of Dr. Holmes's works will be an important contribution to his basic writings on Science of Mind.

WILLIS KINNEAR

Part I

FOUNDATIONS FOR EFFECTIVE LIVING

For too long we have been dividing ourselves as well as the universe in which we live into small unrelated segments. We have been so busy doing this that we have overlooked the fact that everything is part of one stupendous whole. We have separated the spirit from the mind, and the mind from the body. We have isolated living things from that which causes them to live. The stars and the atoms we consider apart from the purposive Creativity which creates and sustains them.

There comes a time when it is necessary to try and put things back together again. We need to start to correlate and integrate the knowledge we have into a unified practical system of thought for our greater benefit in everyday living.

The ideas and wisdom expressed in the following chapters will enable you to more fully express the wonderful and complete person you are.

PHILOSOPHY

Something to Think About

Philosophy means the love of wisdom. The study of philosophy is an inquiry into the knowledge of general principles, a search after truth. Since there are many kinds of wisdom and many truths, it follows that there are many philosophies. From its broadest viewpoint the average man's philosophy is his opinion about life. The philosophy of a religious man is his opinion of the relationship between God and man. The philosophy of a businessman constitutes his speculative thought about economics. Philosophical knowledge is an attempt to establish for us a rational explanation of things as they are.

We have two general philosophical outlooks on life: one is idealistic, the other materialistic. Either one may or may not be practical. In the highest use of the term, philosophy is supposed to be ideal; hence, we have the term "idealistic philosophy" which in its extreme form means interpreting the universe purely in terms of ideas. The materialistic viewpoint of life interprets it entirely in terms of physical processes.

Until recent years the study of philosophy was held to be entirely speculative thought, a sort of Utopian dream. Those who pursued its study were considered impractical dreamers; marvelous perhaps in their mental deductions, but nevertheless pursuing a useless cause in a world of pragmatic values.

The modern philosophical outlook, however, is different. The quest after truth is now so universal that every man's mind is stimulated to inquire into the reason for things, and to study the relationships existing between the world of everyday life and action, and those higher values which we all sense. The study of philosophy is no longer looked upon as an idle speculation, a useless mental performance, entirely impractical, but is now viewed as one of the noblest pursuits to which the mind may give its attention. More books are being written on philosophy today than in any other period of history.

There is an earnest and an insistent desire on the part of ever-increasing numbers of people to discover the reason for things and the relationships existing between them, particularly in the realm of idealistic philosophy. There is an effort to discern the relationship between the Creator and creation, the invisible Cause and Its visible effect; between God, or the universal creative Spirit, and man—man being the only form of life we know of having the power to consciously and definitely sense the necessity of there being such relationships.

There is an apparent tendency in recent years among many of our scientists to turn to philosophy for a fuller explanation of their scientific findings. Today we find the study of philosophy not for those who turn from the practical values of life to daydreaming, or the courtship of mental hallucinations, but necessary to those who, having some knowledge of scientific principles and facts and some understanding of the practical values of life, still believe that there is a synthesis or a unifying Cause back of all facts.

It is from this viewpoint that we approach the study of philosophy. Like all other inquirers into truth, we have certain fundamental assumptions or beliefs which we seek to reconcile to the facts of human experience. These fundamental assumptions or beliefs are simple and few: There is an infinite creative Intelligence which creates all things by imparting of Itself to become that which is created. This original creative Cause is an indivisible unity—in Its own nature changeless and eternal—and from It proceed laws which sustain the visible universe.

It is the nature of this original Cause to continuously express, to eternally do new things; yet in doing these things It can never contradict Its own nature. The expression of this infinite Spirit in an ascending creation is what we call evolution. All things, ourselves included, are some manifestation of It; hence all things have a direct relationship to It. Since all things emerge from It and are sustained by It, and since It is all things, this relationship is direct and immediate. Our consciousness of this relationship is through an inner awareness.

This inner awareness on our part is not only our awareness of It but is also Its awareness of us. Hence our awareness of It and Its awareness of us are one and the same thing; man's consciousness of himself is God's consciousness of man. As man's consciousness expands he becomes more and more God-conscious.

Since God is infinite, the possibility of man's expansion is limitless. Therefore evolution or unfoldment is the eternal process through which Being passes into becoming. This does not make man God nor does man create God; but man at any and every level of consciousness is, at such level, a manifestation of the original Mind. As a drop of water is in the ocean, and in its essence is like the ocean, but still never is the whole ocean; so man is in God, partakes of the nature of God, in essence is One with God, but never is God. Man could never become the whole God for then he would have exhausted the possibilities of the Infinite, which by definition is an impossibility.

The progressive awakening of man to greater ideals and accomplishments, through art, science, philosophy, and religion, is the passing of Spirit through him into expression. It is the nature of this original Spirit to incarnate Itself in and as everything, to quicken all form into life, to create, sustain, promote, and expand; thus does It provide for Itself, within Itself, avenues for Self-expression and the manifestation of Its own infinite Self-knowingness.

RELIGION

Something to Believe

Religion means a belief in an invisible, superhuman power or powers. It is a belief in God or gods. Any system of faith, doctrine, or
worship is some form of religion. So far as we know the religious sense
is universal; all peoples have had some form of worship, ranging from
the simplest forms of fetishism to the contemplation of pure Spirit and
man's unity with It.

All religions teach the recognition of and the belief in an invisible Presence whose power and intelligence are greater than man's. The
more intellectual forms of religion teach that this invisible Presence is
an undivided and an indivisible unit, an omnipresent Reality.

Worship in its highest form is an attempt to identify oneself with the
good, the beautiful, and the true; with love, justice, and righteousness.
Religious emotion is an aspiration of the soul toward God, accompanied by a belief in an overshadowing and an indwelling Presence, and a
desire to unify oneself consciously with this Presence.

Since all forms of religion have in some measure aspired toward this
central goal, howsoever crude many of them may have been, each has
been necessary in its day. The permanent progress of humanity is easily
marked by the growth of its religious ideals.

The vitality of any religion is to be found in its affirmative and constructive beliefs. The weakness of any religion is found in its superstition, creedal pride, and dogmatic assumptions.

People are naturally religious, since through the gift of nature we all believe in some infinite Intelligence or Power. Insofar as any religion stimulates faith, this faith accomplishes definite results in the life, the character, and the outlook of the individual. Any religion which does not stimulate a positive faith in the good, the enduring, and the true, and which does not give at least some inner conviction of our identity with the Spirit, is useless; for religion is a way of life, a sentiment so pronounced that it influences every act and imagination, frees the mind and looses the spirit.

Any religion which is based on fear is negative; its evil neutralizes its good, while too often its good fails to neutralize its evil. Our thought is torn between two opposites, hence becomes the scene of a continuous struggle; faith and failure take equal sides, doubt and fear balance trust and confidence, and man is thrown into a state of complete helplessness.

True religion should teach that there is but one ultimate Power in the universe and that this Power is good, never divided against Itself, knowing no opposites and having none, complete within Itself, yet forever unfolding.

True religion should identify man's mind with this eternal Reality and teach him that his own life is a manifestation of this universal Life; that the highest God and the innermost God is One God; that there are no opposites to good; that all beliefs in the devil, hell, evil, as things in themselves, are myths, phantasies, mistaken concepts. This the religion of the future will do—it will teach the identification of oneself with this universal Being through an inner awareness, a sense which all people have but which few people use.

The new religion will go further than this and deliberately teach a definite technique by which we will be enabled to consciously remove doubt, fear, and uncertainty from our minds and in their place create confidence and trust. For, after all, our approach to Reality is through our own minds and nowhere else. The power of spiritual conviction finds its only avenue of expression through our knowing faculties.

All revelation, inspiration, intuition, and guidance, if they are to find concrete expression, must pass through the mind. The mind is the medium through which all knowledge, all faith, all opinion, all philosophy, and all religion operate. Hence, the new religion will teach a spiritual psychology, an idealistic philosophy, and a system of metaphysics designed to consciously create in the mind a recognition and a realization that the Eternal is one with man, that the creative Intelligence of the universe is available to man, that the dynamic purposive Power which urges everything forward is latent in man, and that he can discover this Divine Presence within him. The religion of the future, then, will of necessity be a universal religion, simple and direct.

SCIENCE

Something to Use

Science is an exact and systematic statement or classification of knowledge concerning some subject or group of subjects. It is the knowledge of facts, laws, and proximate causes, gained and verified by exact observations and correct thinking. The result of scientific knowledge, expressed in terms of law, gives us the ability to do something with a definite predictable result. Because we have many systems and classifications of knowledge we have many sciences, such as physics, chemistry, botany, biology, physiology, psychology. In a general way we may speak of the classified knowledge of any subject as a science.

The laws of science are universal, applicable by anyone at any time and in any place. Scientific laws, insofar as they are understood, are neutral, responding impersonally to anyone, and appear to have no self-determination. Neither could we say that the science of electricity belongs to an Edison nor the science of mathematics belongs to an Einstein, nor that any science belongs to anyone.

The increased knowledge of any science is some knowledge of universal principles which existed in their potential possibilities prior to their discovery by man. The laws of nature are her secrets unlocked by the investigating mind, which, through the intelligent understanding of man, are useful when properly applied, harmful when not rightly used.

It is now believed by many scientific minds that the material sciences can converge into one great synthesis which may be called the science of being; that a greater inclusion will tend to unify and coordinate all truths into one great system of reality, which from the religious viewpoint may be termed "the universe as a spiritual system"—One Spirit moving into many expressions. While viewing the universe as a spiritual system one need not deny the material universe; for the material universe and the laws which govern it are part of the vast system and are necessary to it.

The very word "universal" implies that the universe cannot be divided against itself. If the discovery of a new law contradicts the established facts of an older ascertained law, either the facts of the old law are false or the facts of the new law are false. The universe is so constituted that one law cannot contradict another. However, this does not mean that one law cannot transcend another. There is a law which says that anything heavier than air will fall to the ground, but by the application of the law of aerodynamics that which is heavier than air may ascend. These two laws do not contradict each other—each is a part of a whole and a unified system.

When we approach the study of the Science of Mind in its practical application we are not denying material or physical laws; we are simply introducing the use of a higher law—the law that the higher form of intelligence governs the lower, but all is part of the unified whole. The laws of psychology or metaphysics cannot neutralize or wipe out the laws of physics, nor is there any science of mind which can do away with the physiological or psychological laws of our being.

As an example let us consider the act of prayer and faith in its relation to physical healing. Many people have been healed of physical diseases through prayer and faith. The denial of this fact would be an admission of one's ignorance of such events. If the universe is an undivided system, containing as it does many laws, and containing as it must many gradations of intelligence, then it follows that when through the act of prayer and faith one is healed of some physical disability, this healing is accomplished not through the suspension of any physical law but through the recognition of the One Law which governs all. We cannot believe that God or the intelligent Life-Principle would or could violate one of His or Its laws because of any man's petition.

We cannot believe that prayer or faith changes the natural order of the universe but we do know that the act of prayer and faith does produce definite results. Hence we are compelled to admit by the very evidence of spiritual healings that something else is involved in the process.

Here is one of the apparent riddles of the universe and of our own existence. Are we living in a spiritual universe? Are we living in a mental universe? Are we living in a material universe? The extreme idealist will say we are living in a spiritual world, in a universe of pure ideas—all is mind, there is nothing else. The extreme realist will say we are living in a material universe in which mind plays no important part and in which Spirit, viewed as infinite Intelligence, plays no part. Between these two positions there appears to be a gulf which cannot be bridged. If we are living in a universe of Spirit or mind alone, then the material universe is an illusion. If we are living in a material universe alone, then mind or Spirit are fantastic concoctions of our imagination.

But how can mind be a fantastic concoction of our imagination since we are using it this moment? How can the material universe be an illusion unless mind itself is an illusion and unless all is illusion? And how can Spirit or universal Intelligence be a myth unless we, It, the material universe, and all of our mental reactions are but dreams; and to complete the argument, how can there be a dream without a dreamer?

This gulf is easily bridged if we conclude that the spiritual, mental, and physical do not contradict each other, are not divided against each other, but are one in essence; they have One Source, and function according to one great body of Law.

Let us create this new synthesis in our imagination and see what we have. If we consider that in essence the universe is one of pure Spirit, infinite Intelligence, conscious Purpose—which also acts as, and is, the source of inviolate Law by means of which It becomes universally manifested through Its energy becoming what It creates—then we find that there is room for all things. We do have a spiritual universe, we do have a mental universe of conscious thought, as well as a physical universe of tangible things; in essence they are all the same—they are but different aspects of *that* which we call God or infinite Spirit. Spirit is the all-inclusive source; thought becomes the directive factor, with manifestation being the result. But in and through all there is law which functions at every level.

Spirit is universal, Mind is universal, and so is Substance—which is pure energy becoming tangible through Law in the form provided for it by thought or idea. And whether we think of law as being spiritual, mental, or physical it makes no difference, providing we realize that the three work together in perfect unity, being but different functionings of the great Law of God. Spiritual law, mental law, and physical law are all universal and omnipresent, they all work as a unit; however, the higher form always transcends or governs the lower but never by contradicting or violating it. With this concept we can see how it is that the Spirit can govern the mind and that the right mental attitude cannot help affecting the body.

Working from such a basis we can readily see how we can by observation, experiment, and proof develop a definite technique for the practice of a true science of the mind.

SCIENCE OF MIND

Something to Live By

On the basis of our definitions of philosophy, religion, and science, a *science* of mind becomes a definite study firmly founded on our knowledge and our highest ideals and their relationship to the great Reality, or God.

It has been said that "Thought is the activity, not the essence of the soul." The sciences of psychology and psychiatry deal largely with mental and emotional action and reaction more than with the essence. On the other hand, Science of Mind attempts to penetrate more deeply into the essence of the Spirit within man; its theoretical principle is that the real essence of man's mind and life is pure Spirit. Hence, of necessity, Science of Mind must teach *spiritual* concepts and at the same time should include in such teaching the highest and most advanced thought that can be gathered from all sources.

Science of Mind is a systematic study of the creativity of the mind of man, with its conscious and unconscious activities, and of the nature of the Spirit which has created and animates and sustains him.

Mental facts and spiritual experiences are just as real as sunsets and raindrops. One of the highest, most interesting, and illuminating pursuits to which one can give his attention is a consideration of the right relationships between the complex reactions of the mind to its external environment and its subtle reactions to Life Itself, Spirit, the great Reality, or God. We do not think of man's spirit and mind as confined within the body, but of body as being included within and sustained by the mind and spirit; and of body, mind, and spirit as being permeated or one with that higher and finer essence, which is pure Spirit—God.

A correct adjustment of one's thought in its conscious and subjective reactions to that Reality fundamental to all religions tends to produce a state of trust, of subjective harmony, of inner assurance. The physical effect of such mental adjustment is healing, for healing in its broadest and most permanent sense means harmonious action.

Thought which is continuously torn and distracted, uncertain, despondent or morbid, fearful, timid and apprehensive, produces such an inner disquiet that there is a physical correspondence resulting in irritation, inflammation, and malfunction; and, according to the testimony of our most able psychologists, psychiatrists, and doctors, may produce definite and extreme physical disabilities. This being true, they feel that a large percentage of our physical diseases would automatically disappear provided one's thoughts were properly adjusted in harmony with the environment.

Since religious emotion, culminating in a faith in God, constitutes one of our dominant motives, it follows that a spiritually oriented consciousness tends toward a physical healing; thus it is necessary, or if not necessary at least wise, to build up a true religious sentiment, high ideals, and a faith and confidence in the integrity of the universe. With our present knowledge of mental actions and reactions and with the techniques already evolved by other sciences, we have at our hands means and methods by which we may definitely neutralize wrong mental reactions and place in their stead right ideas, such as hope, trust and faith, a belief in goodness, in love, and in reason, all of which create a confidence in life. Such confidence includes a faith in oneself, and is

sustained through a belief that the self is some part of the great universal Reality which sustains all through the power of Its own Self-existent
Being.

A trust in God is no mere idle myth, nor can we consider such trust
a superstitious reaction to life. The greatest people who have ever lived
have placed their confidence in this invisible Presence and have walked
serenely through life, freed from the fears which assail and hamper the
average man. We cannot doubt the reality of such experiences.

If countless numbers of people have been sustained through a calm
confidence and implicit trust in Divine Intelligence, then we must accept their experiences as being valid, analyze their actions and reactions
to life; and, using such affirmative facts as we may discover, build upon
them the highest and most sublime hope which has ever penetrated the
consciousness of man. What we must avoid, however, is the confusion
which arises from a belief in final revelations, from the belief that all
truth is at last discovered, or that some one person or some one system
of thought has delivered the last word. There are no finalities in any
science, any philosophy, or any religion. Through the continual emergence of the creative Principle any last finality proves to be but the beginning of a new creative series. This eternal spiral, finding its base in
the everlasting Reality, will never cease to emerge.

Science of Mind will never be a closed book but will continue to
gather spiritual truth from every source and every man's experience;
and, combining them, will discover that the result is an ever-increasing
revelation of the nature of the spiritual universe in which we live. Nor
can we believe that any religious ideal or philosophical concept is valid
if it denies the smallest fact ascertained in science. Truth will never
contradict fact but will include it. Hence the religious or philosophical
aspects of Science of Mind must not deny but include the findings of
science through the realization that these three great branches of human
knowledge, these three highways to the One Source of all things, are

partners serving as guides in an endeavor to gain truth. Knowledge alone gives freedom.

Our increased awareness of spiritual truths will make each day a fresh beginning, a new approach to Reality, a spiritual adventure emerging fresh and new from the original creative Principle active within us.

Part II

PRACTICAL PRAYER

Throughout the ages in one form or another, in one way or another, man has thought in what he considered a prayerful manner and has been able to obtain beneficial results.

Many and widely varied explanations have been advanced as to why prayer is answered, as well as to why it sometimes apparently is not answered.

One simple fact does stand out relative to any prayer: It is a certain process of thought as a result of which there are definite, specific results. Regardless of what religious, philosophical, or psychological interpretations we may desire to give to such a process of thought, prayer seems to be a universal fact effective in the lives of all men.

In view of this there must be certain common denominators, which, once known and understood, could enable any man to so guide and direct his thinking that it could become a continuously constructive creative force in his life.

The following pages present certain fundamental ideas, which, properly assimilated and used, will enable you to make prayer the most practical of all endeavors.

THE SCIENCE OF PRAYER

IT IS DEFINITE AND CONCISE

Prayer may be considered as a spiritual mind treatment, and we use the word *spiritual* rather than Christian mind treatment, Jewish, Hindu, or some other kind of mind treatment. We use spiritual as we would use the word beauty; beauty which is the essence of the beautiful. This is why a work of art is spoken of as an object of art. Beauty itself is subjective. It projects itself into a form which is objective, but it is an objectivity of a subjective essence which is felt but not seen. We use the word spiritual in the same sense. It applies to every race, to every creed, and although we happen to be mostly Christians by background and culture, this has nothing to do with spiritual mind healing, either as a spiritual essence or as an active law or science.

We believe there is a science of right thinking which can be taught and definitely used—consciously applied with certainty of a definite result. This is also what we mean when we speak of the Science of Mind. In our way of thinking there is no such thing as a "healer" any more than there is someone who *creates* a garden, or *makes* a rose. We plant the seed; Nature creates the rose. Potentially no one has more power to heal than another. In this respect we always need to fight against superstition. It is so easy for the little truth we have to be clothed by so much superstition that finally we lose sight of its essence.

We need not be superstitious to be spiritually minded. Spiritual-mindedness is a persistent and consistent attempt to feel the Divine everywhere and in all things. It is the capacity not only to believe in but also to perceive, to feel, and to react to a unitary wholeness, an essence, an infinite personalness, a beauty, a love, and I also believe a laughter, which exists in the Universe—the Ultimate Reality. We too often get weighed down by our little virtues. Spirituality is normal, natural, spontaneous, effervescent, never studied or labored.

Spiritual mind healing, then, means exactly what it says—that the One Mind reacting on, in, through, and as the body and environment, will change a situation because we change our thinking within It. ". . . be ye transformed by the renewing of your mind. . . ." The Greeks said that man is pneuma, psyche, and soma—meaning spirit, mind, and body. The science of psychology deals with the mind; psychosomatic medicine deals with relationships between mind and body, or the mind-body unity. In addition we believe there is a unity of the Spirit and the mind, the pneuma and the psyche. Therefore, without contradicting what we may learn from other fields, we add to them and say we believe in spiritual psychosomatics. We really practice spiritual psychosomatics in spiritual mind healing because as we increase our awareness of Spirit, Its nature is expressed in our thinking. If we change our thinking, there will be a change in the body.

Mind and matter are not unrelated; in one aspect mind is intangible matter and in the other aspect it is tangible form. This is no different from Einstein saying that energy and mass are equivalent or interchangeable. He did not say that energy energizes mass, he said it may become mass. Spinoza understood this when he said mind and matter are the same thing. Therefore, in spiritual mind healing we deal with the concept that there is no difference between the essence of form and the essence in form, because the essence of form, in form, is form.

When Einstein said energy and mass are interchangeable, he did not disappear into the picture he had drawn. His identity remained that of a conscious intelligence, analyzing an energy and a mass that has intelligence but not self-awareness or consciousness. It is necessary for us to understand this, for we have an identical concept in the field of mind-body relationships—we do not deny either our body or our mind, but we do affirm Spirit, which encompasses both. We add to, but do not take from.

We understand that mind in essence and mind in form are one and the same thing. In other words, we are not trying to reach a known fact with an unknown or unknowable principle. We are not spiritualizing matter to heal disease, nor materializing spirit to perceive matter and control it. There is no such thing as a spiritual control of a material universe as though Spirit were separate from it, for such a theory involves suppositional opposites and would annihilate fundamental unity.

There is no God who is supervising a human kingdom, and there is no law in nature that contradicts another law of nature. Nature is not in conflict with itself. Nature is One system; God is One; Existence is One. Therefore, spiritual mind healing deals with the concept of disease, not as an unreality in experience, but as a wrong arrangement resulting from man's thought. And thought, rightly arranged, will automatically rearrange the condition on the basis that mind and matter are interrelated and interchangeable.

We believe in spiritual mind healing and our approach to it is very simple. First of all, we believe that the Universe in which we live is a spiritual system governed by intelligent Law—the Law of Mind in Action.

Spiritual mind healing will not be complete until the individual is attuned to the Infinite. It will not be complete until he gets a clearance from a sense of rejection and guilt; therefore, he will have to forgive himself and others. In addition, the individual must come to realize intellectually and emotionally that there is nothing in the Universe to be afraid of. There is no fundamental evil, there is no duality. This is the essence of spiritual mind healing, and as the consciousness perceives this transcendence, it almost automatically sloughs off all other things.

There is a rhythm in the Universe, and if it were rightly understood there would be no conflict. There is a peace in the Universe, a freedom from confusion, which rightly understood would heal all troubles. There is an all-encompassing love in the Universe, which rightly understood would heal difficulties. Everything below the threshold of consciousness is subject to the level of awareness to which our consciousness has evolved. The higher form of intelligence governs the lower. Everything less than conscious intelligence is unconscious intelligence which functions either on the pattern inherent within it or injected into it by the individual mind or the race mind.

One of our greatest errors is that we sometimes think the universe was created, wound up, and is now running down, and that the Mechanic deserted it after He wound it up. God not only created the universe, but also continually expresses in and through it. Emerson said that the ancient of days is in the latest invention. He also wrote that the mind that wrote history is the mind that reads it.

It is our assumption that there is no difference between the thought and what it is going to do. What it is going to do is announced by the definiteness of the thought, but its ability to do it is not injected by the thinker. This is a very important point. For this reason I started out by saying that there are no natural "healers." In the same sense we do not say that a physicist is a natural energizer because he deals with energy. This means that the individual doesn't do the healing, but if he didn't meditate or pray, it might not be accomplished. He doesn't inject himself in the situation as a healer, but what he does is to consciously use a natural energy, intelligence, and creativity at the level of his consciousness, his recognition, and his feeling of it. In this sense the individual is a practitioner, one who uses the Law of Mind.

What, then, would be a technique of spiritual mind healing? The formation of words to conform with an idea—an idea, of course, that harms no one—and with such a conviction that they are true that nothing in your own mind, your own consciousness, rejects what you say; and then identifying what you say with the person, situation, or thing you desire to change for the good. That is all there is to it. It is simplicity itself—but it is so elusive that we look for a greater profoundness, not knowing how profound simple things are.

We of necessity believe that there is an intelligent Principle or Law in the Universe which receives the impress of our thought as we think it, and acts upon it without question, without argument, without rationality. It creates for us in our experience the content of our thought with mathematical accuracy. This is the Law of Mind. To the degree we understand our unity with Spirit, or God, and give to the Law only ideas of good, we expand our thought and free ourselves from the negative consequences of our previous limited thinking.

God is all there is; God is Perfect. There is One life, that Life is God, that Life is our life; therefore that Life is now pulsating in us. It is the everlasting Presence which is both personal and impersonal; personal as Presence and impersonal as Law. There is nothing separate from It. Now as a result of this, the logical outcome of our constructive thinking is the tangible manifestation of the good we desire, the good embodied in our prayer for the person, the affairs, or the situation we wish to help. Since the Law is everywhere and everything is in It, the desired change is initiated in the prayer itself.

The technique of application is very simple. Suppose we are praying or giving a treatment for John Doe. We might begin something like this: "This treatment is for John Doe, he lives at such and such a place. There is only God's Perfect Pattern, and that is his life now. This is the spiritual truth about him, and because it is, all which appears opposite to it is eliminated from his experience." Or we might say, "Every plant, which my heavenly Father hath not planted, shall be rooted up and cast out of his experience." These are but statements to convince the mind of the one giving the treatment; but any statement which will bring conviction is good. No two treatments can ever be alike lest we should listen to ourselves; and we must not listen to what we say but to what we really feel and think, because our speech so often affirms what we should not listen to. Let the child of simple faith within you counsel the man of experience, that the man of experience shall find out what is good and seek to follow it. The simple faith will always tell you just what to say or do.

So, there is no prescribed formula for treatment or prayer, because every time we give a treatment we must expect it to be the only time we are going to give that one. It is a new formation and must be spontaneous. The moment it becomes mechanical it seems to lose much of its power. A technique may be correct, but the fire and feeling and temperament are not always in it, and it is out of the fire of the heart that the mouth must speak. Therefore, do not wonder what words you will use. Treatment follows a Law of Intelligence and its objective manifestation corresponds to our conviction and use of that Law. Treatment is involution, manifestation is evolution; treatment is spontaneous, manifestation is mechanical.

Someone may ask, "How shall we apply this method to the treatment of affairs?" Just the same way. There is no difference between treating somebody for physical healing and treating somebody for the manifestation of needed supply. Both acts are purely mental. We reduce a condition to a mental concept and then correct what needs correcting in the mental concept. We do not deny the reality of things or affairs, but raise our own consciousness to a greater perception and acceptance of the spiritual Source of all substance and supply.

We know that thoughts have the ability of creating new experiences and conditions through the action of the One Mind. For instance, consider a person who is alone and lonely. We arrive at the conviction that there is no limitation in Spirit and no limitation in this person's life for he is One with Spirit, and new experiences are coming to him; he will meet new people, new things, new conditions. As we do this, we are setting in motion for him the Law of Mind which operates upon all things—spiritual, mental, and physical—and he will sooner or later meet whole new sets of circumstances. We must remember that out of the impulsion of our thought a creativity is set in motion which has prerogative and initiative; as the impulsion of our thought is lifted to a higher level of understanding, something new must evolve.

There is but One Creator in the Universe; we individualize It, It individualizes within us as us. There is only One Mind, we use It; One Spirit, we live by It; One Law which governs everything; One Presence which responds to everything. We are individualizations of It with the ability to initiate new causes in our experience. The Universe is not necessarily an endless and monotonous repetition of the same old thing. Every time we think, something new is being done. God is not a static God, and there is no time when creation begins; in the eternal *now*, by thought, Spirit moves upon the Law of the Universe and out of It arises a new creation.

Although it is very important to be specific in prayer or treatment, we may also initiate a new chain of causation just by affirming that something new and good is going to happen. I may send for a packet of seeds that I know nothing about and have never seen. I may never have seen the kind of flower or plant these seeds will produce. I have no mental equivalent of this particular plant in my own mind. When I subject the seeds to the creative medium of the soil they will provide me with that which I did not have an equivalent for. *My equivalent was in the ability to expect and to receive something.*

Remember this, no matter what you are treating—people or conditions—find out what is wrong, know that the opposite thought will erase it. Start as simply as that. You can do it, because nobody can think any better than you can think, and no one has any more authority

THE ESSENCE OF PRAYER

AN EXPANDED AWARENESS

In order to help ourselves and others through prayer, I believe that we have to have a clear consciousness and a deep sense of the inward meaning of what we do. We have to have a realization that each one of us is an outlet of the Infinite because we are an inlet to It. Then I think we have to realize that there is nothing separate from God. When we use the word God we mean the Truth, Life, the Absolute, the Infinite, the Spirit; everything that means that Presence and Power and Intelligence in the universe which *is* the universe.

We are not talking about a theological God, an old man with whiskers combing his beard, soaking the Baptists and dry cleaning those who don't get immersed, or revealing Himself to the Jews and not to the Gentiles, or saving the Adventists and ignoring the Methodists. There is no such God as the God many people believe in, and we should be very glad of that.

By the word God we mean Life, Intelligence in action, the Spirit within all nature, animating everything and animating ourselves. When we use the word God we are saluting the Divine Presence in each other and in everything—the beauty that sees and imagines and paints the glory of a sunset or the softness of an early dawn, the aroma of the rose, the enthusiasm of the child at play, the intelligence of the philosopher, the worshipful attitude of the devotee. This is all God. The moment we draw a line against some part of the eternal Presence which is in all things we shut ourselves off from It. In spiritual mind treatment, or prayer, our purpose is to become actively aware of the unrestricted wholeness of this Divine Presence.

Nothing ever happened to you or to me that need bind us if we free ourselves from the belief in it. This is why Jesus forgave people their sins. He knew that a new world is born every moment; a new spiritual time track, as it were, is created every moment. He knew that there is nothing that can bind man except ignorance of his true nature. Right now, today, any sequence of cause and effect may be intercepted and changed and everything made new in our lives. If this were not true, Jesus never would have forgiven people their sins. If this were not true, no one could be healed physically or psychologically today. Analytical psychology and psychiatry and the practice of psychosomatic medicine would be impossible, no new habits could be formed, no transcendence of ancient experience. There would be no invention in science.

That which has brought comfort to modern man, that which has brought luxury that other ages did not have, is not because the time had come when God decided to give us a gas range or an electric light or an automobile, but because man gradually accepted more of That which was there to be loosed. Out of the God that is, the world is eternally discovering a better God, and that's good.

Whatever in our experience seems to restrict, whatever appears to limit, whatever seems to be the cause of our disturbances must be negated. Now that means that we turn from all our beliefs of bondage, whatever they may be. It doesn't matter who or how many people have believed in them, God the Absolute, God the limitless Infinite, God the eternal Love and Givingness, is right where we are, in fullness. Our own past must not be held against us else we create a new bondage out of the old image.

As we turn within to that Divine Presence, we know that all the ages of the past, all the experiences we have ever had, do not matter today. Here and now we stand forth free from the burden of the past. If there has been what the world calls sin, we are forgiven. If there has been a sense of rejection, we now know that we are included in the Divine Love and Wisdom. If there has been a sense of separation, we now re-unite our imagination and will with That from which we have never been separated, nor could have been. There is One Life, and we are that Life. "I am that which Thou art, Thou art that which I am"—eternal and perfect, forever blessed. Within each one of us, circulating and flowing with the rhythm of the heartbeat of the Universe is but the one heart. There is but one circulation, unimpeded by anything we have done, and that whole system of circulation is the harmony and the joy of the flow and the return circuit of Divine Intelligence and Wisdom.

We are guided and governed and sustained by infinite Mind which knows what to do within us, how to do it, and does it. There is One Mind, that Mind is God, that Mind is in what we are doing. The eternal process of that Mind, forever manifesting Its limitless imagination and activity, is at the point of our own intelligence, thinking in what we are thinking, creating in what we are doing, and being what we are. There is nothing else. And we shall not be bound even by our own mistakes.

We let no doubt or fear or thought of limitation restrict the flow of That which is omnipotent and present and forever blessed. We are animated by the Essence of vitality and energy, we are stimulated by the enthusiastic imagination and will of That which creates everything in the universe, and we abide in the stillness and tranquillity and calm of the infinite Peace which knows no confusion or fear, the eternal Life which needs no resurrection.

Transcendent, triumphant, new and perfect, springing perennially from the heart of the Universe is our own heart and mind and will and imagination. All creation is a proclamation of the Creator. All that is beautiful is the atmosphere of that eternal Beauty and flows in harmony and symmetry through everything and makes one grand music of the spheres—the only Presence in everything, the God eternal. We identify ourselves with this living Presence.

USING THE LAW OF MIND

A RESPONSE TO EVERY THOUGHT

There is a Law of Mind in action, Intelligence taking form through Law; and Its action in our experience can only be a result of motivation by our thought.

This probably confuses many, for most people are a little bit superstitious when they come to think of things spiritual, not realizing that everything in the universe has to be governed by law and order; that there would have to be laws of Mind or Spirit, just as there are physical laws. This is why Jesus said it is done unto us *as* we believe. There is *something* that does it, but only *as we believe;* therefore it responds to us by corresponding with our acceptance of it. Now at first this seems a little difficult and hard to accept and it looks as though we couldn't understand it; but what do we really understand? We do not understand how acorns become oak trees, we do not understand anything other than the *way* nature works. The *why* and *how*, science, philosophy, and religion know nothing about, and these are the only avenues of knowledge we have. If, then, we had the same faith in spiritual law that we do and must have in everything we deal with in nature we would have perfect faith, because we wouldn't doubt and seeming miracles would happen every day.

I would like to establish why I believe that we can use the Law of Mind and use It independently of our present circumstances, The principle upon which Its use is based involves two very simple theories: The universe in which we live is a thing of Intelligence, and of Presence. Sir James Jeans, the great astronomer, said that we could think of God as "an infinite thinker thinking mathematically"; by which he meant there is Person—the thoughts of God and the Law of God. Sir Arthur Eddington, another famous astronomer, said that all physical laws appear as though "they were intelligence acting as law." Now this is exactly what I believe: We as persons live in a Divine Presence as spirit and in a universal Law as action; and we should receive inspiration from the one and give direction to the other. We are surrounded by an Intelligence which receives the impress of our thought and acts upon it. It also could only be the ultimate Creative Agency in the universe which responds to us, much as the image of an object is reflected to us from a mirror. It is done unto us *as* we believe, and we are forgiven our debts *as* we forgive our debtors.

To this we must add one other thought: The subjective state of our thought constitutes ninety percent of our total thought content, maybe ninety-nine percent. All these unconscious thoughts and thought patterns—motivations, conflicts, repressions, whatever you want to call them—are beneath our conscious threshold, but they also help to constitute our entire thought! If we could come to understand that the Law of Mind responds to our entire content of thought, we should see that habitual thought patterns, even though unconscious, would be silently attracting or repelling whether we knew it or not. It is just as though all of our pockets were full of different kinds of seeds and as we walked around they kept falling out into the ground; whether we knew it or not, they would produce growth. We would then look about and say, "I did not sow these seeds." We have done it unknowingly, but ignorance of the Law excuses no one from Its operation.

We must realize that what all the world has believed influences our thought. This is the theory that Carl Jung, the great psychiatrist, developed. In addition to his psychological and medical outlook he also has sound spiritual and metaphysical concepts and he sees the universe as one system. He refers to the sum total of the world thought as the collective unconscious, and what everybody believes in some way operates through everyone else.

In analytical psychology it is recognized that most of our repressed thoughts do not come back into the conscious mind. If so, we should not be surprised that all of us are carrying around thoughts that in some way deny the supremacy of Good. In my estimation, if we could get the majority of the people in the world today to believing and affirming that there need never be another war, there never would be another one. It is the only thing that can stop war, everything else tends to bring it on. This is the only thing that can stop war, whether it is called a prayer of faith or science of mind—it doesn't matter. However, world peace can only happen when the sum total of the people's belief adds up to the fact that it is going to come about.

We do know that one kind of thought can neutralize another. This is very important. Otherwise, if we are full of negative thoughts and they are attracting negative conditions, and if we could not change them then we would be caught in a trap. Fortunately, this is not the case. One kind of thought will replace another. This has already been determined in at least two laboratory projects—at Duke University and University of Redlands. The results indicate that affirmative prayer neutralizes previous negative prayer. These scientific demonstrations indicate that no matter how much anybody failed, if he could affirm success he could neutralize the failure. Isn't it a rather remarkable thing that this finding came from psychological laboratories rather than theological seminaries? It appears to be a paradox, similar to the situation Jesus encountered. He had to find his followers from doctors, lawyers, fishermen, and tax collectors. Why? The priests could not free themselves from old static thought patterns.

I believe we are all somewhat that way. So we find today that some great spiritual truths are being demonstrated in scientific endeavors, and we should be glad of it. I am always glad when new findings in physics, psychology, or medicine have a significance or meaning which exactly parallels what you and I believe and helps to prove it. This, modern science is continually doing. It is now demonstrated—and is no different from what Jesus implied—that affirmative prayer outweighs negative prayer and we may take that to mean that conscious affirmation will neutralize an unconscious negation.

What does this mean?

Suppose somebody has been filled with fear all his life. Fear is sort of a vague thing, often one does not know what he is afraid of, but he is afraid. But if we know that a thought of faith will neutralize a thought of fear in ourselves, or somebody else, and that a continuous conscious affirmative attitude will neutralize a negative one; if we come to know that one kind of thought will neutralize another, wipe it out, then we can set about to change our thinking and our world of experience.

As we entertain new and desirable thoughts in consciousness they in turn become part of the content of the subconscious and gradually the entire content of our thought can be swung over from what perhaps has been negative to what is positive. And as we do this the Law of Mind responds accordingly, and that which is created as our experience comes to reflect the new content of our thought and so we start to live a new life. We give thanks that God, who created all things, has given us the ways and the means to more fully express His Life which is within us, and to discover and experience joy and happiness in all that we are and do.

THE WAY PRAYER
WORKS

As You Believe It Works

What do we mean when we say there is a principle of scientific prayer? What enables a prayer to be answered is the affirmative acceptance that it is already answered! This is not a bit different from what Jesus taught. We are gradually outgrowing our stupidity and gradually catching up to the magnificence and brilliance of the greatest mind that ever graced this planet, that shot like a meteor across it in a few brief years and left behind a trail which all the world seeks to follow.

He said: "I and my Father are one." ". . . What things soever ye desire when ye pray, believe that ye receive them, and ye shall have them." How could it be otherwise? If the universe is a spiritual system governed by Intelligence, and the Law of Mind in action, then it follows that you and I cannot get outside of the universe in which we live. We must obey its Law through understanding It, or in ignorance disobey It. This is why Emerson said: "There is no sin but ignorance, and no salvation but enlightenment." And he was right.

The prayer that accepts its answer complies with the Law of the universe. Why? Because that is the way the universe is organized, and that is its nature. It could not be otherwise and remain self-existent. We are dealing with a natural, spontaneous Power that all we can say of It is, "It is." All we can say of Its operation is, "This is the way It works." All we can do with It is, "Cooperate with Its Law and then Its Power and Energy are available." There is an ancient saying: Nature obeys us as we first obey it. Every scientist knows he must adhere to the law governing the principle he utilizes or nothing will happen.

It so happens and it is so demonstrated that this principle of prayer works! Remember, it was a little child that Jesus pressed into service to multiply the loaves and fishes. Of the great and wise that were there, all said it could not be done. But Jesus knew the Principle with which he worked, his God, and in all this vast throng he had to turn to a little boy to help him, one who did not know it could not be done.

To know that prayer works definitely and specifically is to realize that its creative Power is within us. The Power we do not create. If you and I had to create energy where would we find the energy with which to create energy? "'Tis Thou God who giveth, 'tis I who receive." Every scientist knows that he is a beneficiary of the Divine fact, and that is the way it is. We must *accept*, and not because God would be angry with us if we do not.

To believe is the prime requisite. It is done unto you as you believe is the simple explanation of effective prayer as stated by Jesus. He spoke both from a consciousness of God within him and as a Son of God. He also realized "The Son can do nothing of himself, but what he seeth the Father do: for what things soever he doeth, these also doeth the Son likewise . . . that the Father may be glorified in the Son."

A centurion came to Jesus one day and said, in effect, "I also am a man in authority. I say to one do this, and to another do that, and they do it. I understand the meaning of authority"—in our terminology he meant that he had the mental equivalent of authority—"You need speak the word only, and my servant shall be healed." Jesus turned around, amazed. He was filled with admiration and exclaimed, ". . . I have not found so great faith, no, not in Israel . . . Go thy way; and as thou hast believed, so be it done unto thee. And his servant was healed in the selfsame hour." This was done through natural Energy, Power, creative Intelligence, life-giving Force—call it what you will.

That is the principle of the answer to prayer, delivered two thousand years ago. We are gradually catching up. But up until recently, with very few exceptions, the people who discovered it thought God had patted them on the back and said, "Here is the whole works, anyone who denies your authority, blasphemes." This is nonsense. Is it not strange how difficult it is for the human mind to finally conceive of itself as free, no longer bound, free under the great Law of all life? Every man must finally come to be his own revealer of truth. No man shall enter the sacred and secret precinct of the Most High for you or for me, but each in the silence of his own soul, in the integrity of his own spirit, and the volition of his own choice shall walk into the Holy of Holies and discover God within himself.

This is the secret and simplicity of prayer. The profoundness of simplicity is one of the things that is most often overlooked in philosophy. We have to come right back to simple fact and say the nature of Reality is such, the nature of God is such, the nature of the Law of Being is such, my nature is such, that in some way, whether I understand it or not, I am so much a part of Reality that my thoughts, while they are not creative of themselves, are creative because they deal with *creativity*. And that is the way it is.

Therefore, those thoughts which are affirmative, those thoughts which embody and accept, are like the nature of the creative thinking of God which cannot conceive anything other than Himself. In such degree, then, as I assume this affirmative attitude toward the Universe and embody the meaning of goodness and truth and beauty, so shall they "follow me all the days of my life: and I will dwell in the house of the Lord for ever." How simple! But I can take each of these simple statements and surround it with words that make it as difficult to understand as Plato or Aristotle. Jesus said that it was done unto us as we believe and he didn't try to explain it because he knew it couldn't be explained.

The nature of God, the nature of the Universe and Its Law, our nature and our relationship to this Universe just are, and are universal. And science has learned long since when a principle is deduced and demonstrated to exist there is no argument as whether to label it Methodist or Catholic or anything else. Who cares? It works. And you can benefit from it just as much as anyone else can.

A youngster was drawing a picture and someone asked him what he was doing. He replied, "I am making a picture of God." The wise man said, "But you don't know what God looks like, do you?" The youngster answered, "I don't now, but I will know in a few minutes." He didn't have a guilt complex, so his picture of God was going to be a good one.

In a certain sense, out of the Divine possibility of everything, you and I create each day a better concept of God, drawing closer to the Divine Presence we believe in. We are to believe, to accept, to affirm, and to embody It, not deny It. But there are certain implications. We shall never know that God is Love unless we love. We shall never know that God is Peace, while we are disturbed. Otherwise, it is all a theory. That is the way it works and all the beseeching on earth will not change one bit of it. There is no way to contradict the Law of the Universe. Peace begets peace; love begets love; tranquillity gives birth to tranquillity; opulence, supply, and everything that is the answer to human need is not in a thin dime, but in a concept of abundance that flows evermore.

Because the Universe is one of Law and Order there is an exact, mathematical, mechanical, irresistible, irrevocable, and immutable reaction to our thoughts. It is done unto you and unto me and to all *exactly* as we believe.

Individually and collectively let those of us who espouse the cause of a new spiritual freedom enjoy to drink from the waters of increased knowledge, and in gladness distribute the good we have to the four winds of heaven. Let us keep persistently in our minds that it is our desire, individually and collectively, that everything we touch shall be healed, every person made glad, every situation properly revitalized.

Part III

DISCOVER YOUR PLACE IN LIFE

All too many people go through life without ever feeling that they are in their right place, achieving a satisfactory degree of success, or enjoying good health or companionship. Yet at the same time they see all about them others who do seem to have an adequate share of such things. Does the Universe play favorites?

It may be said that the Universe appears to favor some more than others, but only because an individual first comes to recognize the nature of the Universe and avail himself of Its potentialities.

To what extent does an individual consider himself part of or outside the scheme of things? Does he feel that he is an isolated bit of life waging a futile battle against insurmountable odds in a hostile world? or does he consider himself to be the continual beneficiary of all the good that is available?

Wherever you find yourself today, or wherever you hope to be tomorrow, depends upon what you consider to be your relationship to that which creates and sustains all things. The discovery of a new and better place in life demands a greater concept of Life and the definite application of that concept in a practical way.

The views expressed in the next chapters may enable you to expand your thinking so that you can permit yourself to accept your heart's desires.

START TO LIVE
A NEW LIFE

———

It Is Available Now

Let us never forget that everyone is a center in the Consciousness of God, and no one is more important than another. Every man is on the pathway of an eternal evolution.

We must never deviate from the two fundamental propositions of the ages: The Universe is impelled by Love and propelled by Law. These are the two great realities and their action and reaction constitute the mystery of the Universe in which we live, declaring Its Self-Existence, and filling the mind with wonder and with awe.

When Jesus asked his disciples who the multitudes thought he was, they replied that some thought he was a prophet come to earth again, and some thought that he was the long-awaited Messiah. Jesus then turned to the impetuous Peter and asked: "But whom say ye that I am?" Peter, with one of those quick flashes of intuition of his, said: "Thou art the Christ, the Son of the living God." And Jesus replied that flesh and blood had not revealed this to Peter, but the God indwelling had lifted the veil of sleep that hangs so heavy over the eyes of man and Peter had seen what Jesus came to proclaim: the truth about man himself.

We must penetrate more deeply into the nature, meaning, and wonder of the living Christ, not as a historic Jesus, but as that which lives and moves and breathes today in each one of us. If God is omnipresent, God is both overdwelling and indwelling; the highest God and the innermost God are the same God. No man hath seen God, only the Son hath revealed Him, which Son all mankind is. Not by virtue of any good thing that we have ever done are we that Son; nor by any evil that we have ever done shall we lose one iota of that Divinity. The dismal story of sin and salvation does not belong to the new order of thought which is enlightening the world. "The kingdom of God is at hand."

I have never met and know that I shall never meet one single individual who, having gotten a clearance for himself, has ever denied it to anyone else. I know in such degree as you and I condemn anyone, we are not sure of ourselves. Harmony knows nothing of discord; love has never heard of hate. God is not acquainted with the devil. God is transcendent, and immanent, and omnipresent. It is only as we translate the commonplace into the terms of the transcendence that we shall recognize and realize the immanence; it is only when we elevate the commonplace to the mountaintops that we shall understand and enter into the transcendence. For they are one and the same, equal and identical, even as the Divine Spirit is equally omnipresent throughout the vast Cosmos—not moving, but causing everything within It to move.

Every day is a fresh beginning, every day is the world made new. And when we discover that split second beyond time that Jesus and all the great, good, and wise have told us about—that moment in the eternal present when we are no longer conditioned by the past and when anticipation of the future does not condition the present—we shall be free.

All creation, in my estimation, exists as the expression of God, a Self-Expression of the Infinite; the articulation of That which needs instrumentality for Its own identity. Therefore only as you and I, with wonder, reverence, and enthusiasm, identify ourselves with the living

Spirit can we hope that the living Spirit, through this instrumentality, shall shape the course of our existence and sing the song of eternity in us. Identified with Divine Givingness, the human surrendering itself to intuition shall speak the language of eternity.

This is the greatest revelation we can have. Find one man or woman or child who has become acquainted with the Divine Presence and you will learn more from him than from all the books you can ever read. There is an integrity beyond ours, there is an imagination beyond ours, there is a feeling deeper than ours, and yet we are akin to it. Who listens closely to his own spirit shall hear a song no other person can sing. Who listens to the harmony of his own being, though he be in the desert or on the mountaintop alone, shall compose a symphony which no instrument can be attuned to, for it can be played only on the harp strings of his own heart, his own mind.

There is hidden within the mind of man a Divinity; there is incarnated in you and in me that which is an incarnation of God. This Divine Sonship is not a projection of that which is unlike our nature, it is not a projection of the Divine into the human. God cannot project Himself outside Himself; God can only express Himself within Himself. There is and can be no such thing as a distinct or separate individual that would be separate from the Universe.

An "individual" means something separate from something else. Man is not an individual *in* God, for this would presuppose isolation and separation and disunion. Man is an individualization *of* God. "He that hath seen me hath seen the Father." Unity permits of no division; the altar of God will not accept the gift made in the sense of isolation, of fear, or appeasement. It is only the pure in heart, the childlike in mind, and the meek who can see Him. There is no arrogance in spirituality, for intellectual arrogance is spiritual blindness. The stupidity, the ignorance, the futility, and the littleness of the intellect is a crime against the Spirit, a denial of that sublime Thing within us which waits to take flight to more of the complete, more of the perfect.

What was it that Jesus proclaimed? "I am the way, the truth, and the life: no man cometh unto the Father, but by me." He was not talking about Jesus, he was talking about *you*. Jesus gave us back to ourselves. How are you ever going to consciously reach God other than through your own nature? There are no prophets other than the wise. There is no God beyond Truth, and no revelation higher than the realization of the Divinity within us. That which the ages have failed to reveal, you and I must reveal; each to himself in the secret chamber of his own heart, the secret place of the Most High, where only and alone does one abide under the shadow of the Almighty. This aloneness is not a loneliness; it is the one all-inclusive, all-penetrating unity of everything that is.

This was the claim Jesus made upon the Universe, and we must do the same; identify ourselves with the same Presence, the same Person, and the same Principle. The mind and the spirit cannot help but generate love. Since we are one with all life, we wish to express the most life that we can—your life is my life, my life is your life. I cannot leave you out and understand myself. I am incomplete. I am lame and blind and halt without inclusion. Our littleness, the narrow vision of our spiritual perspective causes the horizon of God's boundless skies to press so close to us that we are suffocated by that which alone can give life. We must reverse the process.

The Eternal, the Everlasting, the Infinite knows nothing about our little ways, our petty thoughts, our little divisions and subdivisions that stifle the mind, the intellect, and the imagination. We have tried to contain the Infinite in a small measure that will not hold It. We have tried to reduce the Eternal to the level of the temporal, and the temporal cannot contain It. In our anguish we have beseeched the living God to save us from limitation, but it is we alone who can free ourselves.

Some day when we come to the great Reality in adoration, having surrendered our littleness, our hopes, our fears, our longings, our heavens, our hells; when we come naked and clean and unafraid, then shall our horizon be extended and the night shall cease. Then shall our valleys be elevated to the mountaintops and God Himself shall go forth anew into creation through you and through me, lighting our path to the indwelling city of God at the center of our own being.

THE UNIVERSE IS FOR YOU

START TO USE IT

There is an old Chinese proverb that says: "Tomorrow's plants are in today's seeds." And our Bible speaks of the time when the plant was in the seed before the seed was in the ground. In other words, they are both saying that everything we see comes from the invisible through some silent process of nature that we know nothing about. Think of the process of the building of the human body; through food and liquids, and by some inner chemistry which is beyond the ingenuity of man, our hair, our feet, our fingers, our internal organs, the blood and bones and tissues are created from some design and by some pattern which no man has ever seen.

No artist ever sees beauty, he feels it; it is an invisible thing. No psychologist has ever seen the mind. All the biologists in the world have no more idea how we can live than a child has. They watch the process, they see the performance, they know what happens, but that invisible thing, the unknown *guest*, they know nothing about. We know very well that within us some invisible Presence, some unknown *guest* animates and sustains; and the moment It severs Itself from the body, the body begins to disintegrate. It is certain that the integrating factor has left.

Somebody said: "Lord, for tomorrow and its needs I do not pray. But make me to do Thy will, dear Lord, just for today." Let's couple that idea with the Chinese proverb that tomorrow's plants are in the seeds of today, and let's couple it with something that Jesus said, because he was the wisest of the wise: "What things soever ye desire, when ye pray, believe that ye receive them, and ye shall have them." Then he said something else equally as interesting: "Judge not according to the appearance, but judge righteous judgment."

For instance, if we were planting an acorn we would not judge according to appearances. We would merely make a little hole in the soil and put in it a small seed no larger than a marble. We would not see an oak tree but it is there in the acorn, in the action of the law that is going to produce it. And even if there never had been an oak tree before, it would still grow. It is the same with everything in life—all of its vital processes are invisible. We do not see them; we do not hear them; in only a very indefinite sense do we really feel them, but we do see evidence of them everywhere about us. In the springtime we see that the seed is bursting forth to produce a plant and the plant produces a blossom and the blossom another seed. And so we find that all of these silent creative processes are going on. That which created the Universe is creating us now. And when Jesus said when you pray believe that you have he was announcing the Law of Cause and Effect that is valid in the world of mind and spirit. For the Universe is one system containing one body of Law, which may be interpreted in terms of what is called spiritual law, mental law, or physical law.

We can choose to plant a seed in the ground and some natural process will operate upon it to produce a plant that is like the pattern in the seed, independently of us. Does this not really explain how it is that faith operates? Everybody is familiar with the idea that faith can produce a result, but how few people ever stop to analyze why, or how, or just what is faith. It is true that faith is an attitude we have toward that Power greater than we are, but it is also a mental attitude that we sustain in our own mind about the operation, action, or reaction of that Power toward us. In other words, faith, if we will strip it of all things but what it really is and view it with complete objectivity and reality, is a way of thinking or believing which admits of no doubt, which accepts a proposition whether seen or not, judges not according to appearances, believes that the future flows out of the present, believes that the future is changed when the present is changed, that the seeds of today produce the plants of tomorrow, and that the thoughts of today produce the events of the future.

I think we should come to believe that the Universe is good. No matter what happens, disregarding everything we may see, the Universe Itself has to be good or you and I wouldn't be here. It has to be constructive or It would destroy Itself. We may be certain that whoever complies with the laws of nature will find the laws of nature complying with him. But somehow or other we haven't quite thought that spiritual and mental laws are just as real as physical ones. And yet today in psychosomatic medicine, in psychiatry and psychology and allied branches of the science of mind, we are definitely discovering how the silent processes of our own emotional reactions and our patterns of thinking are the seeds of what tomorrow will be; the fruitage will be in our physical bodies, in our relationships, and in our environment.

We must know that the Universe is for us and not against us. Therefore it seems to me we should have a quiet sense of childlike trust and faith. Too many people are so afraid of God and the future, and have become so wrapped up with some dismal philosophy, that they feel something bad is going to happen to them. It doesn't need to. You and I do not have to assume the burdens and the obligations and the responsibilities of the Universe. It carries us; we do not carry It. But we certainly have to comply with Its laws. They are creative; they are good.

This is why Jesus said that if you want to be forgiven you have to forgive. And this is only the natural Law of Cause and Effect. If we constructively use It then we have a good reason to expect that something good will happen. If we wish to change our thinking we can change our lives.

If our experiences are the result of our thoughts, then the future, if it is going to be given birth to in the present, will be largely the lengthened shadow of the content of our minds, of our feelings of faith or fear. It is no wonder that the future so seldom becomes better than the past, and often worse as pessimism takes the place of optimism. We have to learn to speak an affirmative language. An affirmative language is creative of good. We must learn to say, "Tomorrow is going to be a good day." Someone may laugh and say, "But look at what happened yesterday?" But did you know that the first boat which crossed the Atlantic driven by steam carried in her cabin a scientific treatise of that day explaining exactly why it was that no boat could be propelled by steam?

It is very characteristic of the human mind to consider that everything that is good, everything that is optimistic, either belongs to some future state or that it is withheld from us, or that we are not good enough to receive it, or that there is some reason why it should not come into our experience. And yet, those whose faith is based on the thought and the philosophy and the experience of one whom we consider to have been the greatest spiritual genius who ever lived, are not reading his words very carefully, for he said: ". . . as thou hast believed, so be it done unto thee."

I suggest that we forget all of the past, and not wonder too much if faith works, but accept; that we start to remake and remodel our own thinking. Here is an interesting thing that happens when we do this. Out of the past comes a sort of a repetition, like a monotonous song being sung: "It can't be this way. It is too good to be true. I don't know how to do it. I am not good enough to do it. Who said it's true?"

You know all the arguments. Where do they come from? It is a well-recognized fact in psychology and psychiatry today that all the morbid and unhappy thought patterns which we have ever had repeat themselves, as they say, with monotonous regularity and that they actually resist any change of thought. Well, let's recognize this as a law of our psychological nature and not be disturbed by it; but, by recognizing it, we then know what we are dealing with; and knowing what we are dealing with, we shall know how to deal with it.

It isn't always easy, but we can determine to do it; and I think there is one first step we need to take and that is to resolve to make our emotions and our thoughts a little more optimistic, a little more affirmative, a little more enjoyable. What difference does it make if somebody thinks, "Well, it's an illusion. It's Pollyannish"? Did you ever stop to think that no one is ever going to live for you but yourself? No one can be unhappy for you but yourself; no one can be happy for you but yourself. And it doesn't make a particle of difference what all the world thinks, if you and I know something constructive about ourselves. We need not fall into the error of believing what everybody around us believes, or in what the world has always experienced.

As we press forward into the future certainly we should carry with us everything out of the experience of the past which was of the nature of love, truth, beauty, faith, reason, and goodness, and everything that has optimism; and certainly we should tend to discard everything that is discouraging. We should create a greater sense of flexibility, of love, a greater sense of tolerance, a deeper feeling for others, for the universe. Every psychologist tells us there are four adjustments: with the self, with the family, with society; then with the universe. How right they are when they say that first I must change my own thinking; then I must make an adjustment to those immediately around me because they are the ones with whom I am most intimately associated; next, it must be with society itself; and last of all, with the universe in which I live. But the interesting thing is the first adjustment with the self; it is the only real adjustment we ever have to make for when this is properly done we are automatically adjusted to all other things.

The seeds of today are the fruits of tomorrow, and we shall be happy indeed on the morrow if the seeds we plant today are seeds of love, and faith, and good will; for "There is no unbelief; Whoever plants a seed beneath the sod and waits to see it push away the clod, He trusts in God."

STARS, ATOMS, AND MEN

RECOGNIZE YOUR IMPORTANCE

It was one of the Greek philosophers who first said everything was made of atoms. Now we say atoms are made of positive and negative charges of electricity—pure energy. No one has seen them, but out of that which we do not see emerges that which we do see. The biggest thing in the universe is just made up out of the littlest things. You put a lot of the littlest things together and the only difference is in the outline or form and not in the substance or the law through which they are created. As far as God, or the Creative Genius of the universe, is concerned there is no big and no little, no hard and no easy, no good and no bad.

You and I right now are living in a universe where the only difference between a star and an atom is in the concept of the man who perceives them. This is the prime relationship. So far as creation is concerned, mankind alone knows a star and an atom; and wouldn't it be strange if we came to see that we alone know heaven and hell, abundance and impoverishment, health and sickness, good and bad? That is why the Bhagavad-Gita says that the self must raise the self by the self. I think Shakespeare understood it also when he said: "To thine own self be true, and it must follow as the night the day thou canst not then be false to any man." Shakespeare did not say "thou wilt not"; he said "thou *canst* not then be false to any man." And Browning, speaking of the soul, said: "What entered into thee was, is, and shall be." In other words, these great thinkers have tried to tell us that we are not separate from God. There is already Something within us which is transcendent and triumphant, not only eternal in the duration of time, but omnipresent in the time in which we live. They did not say, "Man, you are put on earth to save your soul"—not the great ones, only the lesser ones said this. They were the ones who had psychological complexes and psychological frustrations that produced a sense of guilt, which they projected into other people and the universe in order to get a release from their own conflict and anguish.

The great ones were the ones who saw and knew. The interesting thing is that modern science is substantiating their declarations. Modern physics is almost metaphysics. One of the leading authorities in science said the new interpretation of physics makes it look as though everything in the universe is like a shadow cast by an invisible substance. The Bible says "faith is the substance of" *that thing* and will produce its own evidence. And so atoms, the infinitesimal—the little things we don't see—are there all right; but the meaning they have to us as individuals is the meaning we give to them! What is our own vision? What is our own thought?

These men have said that the Universe is in equal balance, so that to each one of us, because each one of us is an incarnation of God, the Universe reveals as much of Itself as we can come to see. This is one of the greatest things in our philosophy. Lots of people say to me, "I don't understand"; and I say, "Wait until you do; keep at it until you do." It is not a spiritual grab bag, but it is nice if you have a stomach-ache to get over it; nice if you have a big headache to get it removed; nice if you need money to get it. I believe in all these things. But how much better it would be if we saw behind it all to the Source. I would rather know that I shall always be happy, which I generally am; that I shall always live, which I know I shall somewhere. I would rather know and be certain that I am in league with That which is both big and little and doesn't know the difference, each is merely an expression of Itself; that the laugh of a child is equal to the building of a kingdom; and the crooning of a mother's love over the babe at her breast is no different from the eternal Heart of the Universe surrendering everything It has in the affection of Its own Self-givingness that It may more completely come into the expression of Its own Love.

All the art and science of the human mind cannot deter, or vary temporarily, its own evolution. Let us not be afraid, let's dare to face things as they are, and not shun the Reality which some day, sooner or later, we will have to face, for we will never be saved from the stupidity of our own ignorance until we do. We are slaves, bound by the chains of our own littleness. We are infinite beings restricting ourselves to the finite sense of things. This the great have known.

Ignorance traps us mathematically and we have to free ourselves from the thralldom of the thought that something is big or little, infinite or finite; until at last we see there is One God over all, in all, and through all. And shall He not clothe Himself in garments of light in what we call big, and seem to be obscure in what we call little? Is there more life in an elephant than there is in a flea because the elephant is bigger? I don't think so at all. And we have to come to realize the atoms and the stars—the infinitesimal, the little—and that which seems to be of great magnitude—the big—are but different expressions of the One that is neither little nor big, and that each one of us must exist here for the expression of the eternal Creator—Mind, God.

What else could we be here for? It is no different from Jesus saying "I am come that they might have life, and that they might have it more abundantly"; or Tennyson saying in *In Memoriam*: "Strong son of God, immortal love, Whom we, that have not seen thy face, By faith, and faith alone, embrace, Believing where we cannot prove . . . One

God, one law, one element, And one far-off divine event, To which the whole creation moves." This is the perception of a poet who feels, by intuition, the irresistible Reality that clothes Itself in every form, sings with every song, writes every poem, creates every invention, and enjoys Itself through our acts. I believe this.

Our ignorance creates our limitation of the Infinite's flow in us. Why else would Jesus say it is done unto us as we believe? We are the measurer-outer. Psychosomatic medicine is proving in its field that the very power that makes us sick can heal us. But we view ourselves so finitely, so isolated, so separated, we do not seem to know that the Power of the Infinite flows through that which is big and little, that the creative imagination of the Infinite is over all, in all, and through all, and that energy and mass, or the invisible and visible, have equality and are interchangeable.

In one sense the stars are not big, the atoms are not little, because fundamentally they can be resolved into the same primary essence or energy. One is made up of a lot of the others. Who can say there is any great and small to the Soul that maketh all? It is absolutely impossible. Neither can we say one man has or possesses more power than another. One man may use more power than another, but we all use the same Power. One man does not have greater joy than another; he may experience greater joy. Every man has all the joy there is. If we could see this we could see that the relationship between the finite and the Infinite is one of identity. Each of us is one with It and as much of It as he incorporates in his own consciousness shall flow through him as power, as love, as joy.

Then, if we find ourselves in bondage, and through ignorance we have created for ourselves a pattern of futility and a future of condemnation, we have to know that there is no condemnation, no judgment, no restriction imposed upon us by the eternal Presence. The Eternal is not static in the temporal; the Infinite is not bound by the finite, nor is God restricted by man. The slightest act or thought of ours, like the atom, can be multiplied into an aggregate of great magnitude. The bigness or littleness, the goodness or badness of our experience is equal to the invisible pattern we have created for it through the process of our own thought. They are the same thing.

UNLIMITED LIVING

FREE YOUR THINKING

The universe is abundant, unlimited in every respect; if it were not unlimited it would have depleted itself long, long ago. Life would have exhausted itself, law would have ceased to function, love would have lost its power to harmonize and to heal, and thought and consciousness would have retreated to instinctive reaction. Instead, what do we find? The fish in the ocean lay so many eggs that if they all hatched the waters would overflow all the lowlands. The stars in the heavens are beyond counting. The grains of sand on the beaches are innumerable. The leaves on the trees continue to multiply. Nature is lavish, abundant, extravagant.

Why? Because God, infinite Intelligence, is perfect, whole, complete, and can never be added to nor taken from. God is all that is. God is the Reality which is limitless in every respect and is the Source of, and is in all things—the same yesterday, today, tomorrow, and forever. But flowing from this infinite and eternal sameness there is always endless change in the form and manner of expression and manifestation.

If we come to know that Life Itself is always the same in essence, including Its Law that governs Its expression, then we shall see that the manifestations of It in and as our experience would have to partake of

Its consistent nature. Although Life goes forth into infinite forms of expression, It of Itself never changes. Suppose we could come to know that there is an order and symmetry in everything; that there is always enough love to go around, enough good, enough beauty, enough health and happiness, then we would know that everyone in the world could enjoy these things without ever exhausting their Source. Then we would have begun to grow up: to think logically; to realize that continued use of a basic principle never exhausts that principle. We can always add two and two and never deprive ourselves of the answer *four*. We need to have a big concept of the fundamental nature of Life, God, the Universe. We need to know there is a limitless abundance of all things good.

I knew a woman years ago who was despondent over her financial condition. She told me her affairs had continued to be chaotic until she realized something was wrong with her thinking. One day she went and sat on the beach—all day and nearly all night. She thought about how many grains of sand there are. She looked up and thought how many stars there are. She was so filled with thoughts of the abundance of nature with which she unified herself that she was able to change her former thinking then and there. Her experiences changed, too. How great is the view! We close it out when we put our little hands in front of our little eyes and refuse to look at things in a big way. We should identify ourselves with the infinite Presence that is universal and whose essence is our substance and supply. The biggest life is the one that includes the most.

God is One, not two. In this One, we are included, not excluded; for we are individualized centers in the Consciousness of God. Since there is only one final Person, God, we all live as personalities in that Person. This means that our personality is the use we are making of a Divine individuality that has been given us, the use we are making of our creative nature. If we wish an abundance of friendship and love, or of any good thing, we should think of the One Person in whom all people live. We should identify ourselves with God who is in every person.

But do we always do this? Do we expect an abundance of love and friendship, or do we deny it and say people don't like us? Of money, or of any other good thing, do we say that we don't know how it can be ours? There is One Source of everything in the universe, which takes the form of the supply we need when we need it. If in the process of the unfoldment of the supply we ought to meet people, we shall. There is but the One and we must go to the One. It is in us. It creates everything. It controls everything. It is everything. Jesus understood this. Therefore, he could find money in the fish's mouth, turn water into wine, multiply the loaves and fishes. But we have to start first with the Divine pattern. All the great thinkers and spiritual geniuses of the ages have believed this. It means that flowing through *me* is something akin to what is in *you*, but it also means we are free to choose and act upon our choices.

If I meet you as someone apart, someone I don't like or someone who doesn't like me, I am making a barrier between us. But if, turning away from everything that appears limited, we meet each other as Divine beings, this will also include us as humans. The greater will always include the lesser. We all have a certain kind of integrity which makes it almost impossible for us to violate, very consistently, that Something in us. Friendship begets friendship, love begets love, peace surrounds us with peace, joy creates joy, and a feeling of the abundance of everything in the universe automatically causes our adequate supply of all things to flow to us.

When this is not happening, what is choking it? Our own thinking! Not always our *conscious* thinking; for we seem to *want* all these things! It is more often an unconscious denial, or an objective appearance which provides a mental denial. This is why Jesus said: "Judge not according to the appearance . . ." The first thing we need to do is to get quiet within ourselves. Consciously deny any sense of fear and uncertainty, and consciously affirm the limitless abundance of God; until finally the unconscious or subjective reaction that had given rise to the reason why our good could not manifest no longer raises an argument. Whether we call this the argument of error or, as the psychologists say, the inertia of our thought patterns makes no difference. These thought patterns can be changed! Every time we identify ourselves with the Spirit within, we are dealing with a certainty, and every word of affirmation will replace a word of denial. In this way we build up within ourselves an acceptance of a greater good.

In order to illustrate this, let us consider the five fingers. There is a flow of blood from the heart down into and through them. If we were to strangulate that flow at the heart, none of the fingers would have any circulation. Let us say that we can never strangulate the heart, which we shall liken to the universal Spirit. It is always active. But down where the fingers are, there can be a strangulation in and about them so there is no circulation. We don't have to establish the stream of flow, but we do have to loosen the bands of fear that restrict the flow so that it will course through all five fingers. In other words, through some pattern of our thinking we strangulate the flow of Spirit, limiting abundance through many aspects of our lives.

There are in the world today approximately two billion three hundred million people. They are all supplied by the same spiritual life blood. They are all using the same Mind and living by the same Spirit. If something could remove every idea and concept of pestilence, famine, insecurity, and the fear we have of each other and of other nations, the Spirit would flow unobstructed. It would no longer be constricted by our sense of limitation. Someday this is going to happen. The only thing that will do it is a realization of the indwelling Spirit. We hear much about insecurity and the need to pray. There is a way of accepting the unlimited Life so that we shall no longer be afraid of ourselves. The only thing perpetuating fear is what Carl Jung calls the individual and collective thought patterns.

We must identify ourselves with the limitless Source of prosperity, love, friendship, happiness, and spontaneous joy, and maintain this identification through new and consistent patterns of thought. I like to be glad. I detest sadness. I know there is a lot of it in the world. I have had much of it, but I don't keep it very long. It is no good. Why should we have to go through life impoverished in a universe that is abundant in all things? Life is not just something to be endured. It is to be lived in joy, in a fullness without limit. We must get rid of old morbid theological concepts. I place no value on anything unless it brings gladness, love, friendship, the ability to laugh, and makes me feel that every person I meet, if I knew him, I would love. He is as good as I am, having the same heart pattern, the same kind of blood stream, the same Divinity.

Can there ever be a freedom of intellect or emotions, or the circulation of substance and supply in human experience until the Divine nature, the Source of all, is recognized and accepted without limitation? We struggle for the affection of two or three people to whom we give the power to destroy our happiness. Passing our doors are thousands who would love to embrace us. Isn't it strange? Yet we see it everywhere in life, the greater good held away because of a denial of the part. Or because we say there is only one avenue through which money or affection or appreciation can come, even though we are a part of and immersed in the limitless Source of such things. It is hard to grow up, isn't it? It is hard to gain spiritual maturity, to see that God is in everything.

The only thing that will release the strangulation hold we have placed on our fuller experience of the unlimited abundance of all good things is for us to wake up mentally and emotionally. We need to escape from our old limited patterns of thinking and from our emotional anxieties and fears, and come to know the most practical thing in the world, the most dynamic truth: God is all there is, and in God there is no limitation. To the degree we stop limiting our thought of what God is, to that extent will we be able to enter a fuller experience of all that God is and can be in every aspect of our lives.

Part IV

THE POWER OF FAITH

———————

All of science is based on the faith that the universe is lawful, logical, and orderly. It is a faith based on the reality of the invisible and intangible which is nevertheless the controlling and directive factor of the physical universe.

At the same time we have a similar faith in the power of the forces of Life to maintain and sustain us. Our heart beats, our blood circulates, our wounds heal. The unseen but ever-present power of Life is continually manifesting Itself in us. We have faith in It, but a faith not too consciously recognized. Yet, when recognized, the faith we have in Life's power to heal has brought forth amazing results.

A faith in the unseen, immeasurable creative powers of the Universe, in and through which all things are possible, is essential. Law does work, there is a beneficial purpose behind things, or nothing would exist. As we become aware of this we are able to develop faith to the point of a fine art and constantly bring into our experience tangible expressions of the unseen creative Power which governs all.

In these chapters you will discover that you can develop a faith that cannot be shaken, and that it is a power that literally moves mountains.

FAITH, THE WAY TO LIFE

CONVICTIONS HAVE POWER

Prayer, the desire to reach out to Something greater than we are, has been common to every age. Instinctively, we feel that there is a higher Power, a greater Intelligence, which responds to us. Our minds reach out with feeling and faith to a Something that is always available.

We need, and must have, a direct approach to Spirit. It is natural for us to reach out from our ignorance to Its enlightenment, from our weakness to Its strength, from our darkness to Its light. We feel and know that the Spirit is right where we are.

Every legitimate desire we have already has an answer in the Spirit, but it is faith or belief which causes It to respond to us. Faith not only lays hold of a Power which actually exists, it also causes this Power to respond as though It were a law operating for us. Somewhere along the line we shall have to surrender our weakness to Its strength, our fear to Its security, our lack to Its abundance. Everyone who has practiced faith knows this.

Why, then, shouldn't we consciously and definitely determine to develop such a faith? We need not ask *how* we should reach out to God, or by what authority, or under what name or sign. All we need do is *to reach*. God has made us all individuals; therefore, when each reaches in his own way he will be fulfilling the nature of his own being. No good can come from waiting until someone tells us just how, because his "just-how" could never be our "just-how." Every man will have to discover his own "just-how." And it will be right. It seems as though it would have to be direct and simple, personal and immediate, reaching out from our feeling of need with an equal feeling that the need will be met—reaching out with faith.

Let us believe in that Something bigger than we are, and come to trust It. It had intelligence enough to make everything, including ourselves; It governs by Law which controls everything, including ourselves. Why shouldn't we have an unlimited faith in It?

Jesus said that the very hairs of our head are numbered, that not a sparrow falls to the ground without God knowing it. Would it not be wonderful to feel that we are cradled in such a Love and Wisdom? to know that Divine Power is immediately available to all of us? And now, because we need It so much, and because we feel we can no longer live without It, we are going to act as though It were right here, always responding to us, loving us in spite of our mistakes. Let's not be afraid to commune with this "Something" that is greater than we are.

Is not this the very essence of prayer? Just saying to Life, "Here I am. I let go of everything that does not belong to God's good man. I accept peace and comfort, today. And I desire to share with everyone I meet. God eternally forgives me as I discard all my weakness and uncertainty, all my past mistakes—I am no longer burdened by them. I know they are now lost in that greater experience of good which is now mine."

One of the tasks of the disciples was *to learn how to pray*. They had watched Jesus in his ministry among the sick and the ignorant, among those common people who heard him so gladly. They had seen new light come into the eyes of those whose vision had been dulled. They had seen a new energy flowing through the limbs of those who had been paralyzed. They had seen the lame walk, the dumb speak, and the deaf hear. And so the disciples asked him to teach them how to pray. Jesus answered them by saying that God was right where they were: ". . . behold, the kingdom of God is within you." He said that everyone who asks will receive. He said that everyone's method of prayer is good; that there is Something that answers everyone according to his belief in It; that God will never ask what you have been doing, or what mistakes you have made, or how good or bad you have been. When you ask, believing, He will give you what you ask for.

Jesus' words were so simple that we overlook their meaning: Something greater than I am, Something bigger, Something I can come to, Something that will listen, Something that understands, Something that will answer.

Next, Jesus gave the most simple prayer ever uttered, and the most effective. It is the only prayer common to all Christian faiths. Countless millions have been helped by it. Why shouldn't we? Perhaps, if we better understood its meaning, we should receive greater help through using it. What did Jesus mean when he said: "Our Father . . ."? That God is the Father of everyone—not just your Father, or my Father, but *our* Father. Being *our* Father, He is always ready to respond to us. We have a direct relationship to God, right now, while we are on this earth. Jesus said that we should come to this heavenly Father just as we would to an earthly one, tell Him what we need, and expect Him to provide a way through which our needs may be met. Jesus made the approach to God so very simple—*everyone's* Father, and *always available.* We couldn't ask for a closer relationship than this; he showed the relationship to be nearer than something outside us—as close to us as our very breath, as near as our hands and feet, for he said: "Our Father which art in heaven," and he had already told his disciples that *heaven is within.* He said, our Father is in heaven, and our heaven is already within, as well as around us. It is the Father within who doeth the works. We have no power of ourselves alone.

This is the relationship we have to God. This is the way we should feel when we commune with God, when we reach out to that Something greater than we are. And we should remember that reaching out is really reaching in, as well as out. If we were separated from God, how could we find Him? But if God has seen fit to implant His own Life in us, then He is as close to us as our thinking; and when we turn in thought to God, we are already communing with Him. Nothing could be more simple or more direct.

And now, according to this marvelous prayer, we are to turn within and find the Divine Presence which is greater than we are, greater than all people combined could possibly be—the one supreme, absolute, and perfect Power. *Our Father which art* means the Power that is, and *Our Father which art in heaven* means that this Power is within us and accessible to us.

Go inside yourself and you will meet God, right where you are, as what you are. The amazing thing is that every man is exactly where Jesus told him to go. He is there already. He does not have to go anywhere; he just begins right where he is. Jesus said we should go inside ourselves. He called this "entering the closet"—closing our eyes to everything outside and thinking and feeling something within. He said, when you have done this, very simply and directly, tell God just what you want.

The next thing he said is not quite so simple, for he added, when you tell God what you want, believe that He is going to give it to you. He was definite about this, for he said that when you ask God for something, you should believe not only that He is *going* to give it to you, but that he already *has given* it to you.

Can even God give us something we don't accept? The sun is shining, but we must step out of the shadow if we are to receive its rays. It all seems too good to be true, and yet, Jesus was able to prove what he was talking about. And it is only intelligent to believe someone who knows what he is talking about so well that he can really prove it. Jesus announced, with the utmost simplicity, that God is right where we are and responds to us; that He is greater than we are, and can and wants to help us; and that He will, when we believe He will.

So, every time we talk to God, let us affirm that God is giving us that which we ask and accept of Him.

AN EXPERIMENT
WITH FAITH

DEVELOP YOUR POSSIBILITIES

We like to try out new things and see how they work. There wouldn't be much fun in living unless we did this, for life is a great adventure; as a matter of fact, is *the* great adventure. Unless new things are happening to us life becomes uninteresting and drab.

When God put us here He made each one of us just a little different, and if Divine Intelligence made each one of us just a little different, as though each one were a new mold, then the greatest adventure in life would be an experiment with ourselves to see what we could do with this thing that is within us.

We seem to be made up of flesh and blood and a hank of hair, a few clothes, and surrounded by certain conditions and situations. We seem to be the product of our environment. But this is a very superficial viewpoint. For while we are thinking of everyone as having just ordinary, commonplace talents, the first thing we know an Emerson or an Einstein appears, or a Buddha or a Jesus. And all the world marvels and says that they were not made of the same kind of stuff that you and I are made of.

This is where we make our biggest mistake, for in reality you will never discover anything outside you greater than you, yourself, are. Even the words and acts of the great mean nothing to us unless we can understand them. The things they say and do have no significance until we grasp their meaning. And we couldn't grasp their meaning unless there were something in us that is already equipped to seize on the truths they taught and make them our own.

When you go to hear a symphony, you don't go just to see others perform, or go to hear a great artist sing or a great musician play. What you really go for is that they awaken within you something that corresponds to and with what they are doing. And they really give you back to yourself. This, too, is an adventure in self-discovery.

Jesus turned water into wine. We believe that he did this because we believe that the Power of God was in him and it is the Power of God that makes the vine and the grape and the juice, and it is really the Power of God in nature that converts the juice into wine. Jesus changed this whole process and immediately converted water into wine because the Power that makes the wine and the water was already in him.

But suppose someone were to say to us: "Why don't you turn water into wine?" What would our response be? Well, we know what it would be—we would say: "Why, I can't turn water into wine. I wouldn't know how. The very idea is ridiculous." But how do we know that we couldn't turn water into wine? Who told us we couldn't? Perhaps we should think about the idea again and try to find out what it was that Jesus understood that enabled him to perform this miracle.

But someone may say: "Well, Jesus was different from other people." And maybe he was. But he didn't say that he was. As a matter of fact, he said, in effect, "What I am doing you can do too, if you actually believe in a Power greater than you are and come to know that you, as a human being, have nothing to do with the process of life whatsoever. You live but you did not create your own life. You think, but you didn't create your own mind. What you are is Spirit, but you didn't make that Spirit."

At once we are confronted with such a stupendous thought that it almost staggers the imagination: "There is Something in me greater than I appear to be, and that Something really isn't myself as a mere human being at all. It is Something that was put there when I was born. There is a Presence and a Power within me waiting for my recognition. But a denial of them on my part makes it impossible for them to operate in a larger way. It is true that they are already working in me, in digesting my food, circulating my blood, causing my heart to beat, giving me such intelligence as I have. It is true that I didn't make any of these things.

"Perhaps I am asleep to the greater possibility. Perhaps I am as someone who is drugged and only half-conscious. If I could only wake up! If I could only believe that the Power which has done all this for me might be able to do a little more, perhaps It could do something beyond my wildest dream. How do I know? It told Einstein how to figure out his equations. It told Emerson how to write his essays. It told Browning how to write his poems. What happened to these people? They must have believed that they could do these things or they never would have attempted them."

And when we think of Jesus, the greatest of the great, perhaps when he first began to experiment with his faith, something said to him: "You can't multiply loaves and fishes. It is useless for you to tell the paralyzed man to get up and walk. There is no sense in your telling Lazarus to come forth from his tomb. You can't resurrect yourself."

How do we know but that early in life Jesus met the same difficulties we do, the same obstructions in his own mind? He said that he had overcome the world; that he had conquered unbelief.

As a matter of fact, I think we would lose the whole meaning of his teaching, his life, and his work, if we overlook this. For certainly Jesus did not say, "I am more Divine than you are. God likes me better than He does you. God has told me secrets that He withholds from you." This is exactly what he never did say. Rather, he said, in effect, "I have overcome the world. I know that no man can take from or add to that which I am. I have come among you; I have lived with you and worked with you and taught you; I have told you about these things which I call the realities of the kingdom of heaven. And I am telling you that everything I do is an example of an adventure and an experiment you all may engage in with the same certainty, the same assurance."

And then he told them it was necessary for him to leave them, physically. They couldn't understand this for they were relying on him. He was the one who knew all the answers. He was the one who was close to God. He was their Saviour. But Jesus told them why it was necessary for him to depart from them, and I think he must have said something like this: "I have really been telling you about yourselves and somewhere along the line the Spirit of Truth within you, the Spirit of God in you, will reveal to you the meaning of everything I have said."

Jesus had finished the greatest experiment with life that any man ever made. There were no longer any questions or doubts, no longer any ifs or ands or buts. He implied: "This is the way it is. Now you prove it for yourselves."

Really, this is the adventure you and I are on. It is a terrific one and it should fire the imagination and the will to action. We are on the adventure of self-discovery through faith, and we are learning the greatest lesson in life—man doesn't live by bread alone but by a subtle Power which flows through everything, a Divine Presence which encompasses everything. Man doesn't live by will or wishing, or hope or longing. Man lives only because the Divine Life is his life.

God comes new and direct to everyone who expects Him, talks to everyone who listens, and acts through everyone who accepts His creativity. The authority or effectiveness of your word, your prayer, your

DYNAMIC FAITH
IS EFFECTIVE!

IT CREATES YOUR EXPERIENCE

Did you ever say to yourself, "I wish that I might never again be afraid of anything"? Or have you met someone who had such a deep calm and peace that you have thought, "How I wish that I might be like that person"? Did you ever, in some still moment, feel as though you could almost reach out and touch something that would make you whole, happy, and complete?

I know you have, and I am sure everyone else has. We are all alike because we are all human beings. You share this feeling with every other person, and you instinctively know that there is something you ought to be able to tune in to which could make everything right, not only for yourself but for others and for the whole world.

What is the remedy for all this? Open your spiritual eyes! Listen with the inner ear! Open your minds!

What is it that you are to open your eyes, your ears, and your minds to? What is it that you must see, hear, and understand? It is this: Life flows into everything, through everything. It passes into every human event and translates Itself through every human act. If you learn to think of Life as flowing through your every action, you will soon discover that the things you give your attention to are quickened with new energy, for you are breathing the very essence of Being into them.

You can think yourself into being unhappy and depressed, or you can think yourself into being glad. Did it ever occur to you that you can also think yourself into being well? into being prosperous? that you can think yourself into success? Well, you can if you believe in the Law of Life, and use It rightly. But you must learn to use It affirmatively. You must learn to identify yourself with your desire.

You can use the laws of nature consciously and decide what you want them to do for you. You may have implicit confidence in them because you know they will never fail. You are surrounded by a Law of Mind which acts on your thought. This is the security of your faith and the answer to prayer.

You must become the master of your own thinking. This is the only way you can realize freedom and joy. Therefore, you will have to turn your thoughts away from lack, want, and limitation, and let them dwell on good. *Make* yourself do this. Learn to think about what you wish to become.

You are a thinking center in Life, and the chief characteristic of the Law of Life is that It responds to thought. Your slightest thought sets up a pattern which is acted upon by Creative Intelligence, causing to be created for you circumstances which will correspond to your thought.

If you think of Life as always bringing to you everything you need, you will have formed a partnership with the Invisible which will prosper you in everything you do. If you think of the organs and functions of your body as activities of Life, then automatically you will be benefited physically.

The spiritual gifts which people have so earnestly sought after are not something that God has withheld from man. Quite the reverse. They are something which man, in his ignorance, has withheld from himself. Life is not vindictive; It is not withholding anything from you.

If you will take time daily to sense the presence of Life within you, to believe in It, to accept It, it will not be long before undesirable experiences which you have known will gradually disappear and something new will be born—a bigger, better, and more perfect you. You will pass from lack and want into greater freedom; from fear into faith. From a sense of being alone, you will pass into the realization of a Oneness with everything, and you will rejoice.

There may be some who think that before they can achieve this they must become profound philosophers, spiritual sages, or men of such deep scientific knowledge that they stand apart from the rest of the world. This is not true. What the wisest have known is only a little more than you and I know. They cannot answer your questions for you; you will have to answer them for yourself. Even the best man who ever lived could not live for you; you will have to live for yourself.

You are some part of God, whether or not you know it or believe it; but you may have hypnotized yourself into thinking that you are incomplete and imperfect and identified yourself with the fantastic pictures of your morbid dreams. But the ropes that bind you are as ropes of sand.

To understand that your faith is operated on by a natural law gives you the key to the situation. But it is not enough just to believe in a principle. This is only the starting point. Principles have to be used if they are going to produce definite results for you, and whether the principles are physical, mental, or spiritual makes no difference.

It is not enough to say that faith can do anything, for most people already believe this. What you have to do is not only to realize that faith *can* do things, you have to find out how faith is acquired and then you have to *use* it for definite purposes.

To merely state that you believe that God is all there is will not necessarily cause anything to happen. But when you believe that God is all there is, and when you have implicit confidence in the Law of Good, and when you use this belief for a definite purpose, then something will happen. And the reason why it happens is that you are surrounded by a creative Power—or a creative Mind, or a creative Principle, whatever you choose to call it—which actually does respond according to your thinking. This is the key to the whole situation.

Learn to make known your requests with thanksgiving and in acceptance. And having done this, in that silent communion of your soul with its Source, believe that the Law of Good will do the rest.

If, then, you can come to see that such a Law exists and that you are using a Power greater than you are, you will at once be relieved of any sense of responsibility about it as though you had to make the Law work. For you do not sit around holding thoughts or trying to compel things to happen. As a matter of fact, this would defeat the very purpose you wish to accomplish. You can no more make the Law of Mind creative than you can compel an acorn to become an oak. You do not hold thoughts over the acorn nor do you visualize an oak tree. What you do is plant an acorn and let nature create the oak tree for you.

You are in partnership with the Giver of all life—God, the living Spirit, almighty and ever present. Therefore, say to yourself quietly but with deep conviction:

> I now accept my Divine birthright. I now consciously enter into my partnership with love, with peace, with joy, with God. I feel the infinite Presence close around me. I feel the warmth, the color, and the radiance of this Presence like a living thing in which I am enveloped.
>
> I am no longer afraid of life. A deep and abiding sense of calm and of poise flows through me. I have faith to believe that the kingdom of God is at hand. It is right, where I am, here, now, today, at this moment.
>
> I feel that there is a Law of Good which can, will, and does govern everything. Therefore, I feel that everything in my life is constructive, everything in my thought that is life-giving is blessed and prospered. It blesses everyone I meet. It makes glad

every situation I find myself in. It brings peace and comfort to everyone I contact. I am united with everything in life in love, in peace, and in joy. And I know that the Presence of Love and Life gently leads me and all others, guiding, guarding, sustaining, upholding, now and forever.

THE USE OF
SPIRITUAL IDEAS

FAITH BECOMES FACT

When we say there is a Power greater than we are, we are talking about a spiritual Power everybody can use, if he believes
in It. Someone may say this is nonsense; but stop to think a moment.
Every time you plant a garden you use a Power greater than you are.
No one living knows how to make a plant or a tree; no one living
knows how a chicken gets in an egg, or an egg in a chicken. We are
three-dimensional beings living in a four-dimensional world which
governs the three-dimensional. We do not have to try to explain the
inexplicable.

There is a Power in the universe greater than we are—an Intelligence acting as Law that receives the impress of our thought as we think
it. It is creative and It always tends to create for us the conditions we
think about and accept. And if we wish to help someone else through
our prayer or spiritual mind treatment, It will create for the person
whom we identify with It. We don't have to worry whether somebody
else believes or not. We should only be concerned about what we believe
and then demonstrate it.

People sometimes ask me if it is spiritual to pray for material things.

There is no such thing as a strictly material universe. Science has outgrown such a material concept; there can be no material universe separate from the spiritual Reality that governs and molds it. There is a Power greater than we are and everything that is visible is an expression of It. All things come forth from It and all things are contained in It, and we are in It and It responds directly to us personally at the level of our conviction that It is responding.

Someone might ask why does not the Power force conviction and faith upon us? It does not force anything upon anyone. Does a garden produce carrots when we plant beets? We have been so afraid of a vengeful God, thinking that we are made to suffer here so that we will suffer less hereafter, that we are all mixed up in our ideas about our relationship to the Infinite. There are certain laws we have to obey on the physical level, and it is the same with spiritual law as it is with physical law, only spiritual law is on a higher level. The laws work just the same.

For instance, there is a law of attraction and repulsion in mind that works just like attraction and repulsion in physics—it always tends to provide for us that which is like our own thinking. Whatsoever things are lovely and of good report, *think on these things,* the Bible says. As a man thinketh in his heart so is he; believe, and it shall be done unto you—this is the secret. There is a principle that responds to us creatively at the level of our own consciousness. To the pure in heart all will be pure. To the ones who see that everything is wrong, everything will be wrong. The ones who criticize everything and everybody will always find something to criticize. But we know that they are trying to justify themselves, they are afraid of themselves, they don't believe in themselves. They have a sense of guilt and rejection and an anxiety and an insecurity within themselves, therefore they are sick. In this sense we are sorry for them, but there is no reason why you and I should have to be like them.

There is no reason to suppose that God is some sad Creature sending thunderbolts to Methodists and candy to Baptists. The Universal loves all of us; It is impartial. There is nothing in nature or in God that with-holds our good from us. There is nothing in the universe that keeps us waiting until we "get saved." You and I believe in a Power greater than we are and we believe It is Good; we believe It is Love, Truth, and Beauty. We believe It responds to us, and if we maintain a certain men-tal attitude of thought It will automatically bring to us those things that make life happy. Life ought to be happy; there is no "weeping" God, of this I am sure.

We believe in something so wonderful that at first it seems impos-sible, yet it is so practical that it touches every moment of our lives. If we can get rid of all the thoughts that say to us we are hurt, sensitive, and unwanted—without being mean or arrogant about it—we shall no longer be hurt or led into situations where people will wish to hurt us. It is just as though all that God is is personal to each one of us. Isn't all the law of mathematics right at the finger tips of the mathematician when he is using it? Isn't all the harmony there is available to the one who sings? All of gravity is holding everything in place, as though all of gravity devoted its entire attention and effort to holding a peanut right where I might put it.

We meet God in ourselves and in each other and in nature and ev-erywhere. But how can we understand a God of Love if we are looking at life with hate? How can we accept a God of Abundance if we think only of impoverishment? How can we experience a life of harmony if we are always in discord? There seems to be a certain psychological mor-bidity about all of us. In the background is the idea that if we suffer in this world then we shall go to a good place afterwards. Actually, *that* which is the Reality comes fresh, new, clean, beautiful, lovely, exhila-rant, majestic, dynamic, omnipotent to each one of us every moment of our time. *That* which is the original creative Intelligence, *that* which is alive with Life and aflame with Love is right at the point of our inner listening, right at the point of our envisioning. This is the way it is. We did not make it this way, but we can thank God that each one of us has access to the infinite and ineffable All.

It all is as obvious as planting sunflower seeds and getting sunflowers. Jesus understood this—kind for kind. We cannot jump off a cliff and expect the law of gravitation to suspend its action just those few moments for us. We do not expect the laws of nature to disobey themselves to please the scientist; but somehow when we come to mental or spiritual things we expect the whole order of the universe to reverse itself, that out of the chaos and confusion of our thought we should be able to have an experience of peace and happiness.

It is fundamental to our wholeness and to our well-being that we must learn to affirm what we desire. We must learn to enthusiastically expect those things of good which we wish to experience. Everyone can pray an affirmative prayer; and we do not have to wonder if the Law of Mind will operate for us. It cannot help it as It acts by reflection. As we advance in our demonstrations of this most fascinating of all sciences we shall discover that the only way to change the outer condition is by inwardly changing the nature of our thought, which is then reflected as the condition.

We must remember, too, that we carry around the thought habit patterns of the ages. But we may be sure that there is a spiritual integrity within us such as we shall discover nowhere outside ourselves. Here we shall meet life; here decide that we may neutralize negative thought patterns by denying them; here accept the Power greater than we are, knowing that no matter what our mistakes It holds nothing against us—ever. Our part is really to wipe the slate of the past clean of fear and doubt and unloveliness and write a new song of acceptance of Life and Love, knowing that they forever hold us in their embrace.

Let us no longer be morbid over the past, nor afraid of the present, nor insecure about the future; but, looking in, up, and out, let each see himself as a Son who knows he is beloved of God.

Part V

HOW TO LIVE
SUCCESSFULLY

Properly viewed, we are always successful in all things. That is, we always seem to experience the ideas which dominate our thought, regardless of what those ideas may be. They could be of accomplishment or failure, it doesn't matter, for if we have had a fulfillment in our experience of what we have thought about most, then we have been successful.

There is always a logical sequence of cause and effect. We cannot expect our experience to be different from the mental patterns we have established for it. We cannot be healthy if we constantly think of illness, neither can we possess wealth if we let our thoughts dwell on poverty. There is a definite correlation between thought and experience which nothing can violate.

To change an experience from bad to better, we change our thinking about that experience, establishing thought patterns of what we want rather than what we don't want. Successful attainment of better experiences in living depends on the manner in which we are able to manage our thinking.

These closing chapters can show you the way to a better life than you have yet dreamed of.

THE WAY TO SUCCEED

THERE ARE DEFINITE RULES

There are needs which the human mind has and which every man has in common; one of them is the need for success. I would like to develop the reason why I believe this to be so.

Science of Mind is a practical philosophy. It is based on the wisdom and deep abstract concepts of the ages but never departs from an intelligent perspective of life and gives us a great latitude for personal action. We believe that there is only One Mind in the universe, One ultimate Self or Spirit, and we live in It and by It. We believe that all law is an activity of this Intelligence. The Bible tells us that "In the beginning was the Word, and the Word was with God, and the Word was God. . . . All things were made by him; and without him was not any thing made that was made." God is all—God is everywhere—God is everything.

Throughout the ages people have prayed, and we believe all prayers have been answered in such degrees as they have been consistent with the nature of Reality. We function in or manifest God's Mind at the level of our individual perception. There is at the center of your being and of mine an inner Presence always seeking a greater expression of Itself.

Now we believe that we can sit in the silence of our own thought, give a treatment, say a prayer, affirm something, or accept something, and as a result of what we do mentally something happens in our experience. This does not mean that our thought causes something to happen, but rather that we have permitted something to happen by the action of a Power greater than we are flowing through it.

We have to understand what the wise and the good have always taught: The universe is a living system of intelligence, will, imagination, and freedom, but always acting in accord with law. There seems to be no other explanation of life and the world as we know it. Whenever a prayer has been answered it has been answered according to our belief in it and through a corresponding action of law.

There is within us, now, the possibility of greatness, the possibility of limitless success in life. There is nothing unspiritual about this concept, for you and I live in God, by God, and with God. Whatever the ultimate Power of the universe is, It is One; and since It is One It is undivided, therefore It is here. Since It is here, It is where we are and what we are within ourselves, and only within ourselves shall we discover God. That is why Emerson said we cannot be satisfied except by the triumph of principle that is within our own mind. There is no division, no separation; God is Life as well as Law.

You and I always have immediate access to God. We may always initiate a new cause, a new pattern of thought, decree a thing and have it happen, providing it is in line with the nature of Reality. Our thought as prayer cannot make the world become flat, it can only flatten our experience of it. Our thought has to be naturally consistent with the Law of God. We do not have to accept dogmatic statements about this, instead we must prove it for ourselves.

There is only one human race; one heart beats in every human breast. Back of you and back of me, however inadequate we may appear, is the potential of the Infinite, surging through us to express as life, truth, action—as successful living. There is no law of God that deprives us of experiencing a greater degree of His nature. I do not believe the Infinite could possibly impose limitation on Its creation without limiting Itself, which of course would be impossible. But I believe we are all coming up through ignorance to a greater enlightenment.

Jesus, the most exalted of all the great teachers and prophets the world has ever known, stated simply and most effectively a principle we are always consciously or unconsciously using: ". . . as thou hast believed, so be it done unto thee." He implied there is something that responds to our belief *the way we believe it.*

In this concept rests the idea that we experience what we accept. However, we do not say to someone, "You must believe this, too, because we believe it." We should not believe something just because someone else believes it. It is not what you and I believe that makes truth; but we are fortunate if what we believe is truth, for then all the Power of heaven and earth is allied with us. Sitting quietly, announcing that God is all there is, each may say, no matter what the present appearance may be, "Good and only good shall come to me."

There is nothing in the outer world that can attach itself to us unless we mentally attach ourselves to it first—in ignorance as a rule. We are held in bondage until we consciously seek the enlightenment that sets us free. Successful living has nothing to do with mental suggestion; it has to do with inward knowing. To know is to experience. There is no other way to be certain. Until you and I realize that we can decree the thing and then experience it, we shall not understand the only real security there is in the universe. Times may change, people may come and go, but the One who changeth not abides with us eternally. We are immersed in a living Presence which is God, personal to each one of us. You and I must come to know God as an immediate experience and as always creatively active in our lives.

I find nothing in logic or reason to contradict this idea. We have this need of God, this need of consciously feeling the warmth and color, the action and intelligence and enthusiasm of the Universal at the center of our own being. Some people are so used to thinking of a reluctant God doling out gifts that it is hard for them to understand that to have prayer be effective they must believe the prayer is answered when they pray it. But time and experience have proved this to be true to millions of people. Something responds to us the way we believe. God is real.

We must come at last to believe in our own word of affirmation and acceptance; not only to put our hope into words, but also to accept the realization of that hope. Any person who will do this consistently, who will continue to announce his good and to believe in it, most surely will find the seeming barren areas of his life awaken to new creativity. To keep an integrity with our own soul, to trust ourself though all men doubt us, yet "make allowance for their doubting, too," is to let go of all that denies the magnificence and beneficence of God. It is to lay down the fear of the unknown and to take up the challenge of confidence in the Invisible, and to consciously place our hand in the hand of the Infinite, accepting the love and light and truth and peace that is at the center of our being.

So shall we find that our word ever accomplishes that which is good and always prospers that thing whereto we direct it.

HOW TO
BUILD SECURITY

It's an Inside Job

Everyone is looking for security, and often we think the word "security" means that we have money enough to pay the bills. It does certainly include that. But there is a deeper security than that, a security that comes only through a deep and abiding faith in Life; a deep and abiding faith in ourselves, and a deep and abiding faith in God. There is no security in life without this faith. That is why a person is not healed of a neurosis without attaining some kind of new faith. There is no permanent healing of anything in life without a restoration of faith. There is no gratification or feeling of safety without faith. Why is this so? I do not know, but I have a theory about it.

My theory is very simple. Every man is on the pathway of an endless evolution. There is Something that impels him; there is a spark of Divinity that shapes his ends, rough hew them though he may, as Shakespeare said. Everyone has an urge to live, to sing, to dance, to accomplish something, to love something, and to give. The moment we stop the loving and the giving we are forlorn—we are unhappy.

I think we belong to God, we are *of* God, the very essence of God. Spirit, I believe, is incarnated in everything and in everyone. There is only One Spirit, but innumerable incarnations. We are, as Browning said, a God though in the germ. I am sure millions of people hold this view, but not everyone understands it, or they do not think about it enough. If we are not willing to think, we are wasting our time. Think! Someone said, "Keep faith with reason for she will convert thy soul."

It is unreasonable and illogical to suppose that the supreme Life would create something that It could destroy. When Jesus was asked about God's relationship to the dead, he answered as we would expect an inspired spiritual genuis to answer: "God is not the God of the dead, but of the living . . . for all live unto him." Now that is logical; it is rational and reasonable and sound. God is Life, and cannot produce death. God is Peace, and cannot produce confusion. God is Love, and cannot produce fear. You and I have to come to believe this if we would know security.

You see God has entered into you and me. We could not find anything in us that is really separated from God, except our belief. We seem to have that freedom. And if this is true, how can we hope to have security unless that security is based on our own unity with God, on our own Divinity? "Hear, O Israel; The Lord thy God is one Lord." There is only One. That is why Emerson said that "there is one mind common to all individual men."

Your mind is God's Mind in you, as you. Your spirit is the Spirit of God in you, as you. This you did not make. *It is*, and will not be changed. This is the great secret that Jesus taught, as have all of the other great teachers of man. In essence no race, no person, no form of life is external to our own. We cannot exclude any facet of life and have a universe left. We will only have a fragment of a universe in which we will blindly stumble around.

God is our life *now*. It is not a life that we are going to attain some day. It *is* our life. We are not gradually becoming unified with God; we cannot be separated from God! We shall never have to unify with

God, but we shall have to recognize that we are not separated from God. Then, that in our experience which appears to be separated will flow together; it will rush together, as the mountain torrent rushes across the valley to join the ocean of its infinitude.

There is Something in you and in me that foreknows these things; no one taught us or caused us to remember that celestial palace whence we came. But how can we hope to have a sense of security if we separate ourselves in belief from That which alone can give it? Who hath power to give us life but God? Science cannot bestow it. The various branches of learning are fine and wonderful, but they do not give us life—they only tell us about it. There is no security unless we have a deep and abiding faith in Life; a faith which permits Life to flow through us, but only at the level of our understanding and acceptance of It.

What inhibits It? We pretty well know now. We are born with a desire to love, to laugh, to sing, to dance, to create. Without being technical about it, we are born with an emotional craving for self-expression. Life is action, movement, and enthusiasm. Unless we keep doing new things, we will not have the interest to do new things. This is the secret of growing up mentally, emotionally, and spiritually. We shall never recapture yesterday, we shall never catch up with tomorrow for it eludes us; but today is ours! This day in which we live, this hour, this moment is one from which we should distill all the joy there is, all the enthusiasm.

Do you know that people who are unenthusiastic are always tired? It is now definitely known that, unless there is a physical infection, most weariness is associated with ennui which comes psychologically and emotionally because the individual isn't interested in others, or in living. It is definitely known that those who stop living for others, stop living. The emotional energy, which is the greatest creative force we have, is designed to go out and express itself in wholesome action. This energy is as real as the energy of physics. If it is inhibited it still remains in a dynamic state and the result is a discharge of energy in what we know as an inner conflict or complex.

I believe that everything that exists is an expression of God, and that is why we are here. There is an inner Something in man that belongs to the Universe and we have to get rid of all that inhibits It—every sense of rejection and guilt and insecurity and anxiety. The security I am talking about is the kind that not only warms the heart and makes glad the mind, but feeds the soul. We belong to God. There is That within us which will last forever. "I am That which Thou art." There is no other security.

What joy we would have if we would just see God in each other and in human events! If we know God is our substance, we shall have supply. If we know God is our friend, we shall have friends. If we love everybody, there will be enough people to return that love to us. This is security, and there is no peace of mind not based on this security. There is no final peace but love; there is no final security anywhere in the universe but a faith in Life that proves itself. Truth demonstrates itself without effort. We are begirt by spiritual laws which execute themselves, as Emerson said.

So there must be a deep sense of love and givingness if we are going to have a real security and peace of mind. There is in us a primal Cause, an ultimate Reality, a cosmic Wholeness, a God from whom all things flow and in whom all things move and live.

We are not all of God, of course, but everything that we are is made out of God because there is nothing else it can be made of. The Universe holds us forever in Its warm and close embrace. When you and I turn to that Divinity within us we shall feel something and we shall know something which every endeavor of the ages has sought after—the living God. Engraved on the scroll of the Universe is the inextinguishable imprint of our own individuality—the name of the beloved Son.

Here and here alone is security; here and here alone is peace. But not in splendid isolation shall it be found. It is in the wind and the wave, the song of the child, the crooning of the mother, the beauty of the sunset, and the golden glory of dawn's rise over the mountaintops flinging its light into the newness of another day. It is not just in religious adoration, but in the stillness of our own heart that He speaks.

THOUGHT AND
PHYSICAL HEALTH

S cience of Mind is a real science, a practical, workable science which can be taught to and understood and used by anyone. It is the newest of all sciences and the most effectual.

In Science of Mind we do not deny that people are sick. We do not have to deny one truth to affirm another. We believe in the application of medicine, surgery, sanitation, diet, proper exercise—everything that belongs to the plane or the level upon which the various aspects of life function. It has been my endeavor to make Science of Mind a bridge between the world of experience and the indwelling Spirit, between what ails us and what can make us well, and this includes psychosomatic medicine and the physician. We are the first metaphysical group that has ever recognized the wholeness and unity of all things and that is why there are so many leading physicians and surgeons who adhere to and use the principles of Science of Mind.

We believe that man is a spiritual being right now, living in a spiritual universe right now, and that every man is an incarnation of God—right now! All of the Power and Presence, all of the Wholeness in the universe is available to man right now. There is nothing but God. I believe the time will come when this idea will be taught from the kindergarten level on up.

There is a spiritual man who never gets sick; if he did, neither medicine, surgery, nor prayer could heal him. There is nothing you and I can do objectively, subjectively, or spiritually to change *the nature of God*. ". . . the Lord he is God: there is none else beside him."

The ancient Chinese said that man has three bodies; a physical, a mental, and a spiritual body. It was believed that his physical body could not be well unless there were circulation. It was only about three hundred years ago that the circulation of the blood was discovered. We now know that there must be circulation, assimilation, and elimination if there is going to be physical health. The ancient Chinese recognized that where there is no circulation there is stagnation, infection, and death. But they also said that man has a mental body and that there can be no physical circulation that is right unless the mental circulates through the physical.

It is within the memory of all of us that there was first introduced the idea of what is now called psychosomatic medicine—psyche meaning mind, and soma meaning body, therefore, we have psychosomatic meaning mind-body relationship. This is a recent thing with us; but the ancient Chinese said there must be a circulation of the mental body through the physical body because they are so closely allied—the very core, sinew, flesh, and blood of psychosomatic medicine. It is believed today that from seventy-five to ninety percent of all ailments and diseases are unconsciously invoked by some mental or emotional action.

And the Chinese also said that there not only must be a circulation of the mental through the physical, but there also must be a circulation of the spiritual through the mental because man has a spiritual body and the mental body cannot circulate through the physical until the spiritual has circulated through the mental. The Bible reminds us that man is spirit.

In Science of Mind we do not deny the physical or the mental, but we say there is also the spiritual. This is our field of therapeutics: We say that man's body is the instrument of his mind or consciousness, but that his mind is at the same time the instrument of his spirit—". . . there is a spirit in man: and the inspiration of the Almighty giveth them understanding."

Future generations will be taught the need of quiet contemplation that they may sense and realize the Presence of God in their minds, in the activities within their bodies, and in their affairs. Let us think about this. We can heal ourselves of most of our physical troubles if we go about it rightly, and we can heal others just as well. We should not think that we have to wait for some spiritually enlightened person to come along or until we attain the ultimate in maturity ourselves.

Jesus was a man who knew God and I think the greatest thing he ever said was, "Neither do I condemn thee." The older I grow, the more I realize that human kindness is the greatest quality on earth. I sense the depth and breadth, and feel the height and wonderful illumination of the man who could say that. But Jesus was also a man of justice for he warned that making the same mistake again would result in the same consequence. The Universe is just without judgment. This is a terrific concept!

All disease is unnatural and does not belong to the *real* person—if it did, no one could heal it. Any doctor will tell you it is the nature of the body to heal itself of every disease, and that it is the nature of the mind to fight off every psychosis and neurosis. If they didn't, no one could be healed. There is no physician who thinks he heals anything or anyone. He only assists nature in re-establishing the normal processes of circulation, assimilation, and elimination in both body and mind.

You and I deal with spiritual mind healing. We believe in the practice of spiritual meditation consciously used for definite healing purposes. We not only believe in it, we know it is true. While we gratefully acknowledge the contribution that is made in every field to alleviate suffering, we do believe in a *transcendence*. We believe there is a Power beyond the physical and beyond the intellect and that It is spiritual. Now, what do we mean by a spiritual Power?

"Shew us the Father, and it sufficeth us," said Philip. "Jesus saith unto him, Have I been so long time with you, and yet hast thou not known me, Philip? he that hath seen me, hath seen the Father. . . ." Jesus was talking about the spiritual man. There is in everyone this spiritual man, this Christ, Atman, Buddha—it does not matter the name we give it. This is the Son begotten of the only Father, and each is that Son right now. "Know ye not that ye are the temple of God, and that the Spirit of God dwelleth in you?"

Spiritual thinking means the realization and affirmation that God is all there is. When we properly identify ourselves with this ultimate Perfection we realize that there is a necessity for us to experience perfect circulation, perfect assimilation, and perfect elimination through our physical body as well as through the body of our affairs.

Each is his own best practitioner, his own best physician, because the Spirit within us is God. It knows all things, sees all things, hears all things, understands all things because It is all things. Therefore, spiritual mind healing means that we identify our consciousness with the One Mind, the Mind that is God. The greatest trouble we have in our work is to convince people that what they are looking for, they are looking with; that the God they are trying to become good enough to understand *is* at the center of their being now, and that the creative word they want to use is the word they *are* using. Though for the most part they use it unconsciously and deny their good instead of accepting it.

If we have to find a good power with which to combat a bad power, where would we go to get it? If my soul were lost, would you know where to look for it? How well Jesus knew this. Emerson knew it also for he said "stay at home with the cause." We have to be still and come to know that we are the manifestation of God. We have a spiritual body right now that is perfect, that is not lame or sick, that does not hurt nor is congested, that has no disease. If we did not have it, neither psychology, medicine, nor metaphysics could help us. All in the world any of us can do is to *adjust that which we seem to be to that which we really are*! Jesus called this knowing the truth. "And ye shall know the truth, and the truth shall make you free."

There is a Spirit in us that bears witness to the truth. Though we may not look it, and often may not act it, we are *perfect* right now. The knowledge and use of this truth of being will make us free of the limitations that our ignorance has brought upon us.

If one has a pain it should be relieved, because it is foolish to think that God wants us to suffer. That is ignorance. We, therefore, do not deny that hospitals are needed as well as doctors and surgeons and nurses. But isn't it wonderful that the great Physician is right where we are, always? Always ready to be called upon by either ourselves or the medical man.

This is the most difficult thing to teach. Nine out of ten people think a spiritual mind treatment is something different from what it is and has to be: the recognition that man's life is some part of God. Jesus knew this and taught over and over that "the kingdom of God is within," that each is a Son of the Most High in whom there is no condemnation. We must come to know the *self* that each is and must be. Then will the glory of this eternal *self* spill itself into the desert of our hopelessness, warm the creative soil of our mind, and flow through our thought into our body in words immaculate.

It is so very simple! There is perfect circulation, there is perfect assimilation, there is perfect elimination, for there is no congestion and no limitation in the Divinity at the center of our being! We should glory and delight in it.

Perhaps some of you are asking yourselves, "What words shall I use?"

Use the words that mean something to you, because the word is a mold for the living essence, making it vibrant with life. Any word that means freedom to you will produce freedom.

Some of you might be saying, "How do I really know enough to speak such words?"

Did not Jesus point to a little child and say "of such is the kingdom of God"? A child is eager to learn, willing to believe, trusting, his imagination is alive and vital. We have to become teachable all over again if we are to learn to experience a finer, higher concept of life.

One of the main efforts in modern medicine is to show individuals that their thoughts are the principal causes of their physical problems; and that once they learn to avoid thinking in a manner that inhibits the natural normal flow of Life through the body it readily returns to a state of health. The body has its roots, its source, its pattern in a spiritual world—in the nature of God which is perfect. But we seem to go out of our way to maintain ideas and thoughts contrary to this perfection which in turn prevents it from being manifested in and through our body and our affairs. Healthful living is available for us to experience when we re-educate ourselves to think in terms of health rather than of illness.

This applies to the entire realm of thinking. Every thought has some effect and helps shape our experience. Our great freedom is that we may choose our thoughts! We need to begin to think anew about ourselves and our relationship to God. Let us practice the principle of beholding our Divine Sonship in ourselves, and in all others as well, until it makes its appearance in all of our relationships. Too long have we misinterpreted life in words of hate and condemnation, of fear and limitation.

There is a perfect spiritual body which is a part of everyone's Divine heritage. No matter through what other avenues we may seek to meet our physical and mental needs, let us often sit in the silence of our own soul in adoration of the inner Spirit. Let us in consciousness revere the God who never did anything wrong. More often than we have ever done, let us in our thought and feeling say, "Holy, holy, holy, Lord God Almighty within me." Let us surrender the littleness of human conceit and pride and fear and injustice. It can be done, for there is no mediator between ourselves and the eternal Reality.

Remember this: Any word you speak with meaning will have power. Do not try to use words I write, the words of other writers, or even words that are in the Bible. They are good, but the word that springs spontaneously in your own heart and mind is the right word to use in prayer or treatment.

Let us believe as we have never believed before in the imprisoned splendor within ourselves, loosed by our own words. It is God who has willed it, the Law of God establishes it, and our experiences may demonstrate it. The Source of all the good we have so earnestly sought out, we have with us. Our health, our permanent well-being, lie in our realization of our eternal and ineffable life in God. In Him we live and move and have our being; but we must deny everything that denies this and affirm that which establishes it.

Is it not wonderful to know that that which the prophets have prophesied, that which the sages have taught and the poets have written about is true? The more exalted the thought and emotion, the statelier mansions we build. We shall leave the "low-vaulted past" as we build each "new temple, nobler than the last." Let us use our imagination and will and feeling in prayerful attitude and think about God being that which we are, until every mental and emotional congestion is loosened and let go in the acceptance of the glory of something transcendent which comes to us. As we *know* this the body responds, for it is immersed in Something superior to itself.

We are so One with the Whole that what is true of It is also true of us. Life is forever taking form in us. The entire order is one of spontaneous being and spontaneous manifestation. The Law follows the word just as the word follows the desire. This creative process goes on whether we agree that it does or not. Our experiences will change when we purposefully desire to change them for the better.

Going forth into the early morn of a day of new hope, forgetting the old, rising above the doubt and fear of yesterday, let us dare to believe that today there comes into our consciousness something new, something noble, something transcendent, which sings to us of a joy ineffable, of a God approachable, of a hope realized, of a life lived in wholeness.

YOU ARE IMMORTAL, NOW!

THERE IS ONLY ONE LIFE

There are three ways in which the human mind gathers knowledge, so far as is now known. One is by science, which is the knowledge of the laws of nature. Another is by intuition, which includes revelation, inspiration, and all religions. The other way is philosophy, which contains all of the opinions of the ages—what is right or wrong, what is rational, what is logical, what is reasonable. We are interested now in finding the contributions that these different avenues make to our acceptance of immortality.

Every great religion has believed in the immortality and the ongoingness of the soul. The whole system of the ancient Hindus was built on the idea that God—Reality, Truth, Brahma—is only *One*, beside which there is none other, and that every one of us is an incarnation of It; that we are gradually unfolding or evolving into all of It, that It flows through every one of us. We belong to the Christian faith which is a combination of the old Hebrew idea that God speaks from without, and the Greek idea that God speaks from within. We say the highest God and the innermost God is One God.

Now we do not want to believe in immortality simply because some-body became immortalized through the resurrection, which I believe in easily enough. Jesus, I believe, became resurrected to prove the eternal-ity of the soul. You and I are given life, inherent, and we cannot live by proxy. It does not matter how good Jesus was, or how saintly Buddha was, or how great a man one of the ancient Hindus must have been, there is that within each of us which must bear witness to every truth, to every fact, and to every experience; and until it does we are only half-being, half-hearing, and half-knowing. Can someone else play a game for you? If you feel like weeping, can you get somebody to cry for you, real tears? Can somebody else love for you? Of course not! We must meet life individually, as well as collectively, and only the man who does is at peace. It is only in our own integrity that we shall ever see God. We cannot live and be whole because somebody else was a good man. Jesus knew this. He said: "Why callest thou me good? there is none good but one, that is, God." And he called God "the Father, that dwelleth in me." When they wanted to make him a king he said, in effect, that it was expedient that he go away, so that the Spirit of Truth should bear wit-ness to the Divine fact of our own being.

We find Socrates, who was called the Father of Philosophy, and Kant, who was called the Father of Reason, both teaching that God is One and that we are a part of Him. Logic would tell us that there can-not be two infinites—there can only be one finality in the universe. Logic also would tell us how futile it would be if "six feet under and all is over." What an economic waste of energy and time! How irrational the Universe would be! Emerson said we are organs of the Infinite. There is incarnated in each of us that Divine spark which is of the nature of God, and, carrying us through the process of evolution, grad-ually unfolds until we are so unified with Him that you cannot tell where the one begins and the other leaves off. It is the nature of the Father to be inherent in the Son.

Now let us see what science can tell us about immortality. It is now held by some scientists that there is not an atom of our physical body that was in it a short time ago, some say eleven months; but in any event, no one is over a year old as far as the physical composition of his body is concerned. But we do not all look that young, of that I am sure. At the same time, many leading psychologists hold that the mind cannot wear out, although it may appear to become confused. This is interesting, isn't it? What is back of it? Not somebody's opinion, not some sin and salvation theory, not someone's theology, but certain scientific truths, certain universal realities, certain laws of our own being that we ought to consider. Too often our faith must be propped up every few moments, and unless we arrive at a conviction beyond that kind of need, we shall always be exclaiming, "Lord, I believe; help thou mine unbelief."

Behind the thought that the body is not over a year old is another thought: Everything in the universe is in a state of continual flux; new substances appearing all the time—the old disappearing, giving place to the new in all creation. If this is true of our physical body, we have no reason to doubt that it may be true of the structure of the whole physical universe, and that back of it is that Life which forevermore makes everything new. This is not a wild phantasy. God is not old or young, but without birth and without death, and we live and move and have our being in this eternal sea of never-ending Life.

Why is it that the mind cannot grow old? Because there is only One Mind in the universe and we use It. That Mind is God, that Mind is our mind *now*. How could we wear It out or use It up or exhaust Its possibilities? But we can become so confined in our thinking that It does not reflect or flow through us with clarity. There is no physiological or psychological reason, from the viewpoint of God, that anything could ever be used up or exhausted because nothing is static—everything is a continual flow of Life. When we refuse the flow at whatsoever age we may be, we begin to feel "dead on our feet," as the saying goes. This does not mean that God has changed or denied us any degree of life, but that we have blocked ourselves from our Source.

What would happen if we were free from all fear, or doubt, or the unhappiness and morbidity of our retrospections of the past and the unwholesome anticipation of what we think the future holds in store; from sandwiching the day in which we live between two impossible negations? Somewhere along the line we, who are born to be free, must think our way through until we are no longer afraid of the universe in which we live, until a conviction has dawned in our consciousness that will bring us a solidarity and an integrity which cannot be shaken.

What proof have we outside our desire, our intuition—which would be enough for me—of immortality? In psychological laboratories they have demonstrated that we can experience many of the activities of the organs of sense without using the organs. We can see without the eyes, hear without the ears, speak without the tongue, communicate, travel without the ordinary methods; there is something in us that can function without the body and without the brain. It is not that we do not need brains, but the brains do not think—they are but the instrumentalities of That which is above them and superior to them. This is why Jesus said: "Before Abraham was, I am . . . Destroy this temple, and in three days I will raise it up."

Many who have begun to investigate such facts to disprove them have come to devote all their time to proving them. There is no question but that they have scientifically disclosed beyond the possibility of chance the ongoingness of the soul. This is why Jesus said to the thief on the cross beside him: "To day shalt thou be with me in paradise." Now if it is true that there is That within us which transcends the use of the physical senses, could it not mean that we are immortal now? The materialistic concept of life has been completely annihilated.

This is the great truth of our being: We are forever individualizing the Spirit, the Spirit is forever unifying with Its own individualization;

which means we live in God and God is what we are. Why, then, if these things are true, should we not enter into the spirit of our immortality right now? Carl Jung, whom I consider one of the greatest psychologists, has said that he never knew a case of permanent healing without a restoration of faith, he never knew a person who could be happy the latter part of his life unless he believed in immortality. Why? Because he has nothing to look forward to. It is only in the attention we give to the present, and the certainty we have of its expansion into what we call the future, and the continuity of ongoing, that we would have any joy at all.

Why, then, do we need to feel we must wait to become immortal when it is something we may see and feel and know and understand right now? Growing old is refusing to grow every day, a waiting until that final moment when we step into the larger life. We should be children playing on the shores of time. We miss our friends, we long for the touch of a vanished hand, or the sound of a voice that is stilled. We would not have it otherwise. But there is no hopelessness; there has been but a loosing and liberating from what is no longer needed.

But suppose, right now, we become resurrected and, one by one, remove out of the tomb of memory the fears and morbidities and uncertainties, the hates and jealousies and animosities—everything that is vindictive—and resurrect only that which can bring joy into life. Why is it that down the avenues of evolution, in the begetting of all the great religious systems, which are so good otherwise, they had to drag the corpse and morbidity of sin and punishment and chagrin up the pathway to eternal God and blot out the light of heaven with a shadow of fear?

We should resurrect ourselves, even as Jesus did, to the joy and simplicity and spontaneity of Life. God is no taskmaster. The eternal Law of Love cannot hurt. That which is Light will never produce darkness. Heaven will never descend into a hell, and a hymn of hate will not stimulate the mind to the harmonies of Life. For our resurrection today must leave the corpses of our dead yesterdays in the tomb of their own obscurity. We must live more abundantly in the God of heaven and earth—awake to God within us this day. Jesus has left us the hope which must be realized. You and I must and shall come out of our tomb of ignorance and disbelief. How glorious shall be the dawn!

LIVING
WITHOUT FEAR

FOREWORD

This is the second in the series of Annual Editions of *Science of Mind* magazine to bring together the miscellaneous writings of Ernest Holmes.

The material in this Edition is taken from the earliest issues of *Science of Mind* magazine. Many of these articles were based on Dr. Holmes's lectures during what was probably his most dynamic period as a teacher of modern metaphysics.

A great deal of the material in the early issues of the magazine was incorporated in the revised edition of the textbook, *The Science of Mind*. However, equally valuable material was of necessity omitted due to limitations of space. Some of it has been brought together to make this book. From one point of view this might be said to be a supplement to his textbook.

For over thirty years this material has been unavailable to the reading public, and it is hoped that now that it has been brought to light it will offer new hope, inspiration, and instruction to many new and old readers. Here we find Ernest Holmes presented to us in the same manner that first established him as one of the great religious philosophers and spiritual leaders of our day.

WILLIS KINNEAR

INTRODUCTION

We spend most of our lives trying to avoid what we do not like and seeking to experience more of those things that bring us pleasure, happiness, and well-being. However, in doing this we find ourselves in an almost continual state of fear in one or more of its many forms. We fear what we do not like, and also fear we will not have what we do like.

Worry, crisis, and anxiety seem to plague most people, often to the extent that life is something to be suffered through rather than to be lived with joy. This does not mean that we shall ever be free of all problems, but rather that life and living present a continual challenge, which we should learn to master instead of allowing it to master us.

No one imposes fear upon us, rather we create it for ourselves in our own thoughts and emotions. What we need to realize is that we have just as much freedom to eliminate fear as we have in creating it.

That there is an obvious need to secure our freedom from our self-created and self-imposed fears is found in those sciences which deal with the mind and the body. Any evidence of fear in our thought, whether it be large or small, can have subtle and far-reaching consequences. Unless properly handled the entire process of thought can become unbalanced and misdirected. Similarly, fear seems to be able to affect the function and structure of almost every part of the body.

Two questions immediately arise: To what extent can we afford to let ourselves become subject to the destructive thoughts of fear which we have established for ourselves? What can we do to free ourselves from them and replace them with other thoughts and ideas which will contribute to our welfare?

The escape from fear does not involve a retreat from living, but it does mean that our reactions to experiences should not be allowed to overwhelm us but should lead to constructive action. This implies that there should be a renewing of the mind so that its reactions to life are not negative, and that a watch should be maintained on our processes of thought so that they are maintained on a positive, constructive, creative level.

If a person seeks to free himself from limitations which his fears have imposed upon him, it will also be necessary for him to free himself from those ideas which have nourished and kept the fears alive to wreak their damage.

The purpose of the material in this book is to show you the pathway that may enable you to start your journey to a new freedom, a freedom from fear, and a greater participation in all those things which make life more worthwhile.

You can find a freedom from fear, and you can discover the ways and means to achieve more of what your heart desires. The journey can be made, the goals can be achieved. But it is something that no one else can do for you, for the attainment rests in the processes of your own thought.

The challenge in life and living is to what degree we can learn to think constructively. This book can show you the way, but the actual traveling of that way is up to you. And in your journey from fear to freedom you will be making the greatest discovery any man can make— the discovery of yourself!

W.K.

FREEDOM FROM FEAR IS POSSIBLE

From time immemorial it has been almost instinctive for man, when confronted with fear, to turn to what he has considered a Power greater than himself; to seek release or protection from situations and conditions which have threatened what he considered a normal, natural existence.

This turning to a greater Power has been common to all men, at all times, and is an inherent aspect of all religious beliefs.

Primarily it is an act of thought, but it is also accompanied by action commensurate with the nature of the thought. This act of thought has been called many things, but is commonly identified as prayer. However, much that has passed as prayer has been ineffective in establishing the freedom sought.

What we seek to determine is the nature of man and the prayer which produces desired results.

GET RID OF
SUPERSTITIONS

cience is defined as "knowledge of facts, laws, and proximate causes, gained and verified by exact observation and correct thinking."

Superstition is defined as "a belief founded on irrational feelings" and as "a belief in a religious system regarded (by others than the believer) as unreasonable."

Supernatural is defined as "that which is outside the range of the accepted course of nature; that which transcends nature and includes the Creator."

Nature is defined as "the system of natural existences, forces, changes, and events, regarded as distinguished from, or exclusive of, the supernatural."

From the above stated definitions we gather that science is that which we know something about or have a definite knowledge of. Superstition is an unreasonable belief, especially in regard to religious convictions and our ideas of God. The supernatural is that which we do not understand or have any definite knowledge of, but might be that which includes the Creator, while nature means natural existence.

It appears from these definitions that the dictionary defines the supernatural from a superstitious standpoint, for it clearly states that the supernatural is outside the range of nature but includes the being of God. The definition is not scientific but superficial.

We are living in a scientific age, therefore in an age of a more or less exact knowledge of many things. But can we say that we have exact knowledge of ultimate causes other than that gathered from their effects? *We do not see the cause of anything.* All that we do see is the effect of invisible causes.

We are daily confronted by a creation the cause of which no man sees. This cause is what we mean by the supernatural or that which transcends nature. And man has given to this cause the name of God or Spirit.

Of course we have the right to assume a cause when we see an effect, for there can be no effect without some cause from which it rises. If superstition is that which is outside the range of our accepted ideas of nature, but that which might include the Creator, then it follows that most of our ideas about the Creator must be superstitions.

Now is it, or is it not, superstitious to believe in God or Spirit? Can the scientist call the religionist superstitious? or can the religionist call the scientist superstitious? The religionist believes in a God higher and more powerful than the natural world as we now understand it. The scientist believes in a power which transcends the material world but is part of ultimate Reality.

Suppose we combine the beliefs of the scientist and the religionist and see what we will have. We will have God, the Intelligence above nature (which the scientist says we do not understand), and we will have nature and natural causes which we understand only in part.

It would seem as though there were room for both the scientist and the religionist. The religionist believes in God, the scientist also believes in God, and there need be no conflict between the two. But both the religionist and the scientist may easily become *superstitious*. The religionist is superstitious when he believes that God works outside of nature or contrary to it, and the scientist is superstitious when he believes that there is any natural existence which is exclusive of the supernatural.

Science of Mind teaches that the supernatural world is the spiritual world and at the same time the spiritual world permeates the natural world. One is the cause, the other the effect. Both are true and each is necessary if there is to be any creation.

Creation is a fact, therefore the Creator also must be a fact. By the Creator we mean the intelligent Principle running through everything.

How do we know that there is such an intelligent Principle? The answer is simple but conclusive: because we are intelligent enough to recognize Intelligence!

The dictionary defines God as "the one Supreme Being, self-existent and eternal; the infinite maker, sustainer, and ruler of the universe." It is an axiom of pure reason that there must be and is such an infinite power in the universe. God is an undivided whole, therefore omnipresent. God, then, is not only above but is also in His creation. The natural is permeated with the supernatural; it causes, flows through, and gives rise to conditions. God is not only *above* what He does; He is also *in* what He does.

The scientist, observing the natural world, is watching God at work. And as God always works through Law (for this is His nature), the scientist is studying a world of law which he is more or less able to understand.

Let us consider evolution and growth as the series of steps by which a single cell develops or grows into a multi-cellular organism, either in the development of all life or in a single life. We do not see that which does the evolving, but its result—the thing evolved.

Law is the rule by which certain actions take place; everything in the universe is governed by exact laws, otherwise the universe would be a chaos. We do not see any law, we see what it does and how it acts. *Law is a part of the invisible government of the universe.*

In dealing with facts and actions of every kind we are dealing with law, and insofar as we understand the law governing any fact or action, we understand the action. But we understand the actor only through the act. Causes are partly revealed and partly concealed. Any given cause is ascertained by a careful observation of its effects. In proving effects we establish causes in understanding effects we penetrate the nature of causes.

It is certain that there can be no effect without a cause; it is just as certain that there can be no cause without some effect. Science deals with effects and in this way penetrates into causes. In the effect, it is dealing with the natural world; in its idea of the cause, it is dealing with the supernatural or spiritual world.

Science of Mind takes into account both the cause and the effect. It affirms both, each in its place. It does not deny the one and affirm the other, but it does affirm that the one is the cause of the other.

We are living in a universe of spontaneous Intelligence and of absolute Law. Of this we are certain, since we, ourselves, have spontaneous intelligence but are, at the same time, subject to exact laws.

But the question might be raised: How can spontaneous intelligence be subject to exact laws? The answer is that it is the *nature of being* to be this way. The answer is both sensible and adequate. Law is necessary to the universe. It could not be run without law, but the very fact that we can cognize law proves a spontaneous element in creation.

To believe in a God who transcends law is superstitious; to believe in a law which is outside the nature of intelligence is a mistake. To accept both is the truth. To accept an infinite Intelligence in the universe is the only way to account for our own lives; to understand the Law of Life is to enter into the nature of this Intelligence. *We must accept God as both Life and Law.*

God is self-existent as Life and as Law. God did not make God, hence God did not make Law. God did not make God, hence God did not make Life. God, Life, and Law are One, coexistent and coeternal.

God as Life expresses Himself through Law. This Law, being an invariable part of the universe, can be relied upon.

It would be superstitious to suppose that by prayer we cause God to change His laws or the way they work. God is Law and cannot contradict His own nature. But, if God is Intelligence as well as Law, it would be a mistake to suppose that this Intelligence cannot respond to our intelligence. This response would not be supernatural but Divinely natural.

When the scientist calls upon the Intelligence within him to direct his thought, he is calling upon God, for the Spirit is everywhere present in Its entirety. The scientist who is truly religious will always surpass the one who discounts the possibility of thinking God's thought after Him.

To suppose that God helps some and not others is superstitious. To suppose that God is ready to help all is both scientific and sensible. It is the nature of God to express Himself. This we know because it is true of our own natures. Whenever our minds are receptive to the Divine influx there is a flowing of God through us, according to exact Law. To deny this Divine inflow is to deny our own natures and shut the door to our own possibilities.

When the scientist thinks, he affirms Intelligence; when he discovers how things work, he affirms Law. Intelligence is spontaneous, Law is automatic. God works through Law, therefore all Law is of the nature of Truth and Reality, whether it be the law of evolution, of chemical reactions, or of gravitation; or whether it be the most subtle law we know of, the "law of mental action and reaction."

There is no law known but that we can affirm it to be a part of the Divine nature. We do not deny Law but that which contradicts Law. We affirm Intelligence and Law as necessary to creation, and we affirm creation as the result of Intelligence and Law.

Abundance cannot produce limitation nor can freedom give birth to bondage. Perfection cannot create imperfection, nor completion create incompletion. That which to us appears incomplete and imperfect is the result of an incomplete and an imperfect understanding of Reality. We are but children in the process of an eternal evolution.

If God is already perfect, free, deathless, and complete, it would be impossible for this Perfection to cognize anything less than Itself. We do not change the nature of Reality through prayer, and it would be superstitious to suppose that we do or can. But, through prayer and meditation we enter into the nature of Reality and partake of this nature. Not that God changes, but that we change our attitude toward God.

The scientist does not pray that the principle of his science may be true, but that he may enter into an understanding of a principle which is already true. As he enters in, he partakes. The religionist should not pray for God to be God, but that he may enter into the Divine nature. The nature of Reality is immutable Law and Order and it cannot be changed by prayer, but when we stand in the shadow of the Almighty we shall no longer be blown by the winds of chance. There is a warm responsiveness from the Spirit to all who contact It in the right way. But this is always Its way. Not our way, but the way of Truth.

We cannot pray to the Principle of Perfection to feed and clothe us and in so doing alter Its exact Law of Cause and Effect. What we can do is to avail ourselves of the Law of Abundance, then we shall experience plenty while the nature of God remains unchanged. There is no special creation. All is Law and all is Order and everything is Divine when rightly understood.

WHO AND WHAT YOU ARE

Man is a triad—a threefold unity. He is physical, having an objective body; mental, having a conscious, emotional, and subjective reaction to his environment; and spiritual, having a self-knowing mind.

The full nature of man constitutes the law of his being. He is a little world within a big world, but he is largely ignorant of his true nature and this ignorance brings upon him the very bondage, limitation, and fear from which he suffers.

If we were able to remove the entire realm of consciousness from man there would be nothing left, or if anything *should be* left we could not know it. We realize then that the entire being of man, insofar as we can understand his being, must consist of different states of consciousness. Man lives in his states of consciousness, moves and has his being in them.

Whatever our nature is, we did not create it, we can only use it. As ignorance of the law excuses no one from its effects, and as we are all ignorant of our true natures, we are all bound by this ignorance. This bondage is not an eternal verity, yet it is an actual fact. Enlightenment alone can produce freedom.

The eternal inquiry concerning God is an inquiry into the nature of our own being. It is certain that we have a body, and it is certain that we have a conscious intelligence else this page could neither have been written nor now read. It is demonstrable that the body and mind did not create themselves but have their source in Something greater than they are. Hence we are threefold beings, consisting of body, mind, and spirit.

Now the body itself, evolved through untold ages of time and stages of development, must have started somewhere, somehow, with an original concept which man did not create. This original concept must have been an idea in the Mind of God, hence it must be a Divine idea and Divine ideas must be perfect. Therefore it follows that whatever the true idea of body is, or shall be discovered to be, it must be perfect. As yet we do not understand this perfection, although we dimly sense it. In such degree as the mind senses this perfection the body responds to this spiritual awareness and becomes harmonious.

This is not a matter of creation on the part of the individual mind, but is an awakening. All evolution is an awakening and development to a greater possibility, resulting in an unfoldment of an inherent potential. Since man lives in his consciousness, it follows that a change of consciousness will produce a change in outward manifestation. Hence we arrive at the idea that man lives in and by his beliefs and opinions, and that, could he change these beliefs and opinions, there would be an outward manifestation corresponding to the inner change.

A theory basic to effective prayer and Science of Mind is that in reality we are *now* perfect, even as God is perfect, and that this perfection appears outwardly in a ratio corresponding to our spiritual perceptions. We have reached that place in the evolution of our consciousness where the mind begins to grasp a higher order of being. We do not know what the future holds in store, but that it has a new order for humanity there can be no doubt. The old order is rapidly passing and millions of people today are endeavoring to sense their relationship to the Universal. The persistent study of man's nature carried on through the last one hundred years has developed an understanding of truths which will completely revolutionize not only human thought, but its corresponding reactions. Never before has there been such an inquiry as is now being carried on. We are gradually shifting our mental concepts from a material to a spiritual basis. The time will come when all people will look upon humanity as individual incarnations of the universal Spirit, which is God.

The nearer we approach this position, the more we shall withdraw from a false concept of our own being. Man is a spiritual being, using the Law of Mind, living in a world of objective form, and being surrounded by an unfoldment in his experience which is the counterpart of his persistent pattern of thought.

Like produces like. "Do men gather grapes of thorns?" Man's nature is drawn from that universal Nature which is not only the sum total of all individual life but which is also the essence of Life Itself. This ultimate and intelligent Causation is what we mean when we say "God."

That there is a direct relationship between the Universal and the individual there can be no doubt, and that man is the product of the Universal no man can deny. That God or the First Cause is complete and perfect all thinking people have affirmed. Intuition, revelation, and investigation combine to prove the fundamental premise that the First Cause is complete within Itself, and that we have access to It through our understanding.

The entire evolution of man is the result of gradual awakening to truths which have eternal existence. Evolution is not a cause but an effect. The cause of evolution is Intelligence, the effect is manifestation. As man's body is part of the one great body of all physical life, so is his mind one with the infinite Mind. From this infinite Mind he draws inspiration, knowledge, and wisdom—the direct revelation of Reality through him.

There are numerous channels by which he has access to this infinite Mind. Intuition is the direct inner perception of Truth, while science, by careful investigation, works its way back through appearance to ascertain the cause. However, each discovers a universe of order governed by immutable laws. How could man either perceive intuitively or investigate scientifically unless his consciousness were already *one* with that which it conceives or understands?

The advance made in human progress, through the acquisition of greater truths, is a continual proclamation of the spirit in man as it penetrates more deeply into the nature of that Being which spreads the evidence of Itself throughout all creation and proclaims the exactness of Its Law. The higher discoveries in science have led man to a point which transcends all material form and then arrives at ultimate conclusions, even through pure mathematics, announcing that all movement, all creation, even every creative act, starts with an original unit which is pure Spirit or absolute Intelligence.

RECOGNIZE YOUR
INDIVIDUALITY

To be an individual means to exist as an entity. Rightly understood, God can be considered as the infinite Person; hence Spirit is the infinite Essence of all individuality. Within the One Supreme Mind, since It is infinite, exists the possibility of projecting limitless expressions of Itself; but since the Infinite is infinite, each expression of Itself is unique and different from any other expression. Thus the Infinite is never divided but has infinite manifestations.

While all people have the same origin, no two are alike except in ultimate Essence. One God and Father of us all, but numberless sonships. Each sonship is unique in a universe of Wholeness. Man is an individualized center of God-consciousness and spiritual Power, as complete as he knows himself to be, and he knows himself only as he really comprehends his relationship to the Whole.

Our individuality externalizes as personality at the circumference of our existence and experience. At the center of our being is the point of individual contact with the infinite Source, of the unexpressed and unconditioned, the Absolute, God. There is a reservoir of life and power as we approach the center which is loosed and flows through to the circumference when we realize the unity of the Whole and our relationship to It. God is incarnated in all men and individualized through all creation without loss to Himself.

Each of us, as a unique individualization of the Infinite, is complete. No two people look alike, act alike, or think alike. No two faces have the same expression. Our fingerprints are different. The emotional reactions of each are distinct and individual. All this, in order that individuality may not be lost in the great shuffle of life. God would not be a creative God if His creations were monotonous repetitions.

The more completely we recognize our individuality, the more unique Our personality. Due to this we commonly speak of persons as being "individuals." A psychological reaction against our machine age is an instinctive gesture of a person protesting against anything that would seek to replace the necessity of more fully expressing his individuality. As we seek to develop our personalities we should at the same time try to unify them with all others.

Some find their approach to expressing the Reality at the center of their being through art, science, or literature, some others through prayer and meditation; but all do it by extended recognition and increased inner awareness. The voice of the Spirit speaks to and through all; it is a universal language speaking through many tongues.

Emerson tells us to watch the spark which illuminates our own consciousness. This spark is shot from the central fires of the universe and gathers brilliancy within us as we fan it with our awareness of it.

Individuality is the thing behind our personality. Personality is what we make of our individuality. The uniqueness of our personality springs from our individuality, which is entirely God-given.

We think of Jesus, the "wayshower," as a divinely inspired personality, a teacher of man, a lover of humanity, and a spiritual genius. The conscious knowledge of God which impregnated the mind of the man Jesus we think of as Christ, or Christ-consciousness. To worship this personality is idolatry, to believe that God gave more of Himself to this man than to other men is superstition, to think that the word of

Jesus had the power to change the natural order of Reality or refute natural laws is ignorance.

As other men, Jesus was a human being, but he was a spiritual genius. Just as we have had geniuses in every field of endeavor, so we have had spiritual geniuses, those who have seen more deeply into Causation than others. Jesus, as a personality, has long since passed to other fields of activity, but the conscious knowledge of God which endowed this unique man with what may be called the Christ-consciousness, remains as a potentiality for all of us.

We are beginning to understand more of the meaning of this Christ, this Emmanuel or God-with-us, the direct relationship of the Universal to the particular, of the Infinite to the finite, of God to man, of the heavenly Father to the earthly son. The forming of this Christ within us is the incarnation of the Almighty, consciously received, and the power attending this new birth is the result of opening a greater channel in our own minds through which the originating Cause may flow.

The greatest teaching of Jesus was the necessity of belief or faith. What should we believe in and how can we have faith? His answer: Believe in God or the universal Spirit; have faith that your belief in this universal Spirit will produce a definite and tangible result in your experience.

It seems impossible to have belief or faith while we doubt or are afraid. Hence the enemies to be overcome are our denials of the good, the beautiful, and the true. "To err is human," and that part of us which is human seemingly is continuously in error, is fearful, timid, uncertain; it needs and must have knowledge of a new source of freedom.

The only possible "salvation" is for a new birth to take place in the mind; it is the mind that needs to be reborn to a greater recognition of the Divinity within it. Hence we are told to be "transformed by the renewing of the mind." The mind must shake off the adversary which is the denial of good, and, looking upward, must become impregnated with the great affirmations of Life Itself.

THE LAW OF
YOUR LIFE

As we approach a consideration of Science of Mind in relationship to our daily living we need not consider it as being deep, abstract, or probably beyond our ability to fully understand. Although it necessarily is founded on great truths, at the same time it is very simple. All too often we tend to complicate our thoughts and ideas rather than keeping them simple and usable.

Let us remember as we progress to keep our minds open to new ideas and be ready to accept old ideas which have been shorn of their worn-out cloaks. We want to be happy and willing to learn more about ourselves, to discover more of that Life of which we are a part, and at the same time to ascertain the nature of the Law through which It makes Itself manifest.

We do live in a spiritual universe, a universe that is intelligent and creative, and it is a thing of law and order. It is God's universe, a Divine idea and thought that has become manifest, God becoming that which He has created through the Law of His nature. It is one stupendous Whole, with God as both cause and effect. Idea and manifestation, and the Law by which one becomes the other, are all one in the inherent nature of God.

Man is an individualized center of God-conscious life, a point in the infinite sea of life, and an intelligent, self-knowing point. Man is the outcome of God's desire to express Himself as individuality. The whole meaning of experience is to promote this individuality and thus to provide a fuller channel for the expression of the supreme Spirit of the universe.

We note that through the ages people have been healed by the prayer of faith, which is a practice of every religion. There is a Law governing this possibility else it never could happen. It is the business of Science of Mind to view the facts, evaluate the causes, and in so doing provide a definite knowledge of the Law which governs the facts.

The universal Mind contains all knowledge. It is the potential ultimate of all things. To It all things are possible. To us as much is possible as we can conceive, according to Law. Should all the wisdom of the Universal be poured over us we should yet receive only that which we are ready to understand. This is why some draw one type of knowledge and some another and all from the same Source—the Source of all knowledge. The scientist discovers the principle of his science, the artist embodies the spirit of his art, the saint draws spiritual awareness into his being, all because they have courted the particular presence of some definite concept. Each state of consciousness taps the same Source but has a different receptivity. Each receives what he asks for, according to his ability to embody. In this way the Universal is infinite, the possibility of differentiating is limitless.

We waste much time in arguing over things that cannot be answered. When we have arrived at the ultimate, *that is the ultimate*; it is the way the thing works. Therefore we have a right to say that there is a Law involved and that this Law executes our word or prayer. We discover laws, find out how they work, and then begin to use them. Therefore we say it is the nature of thought and of creative Law *to be this way*.

I would say that Law is an attribute of God. God did not make Law; It co-exists with the Eternal. The infinite Law and the infinite

Intelligence are but two sides of the infinite Unity; one balances the other and they are the great personal and impersonal principles in the universe. Evolution is the out-working of that which is tangible and mechanical, and involution is the in-working of the conscious and the volitional.

We can no more do without religion than we can do without food, shelter, or clothing. Indeed, the religious instinct is so firmly implanted that it is inseparable from life and living. According to our belief in God will be our estimate of life here and hereafter. To believe in a God of vengeance is one thing, but to believe in a God of Love and a just Law of Cause and Effect is another.

We live in a universe of Spirit and of Law. From the one we are to draw inspiration, from the other we are to utilize power. Each is a complement to the other and both are necessary to existence.

To believe in a just Law of Cause and Effect, carrying with it a punishment or a reward, is to believe in righteousness. To believe in eternal damnation for any soul is to believe in an infinite monstrosity, contradicting the integrity of the universe, and repudiating any eternal lovingkindness inherent in God.

To feel that we suffer for our mistakes is justice, but to feel that our mistakes are eternal is to be already in the suppositional hell of a false theology. A sin is a mistake, a mistake is a sin; both will ultimately be done away with.

To believe that evil draws as great benefits as goodness from the storehouse of God is unthinkable, and to feel that some are foredoomed forever to be evil is also unthinkable. It denies solidarity to the universe and creates a house eternally divided against itself.

All Truth is our truth. No man robs us of our own soul, and our spirit is already one with the eternal Goodness. Everyman's belief is good insofar as it is in line with Reality. We have no controversies with anyone. As we claim freedom, so we extend its privileges to everyone else; we will give and accept on no other terms.

We study the thought of the ages and are not ashamed to admit any falsity in our own thought. We are after the Truth and shall be satisfied with nothing less than that Truth which proves Itself to be really true. We are scientific searchers for that Truth which makes man free, and we know that we have found entrance to It.

The past is behind and whatever doubt it may have held is gone with it. The future is before, bright with prospects; the eternal sun of righteousness is ever ascending, never to descend. Let us look toward the high goal of lasting attainment, fearless and happy. Let us live in the present, looking neither backward in horror, nor forward with apprehension, but looking into the present with joy—"abiding in faith."

PRAYER IS A SCIENCE

There are too many instances on record of a direct answer to prayer to discount the fact. Prayers have been answered directly, specifically, immediately. We are confronted with a fact and not with a theory. We are not seeking to find facts with which to prove some theory, but rather to find a correct theory which fits the facts.

Prayer has been answered in many thousands of cases; the answer has either been through the caprice of some deity, or through the action of some definite law. It is unthinkable to suppose that God, the Creator of all life, gives to some while withholding from others. We cannot believe that God is pleased with some and displeased with others. So we must believe that prayer is answered according to law, and that should we discover the right use of this law, all our prayers would be answered.

What does one do when he prays? *He talks to God.* Where does he talk to God? He talks to God in his own mind, through his own thought or feeling. It is quite impossible for one to talk to God outside himself, for he cannot go outside himself. Whatever God he talks to is in his own thought or approached through his own thinking, feeling, and knowing.

The man, then, who asks God for abundance, asks God in his own mind. God answers through his affairs. But some have asked God for money for some worthy purpose and have not received an answer to their prayers. Indeed, to be perfectly truthful, can we suppose that God is or can be more interested in one good deed than in another? This would be dangerously near making the Divine Being more limited in thought than we are.

But the fact remains that many men's prayers relative to worthy purposes have been answered. It must be that *the answer to prayer is in the prayer when it is prayed* and not in the inclination or the disinclination of God to answer some and not others. God answers prayer according to law and order, the immutable Law and Order of the universe.

Prayer is a thought, a belief, a feeling, arising within the mind of the one praying. This feeling becomes a complete belief and a perfect acceptance when the mind is most completely in tune with the Infinite. The mind is the most completely in tune with the Infinite when the emotions are the most constructively aroused. The highest faith comes from the greatest spiritual awareness.

The prayer of faith is answered because the prayer of faith admits of an answer while the prayer of unbelief does not admit of one. Perfect faith is an unqualified acceptance of the desired result; and this acceptance is a mental attitude which cannot be shaken by any objective evidence to the contrary. The prayer of faith looks through the apparent condition to a perfect fulfillment. Prayer is a mental attitude aspiring toward God as the great Giver of all. Faith is the acceptance that God has given or is now giving. Prayer and faith are both mental attitudes. A continual prayer of faith repudiates all that contradicts the desired end and culminates in positive acceptance.

When prayer removes distrust and doubt and enters the field of mental certainty, it becomes faith and the universe is built on faith.

The mind will soar to new heights when fired by a potent constructive emotion. This explains why people with high spiritual emotions generally receive the most direct answers to their prayers. It matters not what stimulates the emotion so long as it is constructive and agrees with its ideal. The intellect is a cold thing and a merely intellectual idea will never stimulate thought in the same manner that a spiritual idea does.

It so happens, or the universe is so organized, that it is quite impossible for us to arouse the highest emotions and the most creative ones without using the highest ideals. These ideals are always what we call religious or spiritual. But spirituality and religion are not to be thought of as either unnatural or supernatural. Spirituality means dependence on the Spirit. Religion concerns beliefs in God. Both are normal and quite natural to the average person.

God gives some more than others because some accept more than others. The Divine Giver Himself knows nothing about size. Prayer should build up a greater acceptance of God's Life, Truth, and Action, and when it does the response will be commensurate with the higher acceptance. When the whole emotion is aroused and the mental acceptance is complete, the answer will be certain. The Law has not changed, but has responded in a different way.

In an effort to discover more fully the nature of prayer, it becomes a matter of finding out more about the processes of thought and emotion which are the ingredients of prayer. In order to do this it is a case of ascertaining the nature of mind in action, which easily and quickly resolves itself into a science of mind.

THE BASIS OF
SCIENCE OF MIND

Science of Mind in its broadest and truest sense includes all there is in science, religion, and philosophy. Science of Mind is not a personal opinion, nor is it a special revelation. It is the result of the best thought of the ages. It borrows much of its light from others, but in so doing does not rob anyone, for Truth is universal and never personal. We need the entire revelation of the whole world, and even with this we shall have little enough.

The universe is impersonal. It gives alike to all. It is no respecter of persons. It values each alike. The philosopher, the priest, and the professor, the humanitarian and the empire builder, all have caught some gleam of the eternal glory and each has spoken in his own tongue that language which is, of itself, universal.

Science is a knowledge of facts that are provable. *Science is not opinion but knowledge;* a demonstrable truth of which there may be a practical application. Science reveals universal truths and gives them to the world as practical values and usable facts.

Science of Mind does not scoff at the words or works of medical science, for instance. They both work to help and heal humanity. Science of Mind is a complement to medical science and when so understood and practiced will help heal the world of its physical infirmities. The world of knowledge needs to be knit together and not pulled apart. We have no objection to any form of healing. What we insist on is that there can be no *permanent* healing of the body without a correspondingly permanent poise in the mental and emotional life. Psychosomatic medicine has shown that mental disturbances, conscious or subjective, produce physical reactions in the body. If the body is to be permanently well one's mental life must be creative, peaceful, and happy. This is the purpose of any mental healing, whether it be approached from the psychological or the metaphysical angle. Psychology and metaphysics are but two ends of the same thing; they meet somewhere in consciousness and merge into a perfect unit.

Science of Mind teaches that there is a favorable physical reaction, an effect, which follows a pattern of thought incorporating ideas of health, for the Law of Cause and Effect governs everything. Similarly, it is held that right thinking will result in a greater experience of success and abundance. A successful man thinks success and the Law of Mind that reacts has no other choice than to produce an effect corresponding to the causative idea.

The road to freedom lies, not through mysteries or occult performances, but through the intelligent use of natural forces and laws. The Law of Mind is a natural law in the spiritual world. We need not ask why this is so. There can be no reason given as to why the Truth is true. We do not create laws and principles but discover and make use of them. Let us accept this position relative to the Law of Mind and Spirit and see what we can do with It rather than how we may contradict the inevitable. Our mind and spirit is our echo of the "Eternal Thing" Itself, and the sooner we discover this fact the sooner we shall be made free and happy.

God, the universal Life-force and Energy running through everything, is an intelligent Presence pervading all space; a beginningless and endless Eternity of eternities; a self-existent Cause; a perfect Unit, and a complete Wholeness.

The unthinking would believe that God is a Spirit who keeps books and checks up on the wrongdoings of each individual member of the human race, and that He sends some to heaven and some to hell and all for His glory. Each, according to his own light, has believed in the kind of God who best fitted his personal ideas, or in the idea of God that has been imposed upon him by ignorant or superstitious leaders.

But ever there has been the voice of those crying in the wilderness of superstition, ignorance, doubt, and fear; the voice of those who have thought the thing through to conclusions that have been independent of race beliefs, of the subtleties of religious dogma, and of theological superstitions. These have been the wayshowers of humanity and millions have lighted candles from their flames. But the world progresses slowly; evolution and the growth of knowledge and wisdom is a process of time and experience.

In olden times an intelligent few understood much deeper truths than were known by the multitude, but the common people were thrown a few crumbs from the tables of those who were "in the know." These crumbs were shrouded in mystery, symbol, word picture, and parable. Perhaps this was the only way in which wisdom could have been taught at all.

In principle the great religions of the world do not differ as much as they appear to. Stripped of their accumulations of adornments and observances, and incrustations of interpretations, it is found that each acknowledges that there is one central Power, Force, or God, which is Self-existent; and it is from this One Power that all things emanate. All of life flows from It and is a part of It. Nothing can exist separate from It. The Christian interpretation of the ultimate nature of the creative Source of the universe places more emphasis on the life of the individual as being an integral part of the One Life. For this reason an intelligent understanding of the fundamental concepts of Christianity has had a greater appeal to the progressive peoples of the world.

But even in the Christian religion much of its real meaning is hidden by words that are misleading and symbols that but few understand. We could scarcely find a greater riddle to solve than the meaning of the "Holy Trinity." Also, most people either reject the Bible entirely or accept it totally and literally. Both these methods are mistakes.

Religion is a man's idea of God and the Bible is a written declaration of the belief in God held by a great race of people—the Jews. It is, in many respects, the greatest book ever written and does truly point a way to eternal values. But it is only one explanation and cannot be considered the only light on religion; for there are many others, which, taken together, weave the story of Truth into a complete and unified pattern.

The many sacred books of the East constitute other Bibles which point ways to the Truth; but each is only another way and cannot be considered to be *the way*. All races have had their religions and have had their Bibles; all have pointed a way to ultimate values, but can we say that any of them has really pointed *the way?* It is unreasonable to suppose that any one person or race encompasses all the Truth and alone can reveal the way of life for all others. This viewpoint does not apply to other forms of knowledge but seems to be adopted only when dealing with religion, and it is a great mistake.

The world is tired of mysteries, does not understand symbols, and longs for Reality. What is the Truth? Where may It be found? and how used? These are the questions that an intelligent person asks and he must have an answer. He may find his answer in the study of Science of Mind. Shorn of dogmatism, freed from superstition, open at the top for greater illumination, unbound and unlimited, Science of Mind offers the student of life the most understandable and intelligent approach that the world has so far achieved.

Intellectual freedom and religious liberty are necessary to the unfolding spirit in man. Whatever is true is free to all alike. We cannot cover the Infinite with a finite blanket. It refuses to be concealed. God has no favorites and knows no privileged class.

Science of Mind reads everyman's Bible and gleans the truths contained therein. It studies all peoples' knowledge and draws from each that which is self-evident. Only that which is self-evident can stand the test of reason and time. Without criticism, without judgment, but by true discrimination, that which is true and provable may be discovered and put to practical use.

We should take truth wherever we find it, making it our very own. Borrowing knowledge of Reality from all sources, taking the best from every study, Science of Mind brings together the highest enlightenment of the ages.

Part II

GROWING FROM FEAR INTO FREEDOM

Ever since the first cell of life appeared on this planet there has been a continual upward spiral of growth and development. The many manifest forms of life appear to have had a purposive directive factor behind them. This directive factor seems to have had a culmination in man, and even man in his present physical state no doubt will still have future refinements.

We have discovered much about the physical aspects of living things, but about that apparently unique phenomenon in man—his mind— we still have much to learn. What it is, what it can do, and the potentialities latent in it are hardly yet recognized. However, the appearance of mind in man, the ability to think, is the most recent and the culminative expression of the purposive action of Life.

It would appear that for the most part man is still in his infancy in developing the use of his mind. Mind has been given to us, but what happens to its growth and development is largely an individual undertaking—ours is the responsibility to use it and unleash its limitless possibilities. It is in our proper use of the potentialities of the mind that rests our power to release ourselves from fear and discover a new freedom for expressing and experiencing that greater joy of living which is rightfully ours.

UNLIMITED GROWTH

The history of man is a record of the awakening of the self to the Self, the emergence of the universal Spirit through the individual mind. It is as though we had been pushed from the Center of all things and must make the return journey through self-discovery. The greatest lesson in spiritual education ever taught—the story of the Prodigal Son—was given to illustrate this idea.

Man's primal existence was originally an idea within the universal Mind which became individualized as man. Man expresses through personality, possesses free will, for the end purpose that he may choose to return to "the Father's house." Then he no longer is just an expression of God but becomes a *copartner* with the Infinite. He still is subject to the laws of love and of reason, but at the same time is dependently independent; that is, dependent on the Universal but independent in It.

We should deeply ponder the significance of this thought, for it gives the assurance that our future evolution will not be by compulsion but by cooperation. "For the earnest expectation of the creature waiteth for the manifestation of the sons of God." The whole history of human evolution proves this position. Natural forces undreamed of in previous ages are, today, a part of every man's experience; and since we cannot have exhausted the Infinite, we must conclude that the future holds un-dreamed of things for us.

It is significant to remember that since the first man turned his face from the clod, rose to his feet and proclaimed "I am," the universe has silently awaited his conscious cooperation with it. This awakening has ever found its starting point in mental states, or modes of thought. *It is the mind that awakes.*

From the dawn of human history until today this inner awareness has produced a steady and unbroken sequence of accomplishment and progress, and while there have been periods when this evolution appeared to stop or to be broken, it has always started fresh and new. Glancing back over the whole panorama of human existence we cannot fail to see a steady advance. Looking, then, into the possibility inherent in the future and judging the future by the past, we cannot fail to see the necessity of eternal progress.

The natural order of evolution has brought us to a place where there is a quickening of the spirit, a keener perception of the mind, a deeper introspection of the soul; the veil between Spirit and matter is thinning. We are emerging into a spiritual universe, proclaimed alike by the philosopher, the religionist, the scientist, and the idealist, and yet the nature of Reality or ultimate Truth cannot have changed. Two and two were four a million years ago. The awakening is to the mind and spirit, and from this mental and spiritual awakening follow objective equivalents.

As the last one hundred years has witnessed the unfoldment of the physical sciences through the consciousness of man, so has it witnessed a great awakening of the mind to itself. The passing of old orders of thought is but a proclamation of the inauguration of new and higher orders. The unravelings of psychology, the birth of modern metaphysics, the enlarging of religious concepts, the inquiry into philosophic problems, all announce a new birth of the mind, a new discovery of the self, a new consciousness of the intimacy of the mind with the subtle Spirit within.

We shall never know any God greater than the God which our inner consciousness proclaims, for the reason that this inner proclamation is "the Father in us." That Silent Voice, that Divine Urge, that insistent demand made upon our minds, is the original Spirit. The impulse back of our constructive acts is the original creative Genius of the universe flowing through the channels of inner perception in our own minds. Within us this Cause, perennial in Its eternal youth, is ever born anew into creation.

There appears to be one persistent purpose behind the great forward movement of evolution, namely, the outpush of Intelligence, through creation, into higher, finer, and more complex forms. This is one great lesson which science teaches us—that there is an insistent and intelligent Urge in the Life-Principle which impels It to express, and theoretically we might add that It expresses in order that It may become conscious of Itself in many forms.

Theoretically, then, we may believe that the Spirit is forever clothing Itself in form; it is not only Its desire to do this, but by very reason of Its nature It *must* take form. If we were to ask our imagination why this is so, the answer might be that God Himself would remain a nonentity unless He were expressed; that even to the Infinite some form of creative action and expression is necessary.

If we were to further inquire of our imagination what the ultimate purpose of evolution is, the most logical answer it could give would be that the purpose of Life is to produce beings who can consciously cooperate with It; that through such cooperation the evolving Principle Itself may more completely express.

Turning from fancy to fact, we find the facts fitting nicely into the fancy. We feel justified in starting with the assumption that all creation exists for the purpose of spiritual Self-expression; and that man, the apex of creation on this planet, has already reached a place in his evolution where he may consciously cooperate with the Creator.

What the God-intended man may be no one knows, but judging the possibility of man's future evolution by his past, we may rightly suppose that this possibility reaches out and on into limitless fields of self-expression. Man as we now know him is incomplete, and those vague feelings and subtle senses of interior awareness which arise within him are gentle but persistent prophecies of still greater achievements.

The path of progress seems to be persistent and must be eternal; we cannot doubt that the God-intended man will fulfill the most cherished desire of our imagination. It is not of great importance to man's future what processes he may have gone through to arrive at his present place, although it is of great interest and of scientific value to know of his development from the first form of life to his present state. The real problem that now confronts us is not what we once may have been, but, *where do we go from here?*

Man is a self-conscious, individualized center of volition, will, and choice merged into personality. The more deeply we penetrate his nature, the more significant becomes the meaning of that nature. It seems fathomless, boundless, and almost entirely unexplored. If we start with the theory of an infinite potential latent within him—that he has already reached a point in his development where his own conscious determination must, to a great degree, measure the possibilities of his future unfoldment—we shall recognize this most significant fact: Our future progress depends upon our ability to consciously cooperate with nature and its laws and consciously identify ourselves with the Spirit of Intelligence animating nature.

There is an inner urge in our own minds to grow, to expand, to break down the barriers of previous limitations and to ever widen our experience. This persistent urge is a Divine influence, an irresistible force, and constitutes the greatest impulse in human experience. Mostly misinterpreted and misunderstood, and often pursuing devious pathways, it is still the urge back of all accomplishment, the promise of all fulfillment.

There is this question, however, which naturally rises: Why all the suffering, sorrow, and pain; why has tragedy accompanied the journey of man? Again our imagination may answer this question in a somewhat plausible manner. There is no other way through which true individuality can evolve. Man must be let alone to discover himself, else be compelled, arbitrarily, to follow one road, in which case he would be an automaton and not an individual. Perhaps this will solve the whole problem of evil in human experience and at the same time point to a better way—that of learning to consciously cooperate with nature and its laws. This the scientist is already learning to do. This the religionist must also learn to do. Life is not really against us but *for us*, for we cannot imagine a universe divided against itself; but ignorance of law excuses no one from its effects.

We are now equipped with sufficient intelligence to gain the necessary knowledge for our future growth. We must free ourselves from superstition, fear, and uncertainty, and ever seek the inner guidance of that intelligent Purposefulness which has already projected Itself into our form and into our creative imagination. Listening deeply to this inner Revealer, we shall find our footsteps more and more continuously guided.

We are beneficiaries of the Universal, or if we wish to state it another way, "sons of God," and that sustaining Infinite, that originating Cause, that Divine Intelligence which has brought us to this point is to be trusted, but we must learn how to make our thought receptive to It. Thus shall we learn to take part in creating our own destiny, to rejoice in the accomplishment already made, and to look forward to a future bright with hope, filled with limitless possibilities, animated by Divine purposes, coordinated by a sustaining Unity, illumined by an eternal Presence of intelligence, wisdom, and right action.

THINK
CONSTRUCTIVELY

Thoughts are things. This sounds familiar enough; we have all read it many times. But if this is true why can we not think and, through thinking, get what we want? We have been told that we do not get what we ask for because we ask amiss. All this seems very confusing for we also have been led to believe that we should receive anything asked for if we ask believing. It must be that some ideas are more potent than others, that some thoughts have more power than other thoughts, and this is actually the situation.

All thought is creative, but the real constructive creative power of mind comes only from *true* thoughts. True, positive, and affirmative thought has *real* power, for it produces the correct answer. Negative thought also has power for it produces undesired conditions. When we place a positive thought beside a negative one, when we recognize the beneficial one and understand the nature of the harmful one, then it is that we find that the true constructive idea can dominate and have complete power over the destructive one. Thus it is that we are told to know the truth if we are to be made free.

Thoughts are things. Yes, true thoughts are true things, false thoughts are false things. If we think according to the nature of the

Divine, then shall we get what we want? Yes, provided what we wish for is *really* the truth. No, if it is not really the truth. We can never get five by adding two and two although we might believe that we can.

But how are we to know what thoughts to think? What should be the content of our prayers and spiritual mind treatments? How are we to know the false from the true? The answer is more simple than it may appear. Goodness is the truth, and so is beauty and strength and life and love and abundance and loyalty. Even the apparently selfish desires of our hearts are true if they do not contradict the fundamental Truth of the universe, which is unity and goodness and purity.

Our difficulty is not great provided we keep a few fundamentals in view. We have a Divine right to all that makes for a happy life. Abundance must be the heritage of our Divine nature. Our life must come from Life, and peace and happiness cannot contradict Reality. We shall not pray amiss if we affirm these things as part of our experience. Therefore, if we ask, believing, according to the Law of our being we *must* receive.

What we wish for and need is peace, ability, happiness, harmony, plenty, and a greater degree of livingness together with love and beauty. Possessing these we should be in heaven and we ought to be in heaven here and now in our daily living; that is, we should be in harmony with Life. There is no Power in the universe which wishes to withhold good from us—let us forever wipe this idea off the slate of our minds. God is eternal Goodness, hence no evil need befall us either here or hereafter. Life cannot produce death, consequently we cannot die even though we pass through the experience miscalled death.

But what is there left to ask for? Nothing. We need but to *accept* and make use of that which already is and *is for us*. But each shall individualize the gifts of Life through his own nature, and this individualization constitutes that activity which personifies through each of us—the eternal Mind of the universe. This is the play of Life upon Itself and the desire to express which is working through all of us. There can be no life without living, no creator without a creation. And there can be no satisfied man without an adequate expression. There is nothing wrong about desire provided desire is in harmony with Truth. A man who has no desires is asleep and needs to be awakened.

What then if we should desire some special thing that we might enjoy it for a season? Can there be anything wrong with this? Certainly not if this desire harms no one and helps us to express. If, then, we desire some special thing, why should we not ask for and receive it? But how do we ask? *By knowing in our own minds that that for which we ask we now have.* This creates the image of our desire and makes a definite pattern through which the energies of Mind may intelligently and lawfully act, and to which there may be attracted the conditions necessary for the fulfillment of the desire. And according to our belief, receptivity, and full acceptance will it be done.

We cannot live by proxy or attain by pretense. We are dealing with real laws and actual forces when we deal with mental and spiritual laws, and they cannot be fooled. From our own endeavor will come our own reward, only now we know that we are dealing with a Law which is amply able to fulfill the rightful demands made on It and which is intelligent enough to always bring them to pass. With this in mind we shall do our spiritual mind treatment work gladly and cheerfully and with much less effort, for we are no longer struggling against Life but flowing along with It. We are going with the current and not against it.

We should feel equal to any occasion and be overcome by none. We should enter any and all true endeavors with a zest for the game and get a real joy out of living.

THE POTENTIALS
OF THOUGHT

In defining consciousness we find it impossible to conceive of an unconscious state of being, just as it is impossible for one to conceive of oneself as dead, or as not having being. Consciousness, then, is not only the starting point of perception, it runs through all perception and without it there can be no real perceiver.

To really define consciousness seems difficult, yet we all know what the word means for we are conscious beings and cannot imagine ourselves to be in other than conscious states. The movement of any particular state of awareness is a movement of consciousness. The movement of thought is a movement of consciousness.

Prayer, meditation, hope, fear, doubt, all are states of consciousness. To the individual nothing moves unless consciousness is aware of the movement, for if there is a movement without any consciousness to be aware of it, then that movement is without reality, so far as we are concerned.

There is movement in the universe; however we are only partially conscious of many of the movements. These movements and their meanings we but imperfectly understand. The whole history of the human race is a history of the unfolding of consciousness. It is no wonder that many have said that whatever a man can become conscious of he can understand or accomplish. Let us consider what it signifies to *really* become conscious of anything, for it is more than a mere claim, more than an affirmation.

When a child is told that two and two make four, his consciousness begins to work on this problem; he becomes aware of the fact that two and two are four. At first this fact seems external—he must have four blocks laid before him, must be told that one block and one more block make two blocks—that two and two make four. He now understands that four is a real number, having an actual significance in his everyday life. As he becomes really conscious of what four means, he no longer needs to have four blocks laid before him for he is conscious of four without the symbol. He is now inwardly aware. He is now completely conscious of a new idea. It is his. He cannot be robbed of this knowledge for it is a part of him. He becomes partially conscious of the significance of numbers.

If, however, we confront the same child with higher mathematics, we find that he is unable to understand. He has not yet become aware or capable of understanding more advanced knowledge. But it does not follow that he will never become conscious of greater realms of mathematics for he already has a starting point. Thus it is with life and action. We all have a starting point—our mind, our consciousness—and from this point all must travel. The advance in science, art, literature, and all endeavor is an outward and then an inward swing of consciousness. What we can become aware of we can master, and since no man can set any limit to the "measure of man's mind" there can be no limit other than the confines we set ourselves.

That there is a Mind in the universe which is without limit seems a true deduction. That we have access to this Mind seems the only explanation of our ability to progress. That we must be one with this Mind is an inevitable conclusion, else how could we perceive anything at all? That inquiry into any truth is some working of this Mind through our consciousness is apparent, and that all progress is the unfolding of this Mind through our consciousness is the only explanation for our continual progress. That this Mind is a storehouse of untold possibilities we cannot doubt, and that the greatest possibilities of our future lie in the direction of our conscious unity with infinite Intelligence we cannot deny.

A man sits down to write a play, his thought conceives of characters and their actions. The play is in his mind else there is no play. He creates the characters from his thoughts and gives them the only life they have or ever will have. The play is real to another man only when the author's thought is tangibly projected into the visible world. The other man, however, cannot know the play unless he becomes conscious of it, and even though he sees the play actually performed, the only meaning it has to him is that which his thought gives to it.

We are still mostly unconscious of what the great minds have thought, even though we know what they have said. Our own consciousness must supply the only interpretation we can have. If the thinking is deep and we think deeply, the ideas and meanings take on a new color. Our consciousness is striking deeper and deeper. We are more and more aware of the subtle meanings of the great man's mind. We are becoming consciously one with him. A unity is being made and our own consciousness is now an outlet for his. So it must be in our relationship with the great Mind.

Reality is forever hidden from our view. We see, not Life, but that which lives; not Energy, but that which Energy becomes; not Mind, but that which Mind does; not the Creator, but creation. Who ever saw the Power that guides the stars through space, or grasped in his hand the Energy that balances a spinning top? No man has seen God at any time. No man has seen man—the real man—at any time.

We are forever dealing with forces the only evidence of which is the use that we make of them, and we do not think it strange. Why then do we think it strange that there should be power within man himself? Is it not man's mind, the invisible agent, that discovers *external* evidence of power? What if man should discover a power within, more subtle but equally as potent as any of the powers of science which have been harnessed and caused to do his will? Such a power he *has discovered*, but it cannot be analyzed! It must be accepted. This is why we are told that we must live by faith.

This inner power comes not with a blast of trumpets nor a glare of lights. It has been truly said that the pen is more mighty than the sword. Yet the sword has laid low countless hosts, destroyed nations, and established despots in power. But after the sword has been corroded by rust and bent in shame, the words of power—Truth—have lived and conquered and destroyed all enemies. The nearer we approach the Truth the more power we have. Why? Because this is the way of Truth. What is this power? Our consciousness of the Allness of Good, our perception that God is supreme. Where do we perceive this? Within our own minds and hearts.

How much good and how much power can a man perceive? As much as he can believe in and really understand. No man has ever, as yet, plumbed the depths of his own mind and no man ever will, for here is a deep which cannot be fathomed, a height which cannot be scaled, a breadth which cannot be spanned. No wonder Shakespeare said, "To thine own self be true." The self is a hidden reservoir, fed by a stream whose source rises in the Infinite. The Infinite appears to continuously flow out, and the Source and Its flow are one.

Our life's source is the Infinite. The flow through us equals our receptivity to this source. We did not place this Power within us and in the long run we cannot misplace It. Browning speaks of this as a spark which a man may desecrate but which he can never quite lose; and Shakespeare, as that "divinity which shapes our ends," while Jesus speaks of it as the kingdom of heaven within.

There are certain things which we must accept and one of these is that we all have an *inner power*. But let not the boastful brag nor the braggart boast—*the source is the Infinite* and our inner life is forever wedded to It. The still, small voice within proclaims itself only through a consciousness of this unity, and this unity become a power to us only through the good use made of it. Power is silent and deep, calm and undisturbed. Tennyson says that when the outer tempest roars, this inner life has power to walk the waters.

Now since our inner power arises only through our unity with God we approach it only in the desire for good, never in willing evil. Since this inner life is one of unity we cannot approach it while we have a sense of separateness. And since God is really the life of man, man has real power only in such degree as he first recognizes his unity with God.

Who can say what a man might be able to do if he were really in league with the Spirit of Truth, really in touch with his true self? The reward which we have reason to believe in is certainly worth the effort, which effort is a peaceful approach to Reality. And there should be nothing peculiar in the process. Simplicity forever accompanies true greatness, and directness is the shortest distance between two points. One point is the human, the other the Divine. There is nothing between except what we put there. We are too apt to approach Reality by indirection and thus become confused by the shadows of our own misunderstandings.

Again, let our approach be simple and direct. All the statements ever penned by the hand of man will avail nothing if our inner sense of Reality be lacking. A statement is not the way, it is simply a pointer, a guidepost. No man's prayers can be better than yours. No man's shadow can reach any farther than the one you yourself cast. Loose the self, and let the wise follow their own wisdom, but see to it that *you* follow the direct path of your own soul straight to the center of your own life, which is God.

DIRECT THE ENERGY
OF THOUGHT

It is unthinkable to believe in a God who creates man only to set him adrift in a nothingness, burdened with care, doubt, and uncertainty—destined eventually to go to a suppositional hell because he does not know enough to go to an equally suppositional heaven. If we believe in a God who creates man out of Himself, we must believe that since this God has intelligence enough to make man, He has resources enough to provide for his well-being.

We are, we think, move, and act. We observe everywhere the intelligent phenomena of some Cause. This presupposes the necessity of an underlying Intelligence. Nature lies in the lap of an Intelligence and Life, which, without any apparent effort on Its own part, provides both seedtime and harvest. How, then, can we doubt that the Power back of things is adequate and is a Unit?

Originality, consciousness, spontaneity, and volition are evident at every turn in the road of human experience, making it unreasonable to hold a materialistic concept of life. There is but one plausible conclusion that back of everything, coordinating everything, unifying everything, is a unitary Power, all-knowing, all-wise, all-good, all-beautiful, absolute, birthless, deathless, and changeless.

Our popular religions, with their half-gods, are but different resting places of the mind—inns where the weary soul rests overnight on its journey from the extreme outer circumference of materialism to the inner consciousness of spiritual Reality. In the morning of a greater vision, with the dew of Eternity on the grass of experience, the soul ventures forth to find a better God.

Our half-concepts come *as* we need them and remain *while* we need them, to be finally drowned in a greater concept of Reality. Everyman's religion is good for him though it may seem inadequate to others. Religion has ever been an answer to the cry of the soul for something which is real, something which may be relied upon—a resting place for which every person instinctively feels a need.

We are created, we are told, in the likeness of the Eternal, after the image of the Infinite. We sense a Divinity within, a nature hidden in the cryptic interior of our minds which we have scarcely penetrated—a unity with the Whole. The intuitive faculty which we use to uncover Reality is evidence that this Reality is already latent within us.

It matters not if we reach this place through the inductive process of science or through the deductive process of revelation. It is useless for the materialist to say that revelation is a myth, for it can be shown that science is an inductive process leading to deductions, and that all deductions are revelations. All life is a revelation from the cradle to the grave. By revelation is meant the uncovering of that which *already is*, but is new to us.

The most penetrating and far-reaching conclusions ever made by man have announced that creation is a result of the Self-contemplation of God. The Law of the universe propels Mind into action, action into creation—creation being an effect, a result. The creative word of universal Intelligence projects itself into form. When we speak of the energy back of thought, or the power of faith and prayer, we are not thinking of will power, but of original Power. The thought, or the prayer, merely uses an energy which already is. The scientist does not put energy into electricity; he takes it out.

If there is a law of thought, if there is evidence that any prayer was ever answered or that any man's faith has consummated in an objective realization of that faith, then there is evidence of an Intelligence in the universe which accepts the word of faith and acts upon it.

An intelligent person approaches prayer knowing that there is a universal Law which acts on his word, and he uses this Law with the definite knowledge that he is scientifically using a proved principle, a known, definite, and provable force. For to him the presence of an intelligent Law in the universe, which receives the impress of his thought and acts upon it, is an accepted and proved fact.

He also knows, however, that this Law can only respond by correspondence. In other words, the measure of our faith in the Infinite is the measure of our capacity to draw from the Infinite. This is why the Great Teacher said that it is done unto us as we believe. If one can believe in a great good, then that much good can come to him. It is according to our mental acceptance or mental equivalent—according to our faith—that Life manifests through and for us.

Man measures life through his concepts. Automatically, thought has power. If one wishes to demonstrate a spiritual Principle which he may lay hold of and definitely use, let him forego any sense of coercion and become as a little child in receptivity; let him definitely and consciously accept his good and continue accepting until he experiences it. We must subject ourselves to the Law if we wish the Law to subject Itself to us. A good-natured flexibility with oneself and a faith, persisting in the face of anything which would contradict it, is the only way to approach the Principle of right action.

Deep within our minds is the Spirit, which we but slightly comprehend. From this universal reservoir a Power of spiritual consciousness passes through our minds into action. When the mind is peaceful and still it catches a vision of this greater good. While the mind is in turmoil and conflict it cannot receive an image beyond the vicious circle of that small measure in which it has been treading around. Somewhere the walls of the measure must be broken down. We must learn that we can transcend our previous experiences; that we are bigger than we know; that beyond the finite is the Infinite.

We will never arrive at the point of demonstration—experiencing the intended purpose of our prayer—while we believe we have to put energy into Spirit, thus usurping the throne of the original Creative Genius. There is a certain faith to which even our most materialistic scientists find themselves as subject in their realms as we shall ever be in the realms of Mind and Spirit. There is an energy in thought, not because we wish it to be so, but because it is so. Definite and specific thinking draws this energy through our conscious desires and makes manifest these desires at the level of our comprehension of Good.

There must be a conscious belief on the part of the one seeking to demonstrate this principle that his faith and thought are but the avenues through which the Law expresses Itself for him. In the technique of spiritual mind treatment, thought merely uses the Power intelligently. The will is the ability to select a specific thought thus determining how the Power is to be used. Well enough to realize that there is an infinite Intelligence back of everything, but if we have a problem to solve we must *know* that this infinite Intelligence is *now* solving it. This is to be remembered when giving a spiritual mind treatment. The treatment should be concrete, specific, conscious, definite, embodying the general ideas which one wishes to have become part of his experience.

While there is a point of decision and choice in treatment, there must be no outline. If the treatment is the cause, the demonstration is the effect and is already in the cause, as the flower is in the seed. It is written: "I am Alpha and Omega. . . ." Treatment should be given definitely and consciously, with a complete acceptance that there is a Power, an Intelligence, a Law which operates upon our word. Whatever the mind holds which denies this acceptance should be specifically attacked and consciously neutralized. The mind must be cleared of doubt and left open to accept the effect of the newly created cause.

Any experience which proves to a person that his faith can loose an intelligent Power which responds to him will be more salutary in his life than all the knowledge of what the sages of the ages have written. One definite experience which proves the integrity of a man's spirit and its direct relationship to the universal Mind and Spirit will do more for the individual than to know all the teachings of theology. For thus alone can he arrive at the place where he can say: "I know, that, whereas I was blind, now I see."

The energy back of constructive thought is Spirit. Spirit permeates everything. Hence constructive thought calls the best out of any particular experience. One who uses the Science of Mind is a practical idealist, but not a dreamer. While there is in the innermost recesses of our soul a place which dwells in eternal stillness and inaction, there is also a place at the circumference of our being, which, animated by the inner Spirit, goes forth to accomplish. Thus alone can contemplation become fruition, and inner recognition outer realization.

An unexpressed man is incomplete, and the objective universe through which alone we interpret the invisible Cause is evidence enough that the original Creative Genius forever passes from formless Energy, through Law, into manifestation. We would defeat the very purpose of life should we live in a continuous state of meditation or prayer, oblivious to the objective world. The practical values of spiritual perception remain latent until objectified. Any attempt to isolate oneself from the world of action is contrary to the order of the universe, hence futile. The practical religionist seeks to make his dreams come true, and, unless his dreams are subjective hallucinations, they will become actual experiences if he demonstrates his principle.

The average man may spend fifteen minutes to an hour each day in meditation, but this amount of time is of inestimable value in his practical life, for it is here that he joins the ideal to the real, receives inspiration for action and guidance toward accomplishment. In actual practice he tries to sense the union of the Spirit with everything he is doing. His slightest desire is important to the universe since it is some expression of the Parent Mind through him. This gives a dignity to his slightest undertaking and places a greater value on human endeavors. The happiness of the individual life is essential to the universal Wholeness, for thus alone can It find an extension of Itself.

The one seeking to demonstrate the power of spiritual mind treatment in everyday affairs should think of himself as being divinely guided. He affirms that his mind is continually impressed with the images of right action, and that everything in his life is controlled by love, harmony, and peace; that everything he does prospers, and that the eternal Energy back of all things animates everything he undertakes. He should resolutely deny every objective evidence to the contrary and in its place there should come a sense of right action. He should feel within him a unity with the Spirit, with the Spirit in all people and running through all events. He should definitely declare that the spirit within him is the Spirit of God quickening into right action everything he touches, bringing the best out of all his experiences, forever guiding and sustaining. The greatest good which his mind is able to conceive should be affirmed as a part of his everyday experience. From such daily meditation he should venture forth into a life of action with the will to do, the determination to be, and a joy in becoming.

PRACTICAL THINKING

We all wish for better health, greater happiness, and a larger experience in living. There is a Spirit *in* us which desires to be more fully expressed *through* us. This Spirit is conscious Life as opposed to, or different from, Law and Its mechanical action. Man's consciousness of his own existence is the Self-recognition of the Spirit within him.

We do not see this Spirit but we feel Its presence and we see Its manifestations in all our actions; without It we could neither act nor be conscious of ourselves or of anything else. In reality man's spirit is his share of that universal Presence in which all live, move, and have their being, hence the spirit of man is the Spirit of God in man—the two are really one and it is this inner Spirit which wishes to become more fully expressed through us. The *action* of the Spirit, flowing through our mentalities, is the Law of our life.

To use Science of Mind successfully one should be conscious of the indwelling Spirit operating through his own thought, will, and purpose. He should realize that the movement of his consciousness of God in and through him is a reality. Apart from the One Knower there is no knowledge, and separated from the One Life there is no real living.

Man's mind is ever in contact with Omniscience, but his conscious thought does not always know this. Hence he remains in ignorance of that which he inwardly and subjectively knows, but does not bring to the point of consciousness. One should feel that the inner Spirit knows, and that, because this is true, one's objective mind knows. In this way he is led into the right paths of human activity, for *human activity, rightly conceived, is Divine.*

There is but One Knower and what this One knows must be and is so, and this is true when this One knows through what we call the mind of man. The question might arise at this point: "Suppose man should know something which contradicts the Truth?" The answer would be: "Man cannot really *know* anything that contradicts the Truth." He may *suppose* something which is not true; he can *assume* an opposite to Reality, but he cannot *know* that which is not so. For instance, we might believe that two and two make five, but they would still make four. There is a great difference between believing and knowing; we can *believe* anything, we can *know* only that which is true.

Our troubles come, not from wrong knowing, but from wrong believing; they are misconceptions about what is true. One of the intellectual difficulties which we must overcome is our apparent inability to realize that there is an ultimate Truth and this Truth operates through our own mind in Its native and original being and power. But our perception of the Truth is an act of consciousness, as it is the inner perception which must recognize the Spirit.

In practice we start with this premise: The Truth is and is perfect, wherever we find It; being omnipresent It is where we are, where everyone is, and in and through all things. God is *in* and *through* His creation and the creation of God, rightly viewed, must be perfect.

The sum total of human knowledge comes to us through some avenue of the self-knowing faculties. We gain knowledge through science, opinion, and intuition. Science is the result of careful investigation and tabulation of facts, causes, and conditions. Much, but not all, of our knowledge is acquired in this manner. Intuition is a direct perception of the knowing faculty, without data, procedure, or any process of reasoning whatsoever. Our greatest truths come through this avenue. Opinions are our personal ideas about that which intuition gathers and science guarantees. Opinion is the least of the avenues of knowledge.

It is interesting to observe at this point that while the real intuitive perceptions of the ages have remained unchanged and are unchallenged by any ideas to the contrary, opinions are in a constant state of flux. This does not invalidate the findings of science nor overlook the value of opinions. Of course the *principles* of any science, rightly interpreted, cannot change because they are based on immutable laws and laws do not come and go, they are eternal verities and may be absolutely relied upon. As scientific research with its continual new evidence draws us nearer and nearer to basic Reality, our opinions change to meet the new facts and our intuition is opened to receive newer and greater truths. Thus do the three paths to knowledge combine to lead us on to a greater good.

The highest opinions of the deepest thinkers of all ages have agreed that we live in a spiritual universe governed by exact laws. A true philosophic outlook by science will not contradict this position, and the intuitive faculty, when clearly operative, will add its testimony to the same fact.

The spiritual universe is an intelligent organization be-speaking a universal Intelligence running through everything. Our own intelligence perceives this as an ultimate necessity and when our intelligence perceives it as an ever-present fact, we are practicing Science of Mind. The practice of Science of Mind, then, is the exercise of the knowing faculties of the mind functioning on the plane of self-recognition, and must ever be considered from this viewpoint.

It is impossible to separate the mental from the spiritual. The two are one. God is spiritual awareness, whether we think of this awareness as in the mind of man or in the infinite reaches of the universal Mind.

The Truth is not broken into fragments but remains as one unitary Wholeness.

In the application of Science of Mind one should be aware that he is using original Divine Power and that he is using It as definite Law. It is not the law of *his* mind but the Law of the *One Mind*, and this should not be forgotten. He should not feel that he is compelling any reluctant power to do his bidding, but that he is using a natural law in a normal way. The practical use of Science of Mind is a spontaneous recognition of the ever-present Spirit. And deep spiritual awareness does give one a greater ability to heal and to help.

Spiritual mind treatment requires a belief on the part of the individual that the words of his treatment are law unto that to which they are directed, then he should act as though his belief were true. He does this in a perfectly normal way, starting with the premise that Spirit is a universal and perfect Presence, filling all space, molding every creation, and animating every form with intelligent energy. Spirit is the intelligent Life-Principle running through all.

One needs to seek a sense of the perfection of the Divine Presence and to substitute this knowing for ideas of disease, poverty, or discord. In doing this he must often confront negative thoughts with the declaration that there is no necessity for the continuance of a condition contrary to fundamental Good. When the objective belief *in* and the subjective image *of* any given trouble is neutralized by the realization of Good, the condition is met and a healing takes place.

There is nothing which can hinder Law from working. It is never a question of how much the Law will work, but always of how well we can use It. We can constructively use It to the degree our thought and belief will let us, no farther, but always *as far*. The Principle is infinite, but we are only as capable as we know ourselves to be; we can know ourselves to be capable only insofar as we are unified with Truth. Thus does the impersonal become personal.

Spiritual mind treatment, prayer, is more than an act of the intellect;

it is an act of one's whole being, a complete giving of oneself to the realization of Perfection as being an ever-present fact in everyday experience. It carries with it a spiritual sense which cannot be put into words but which must be *felt*.

The thought and the intellect have a definite and a necessary function in spiritual mind treatment, but the final effect, of necessity, must and can only be the result of an *inner realization* that is stronger than the belief which caused the disease or discord. Conviction reaches its own level just as water does. This is a natural law in the spiritual world. All laws are natural, and all causes are spiritual.

To be spiritually minded is our natural impulsion toward Reality; it is normal, and should be spontaneous. To be spiritually minded is to believe in the Presence of Spirit and to trust in Its intelligent response to us in accord with Law. Spirit is but another name for Life. To be spiritually minded, then, is to completely believe in Life and in the responsiveness of Life to the aspiration of the human soul.

We should ever endeavor to sense this universal Presence, and time should be spent in bringing our consciousness to this recognition, for this is the Power that heals and remolds according to a more Divine pattern. Whenever we contact any objective evidence which denies the perfect Presence and the perfect Law we should consider it as an appearance only and not as a part of Reality.

Remember that *thoughts are things*, and that an idea can be erased by denial or by the affirmation of another idea. We must ever strive to cause our thought to rise above the level which produced the discord we seek to heal if we are to be successful in spiritual mind treatment. We will always find that insofar as we do recognize the perfect and the harmonious it will appear, no matter what the evidence to the contrary may be.

Again we are brought back to the fundamental principle of Science of Mind: God is, is Perfect, and is *All*. We should know that behind every manifestation there is the essence of Perfection, which, although it may not now appear, can be permitted to flow through it. We need to go beyond the physical vision, clarify the mind, and purge subjective concepts. Insofar as we are able to do this the rewards of our spiritual mind treatment will be certain. Behind the apparent is the *real*, and when this *real* is sensed the apparent more nearly measures up to it.

To successfully use prayer, or spiritual mind treatment, we do not withdraw from life but enter into all legitimate human activities with enthusiasm, realizing that the Law fundamental to all creation should give joy in the everyday affairs of life. The humble is exalted, each thing has its place in the Divine order, and the expression of happiness in the individual life is as essential to the Divine Being as is the manifestation of the glories of the heavens surrounding us.

In the vast panorama of life we behold the eternal Energy of Mind set in motion through Divine imagery and manifesting Itself in all creation. Thus, and thus alone, is the Spirit manifest on this or any other plane. The budding rose, the flowering tree, the corn ripe for harvest, the child at play, the surging tide, the saint kneeling before the altar of his faith, are all manifestations of the One Life, One Presence, One Power.

THE POWER OF
RIGHT THINKING

The power of our prayer, thought, spiritual mind treatment, is only equal to our conviction of the Truth, our embodiment of Reality, and our unconditioned reliance upon Good. Having accepted the proposition that we are not only immersed in a sea of living and creative Intelligence, but that this original Cause flows through our own minds into new creations, it naturally follows that we should examine our thought to see what we are really believing in.

If the original Mind can flow through us only at the level of our acceptances of Life, which seems certain, then our acceptances of Life automatically decide what is going to happen to us. Clear thinking converts the mind, revitalizes the consciousness, readjusts our valuations, and gives us a new outlook on life. We no longer ask what is the possibility of life, but we seek to determine the nature of our thinking. How much do we think we can achieve? How much abundance can we mentally embody? How much health and happiness can we conceive of? And how great is our faith that our prayer will become our experience? We find that for the most part we have set severe limitations upon ourselves, so we should readjust our thinking to a more positive, affirmative pattern that accepts a greater portion of the limitless good that Life is ever ready to extend to us.

Just as there are laws of matter, so there are laws of mind, for what is true on one plane is true on all. This, no thinking person can deny. If certain factors in physics produce certain results, then certain mental factors will produce certain results. This is a field for exploration and experiment as yet almost entirely untouched; and yet in the laboratory of mind lies a possibility of research as fascinating as that in the laboratory of matter, with undreamed of potentials awaiting discovery.

If we mix the concept of good with the concept of evil, the result will fluctuate between the two. If we mix a concept of peace with one of confusion, the result will be both peace and confusion. If our thought fluctuates, our external world will fluctuate also. Suppose we should try this experiment with ourself, saying: I am now convinced that the ultimate Power is Goodness. I am equally convinced that anything in my present experience which is not of the nature of this Goodness is the result of misconceptions on my own part. Furthermore, I am convinced that through the reversal of my thought and the changing of my concepts my whole external life can be rebuilt, re-created. From now on I only affirm the positive; and disclaim and repudiate, but not combat, the negative. I shall no longer resist evil, but I shall embody only good which overcomes all unlike it. I have neither enemy nor enmity; I shall entertain neither in my thought. There is nothing working against me. Everything is for me and all apparent contradictions to this Truth shall vanish as the mist before the sun.

This mental position would be an experiment in thought, in mind. We would not go through life blindfolded; we would not be declaring that evil is good; not merely saying peace when there is no peace thus hypnotizing ourself by our own suggestion, which is an error we must be very careful to avoid. But we would be demonstrating that an active consciousness of good overcomes evil. This anyone can do who is convinced that the power of right thought is actual and real.

We cannot expect to convert our whole consciousness in a moment, nor is it necessary. But if we take the mental stand that evil and negative conditions are not things in themselves, and constantly and consistently affirm that good alone has constructive and lasting power, is a spiritual entity, and has a real Law to support it, and that good *is* active in our experience, then we will demonstrate our theory, no matter what the existing conditions to the contrary may be.

We must not balance good against evil but must replace, overpower evil by the presence of greater good. In Science of Mind we start with the proposition that pure Spirit, or absolute Intelligence, is perfect Life and perfect Law; that this Intelligence flows through us at the level of our comprehension of It; that clear thinking creates within us an embodiment of this good, which embodiment automatically projects itself into form in our experience. We must know that we are dealing with a Law which need not be coerced but which must be used, and that the conscious use of the Law produces definite results.

The results will be as definite as our consciousness of them, since the Law flows directly through our consciousness manifesting the results. How careful, then, we should be not to mix conflicting concepts in our consciousness, not to become confused by objective situations. We work in our own mind and there re-create the condition, establish a new mental concept of the condition as it should rightly be, leaving the projection of this new creation entirely in the hands of the Law. And if we ask: How can anything be brought into being? or, What is behind all creation, our own lives and experiences included? how can the answer fall short of the proposition that the initial movement of creation starts in pure and positive Intelligence, unconditioned by any external fact?

This pure and original Cause, this absolute Intelligence which is the initial starting point of *all* creation, must be as present in Its entirety *now* as It ever was or ever can be. It must start as fresh through our minds as It did in that supposed dim and distant past when the Primordial Word spoke Itself into being. Creation is not a finished product but an eternal emanation. All life is an effect, a way, an outward manifestation of interior causes, silently working within themselves and shaping things at last to fit the Divine mandate.

Insofar as our thought rises to a realization that creation is an internal process projecting itself *now* through our minds, working through our thought, positive, original, invincible, shall we see why it is that right thinking has power.

Part III

THE PRACTICAL USE OF SCIENCE OF MIND

Probably the greatest single determining factor of our experience in living is what we think. Whether it be a matter of health, supply, happiness, success, harmonious relationships, or any other aspect of our life, in and behind it is the causative, creative pattern of our thought.

Freedom from what we do not want, and our emergence into a life that is more complete with all those things which contribute to the welfare and happiness of ourselves and others, would seem to depend on to what extent we are able to consistently control, guide, and direct our thinking.

Once such a start is made, regardless of how meager it may be, it is a foundation upon which we may build, until the time comes that we know with a confidence and a surety that when a particular constructive thought is entertained in mind there will definitely follow a tangible manifestation of that thought in our daily living.

To be able to accomplish this rests in understanding and using our minds in a specific manner. There is no formula to follow, but there is a technique to be acquired.

MIND IN
CREATIVE ACTION

Whether the mind is in the body or the body in the mind, no one knows. No one knows what the ultimate of matter is, but that it is a formless energy seems to be the generally accepted theory. That this energy takes tangible form throughout all creation is obvious. Form is necessary to the expression of the Spirit, and without body or form It would remain unexpressed.

Theoretically we believe that Spirit, acting through Law upon some cosmic Energy, takes definite form for the purpose of Self-expression. The mechanical processes involved are not essential in a philosophic discussion; hence we view the matter from the standpoint of cause and effect, leaving the ways, the methods, and the means to a more intricate analysis by the scientific mind.

It seems evident that form is the result of some purposiveness in the universe, some force acting creatively through law, the result of which is the evolution of form or the physical universe. This concept has always been held and is continually referred to in most of the sacred writings. In the Christian Scriptures we find such expressions as "in the beginning was the Word" and "all things were made by him" and "the Word was made flesh." There comes from antiquity a system of thought, which has been more or less adhered to throughout the ages, teaching that the pure essence of Intelligence, Spirit, or the Absolute, is the one *reality;* that all nature is a reflection of Its ideas, and that all nature has no other source.

Plotinus, considered to have been one of the greatest thinkers of all time, expressed the idea that nature is the great *no thing* yet it is not exactly *nothing*, since it is its business to receive the forms which the Spirit imparts to it. Some current-day religious groups, harking back to this teaching of antiquity, misinterpret its meaning and proclaim the utter unreality of matter and mistakenly conclude that the physical universe is an illusion. Now the physical universe is not an illusion, although some may conceive it to be such. Plotinus implied that nature is no thing of itself—it lives by proxy, it is the projection of That which is something. But it does have a definite purpose: the expression of the Spirit in tangible ways and in a concrete manner.

To look upon matter as an illusion would be as great a mistake as looking upon it as a thing of itself. The tangible world thus becomes a mirror in which is reflected the countless forms of the Divine and Infinite imagery which we ascribe to the Spirit. The Absolute and the relative are not opposites, each is a complement of the other. We cannot have an Absolute without a relative; we cannot have a relative unless there is an Absolute; they are two aspects of the same thing, one is cause and the other effect.

To suppose that that which is created governs that which creates it is to fall into error. To suppose that the Creator is absorbed in His creation is equally an error. To believe, however, that creation is saturated with the essence of the Creator seems reasonable, and that there is a certain immanence of the Creator running through all nature seems reasonable also. No fact is isolated, *no form can be isolated from the Principle which creates and sustains everything.*

In the mirror of the objective universe we behold the marvelous manifestations of a subtle, invisible Mind or Spirit, and as we enter into communion with Its innumerable forms we are, through them, communing with Spirit Itself.

Forms come and go, but the creative Principle remains intact. The Spirit Itself knows no time, yet all times must be included within It. It knows neither large nor small, as size, yet all form is known to It. If we can learn to supply the material object with a spiritual significance nature will more completely stand open to us—it will not be an illusion but a sublime and a necessary conclusion.

Our conscious, constructive use of the Law of Mind exists to us only as a latent possibility until we specialize It. The declaration that It exists and that we believe in Its possibilities is merely a statement of principles, a proclamation of our faith in the responsiveness of the Spirit to the needs of man; but a proclamation of faith never built a house or drove an automobile. "Faith without works is dead."

The Law of Mind is to be consciously used, definitely specialized. When we have freed ourselves from superstitions regarding spiritual things we shall be ready to approach them intelligently and incorporate them in our everyday living. We should daily seek to do this in our use of Science of Mind. We have a creative intelligence so we should use it. We are surrounded by a spiritual Principle of Law that reacts to our thought so we should consciously avail ourselves of It for definite purposes. Spiritual mind treatment is the act, the art, and the science of specializing the universal Law of Mind for specific and individual problems.

The Law is, but It must be used. Until the time comes when we use this Law consciously and constructively we shall be using It unconsciously and perhaps destructively, for every time we think, we use this Law. We should begin by weeding out all negative states of thought and learn to speak a straight affirmative language. The Universal gives to us through us.

To believe that one is continuously guided in his acts by a supreme Intelligence is a better state of mind and more productive of good than to believe that one is subject to the caprice of fate. Our fate is within our own minds. Destiny is but the objective manifestation of mental states. Success and failure are not things of themselves, they are simply modes of expressing the Original Thing. Thought should be daily directed and consciously controlled.

It is written that God's words are "yea and amen," which means that the Infinite does not argue but meets every man's approach directly, always responding by acquiescence to every man's thought. The physical scientist readily acknowledges a reign of law. The forces of nature are not coerced, they are directed; so the powers of Mind and Spirit need not be commanded but commandeered. They are not reluctant; they are willing. The Universal flow is forever taking place; the turning of this flow into the channels of constructive thought is an individual act.

The simplest approach is always the most direct—believe and it shall be done. Accept and let it be done; convince the mind and no longer deny the greater possibility. "Act as though I am and I will be." We must abandon our ideas to the supreme Cause and wait for the harvesttime with joyful expectancy.

There should be a definite and conscious expectancy. We should feel as though the entire power of the Spirit is for us and never against us. All ideas to the contrary must be resolutely set aside. Remember that spiritual mind treatment is neither wishing nor willing, it is an affirmation of the presence, the power, and the willingness of the Divine to specialize Itself for us, to meet every human need, to heal our bodies, to intelligently guide us, and to bring success into our undertakings. It is not through human determination, not "by power or by might," but by the silent workings of the Spirit through our organized thought that the Divine imparts of Its power to man. We are chemists in the laboratory of the Infinite; what shall we produce?

THE TECHNIQUE OF
SCIENCE OF MIND

A spiritual mind treatment is an act of the mind consciously conceiving the presence of some desired good which one has not before experienced. The principle involved is based on the theory that we are surrounded by a universal Law—a creative medium which is receptive to our thought and acts upon it automatically in an intelligent manner. Consequently, a treatment is the formulating of our thought in such a way as to bring the attention of the mind to the realization of harmony or health, of happiness or success, depending upon the result desired.

It is a fundamental proposition that the universe is a perfect unit and is always in harmony with itself. God is never divided against God; harmony is real, eternal, fundamentally necessary and true. A spiritual mind treatment must inform the mind that whatever appears wrong is entirely an appearance, a misjudgment, or a false conclusion. We do not say the fact does not exist. For instance, we do not say a man is not sick, but rather this: If he can succeed in unifying his thought with Life he will be healed. We do not say a man is not unhappy, but we do affirm this: If he can succeed in uniting his thought with That which must be happy, with eternal Happiness, he will be happy. We may say he is poor and needy, but if he can unite his thought with That which cannot be poor or needy, he will cease being poor and needy.

We do not deny the evidence of any experience because experience is the only means by which we may affirm that we live at all, for without experience there can be no life. We do emphatically state that any experience which is less than harmonious, less than the Eternal Fact, is an unnecessary condition. We experience discord because we wander away from Harmony; we experience limitation because our thought denies Abundance.

Now I am aware that an unthinking individual first hearing of this is liable to say, "Well, that sounds foolish. It sounds very foolish to say that by the act of thinking you can produce anything in the visible world." But if this same individual will pause for a moment and ask himself, "Where would I be, or what would happen if I, the thinker, were not here?" he would at once realize that nothing could happen to him. The moment you take the thinker away there is nothing left, and if we could disjoin the universe from the Intelligence permeating it there would be no universe.

Our inner belief decides what is going to happen to us, but that belief is the result of much ignorance and needs to be enlightened; hence the necessity of meditation, of prayer, of spiritual mind treatment. A prayer or spiritual mind treatment is a conscious, definite centering of thought on some desire, uniting this desire with ultimate Reality, causing the mind to perceive that this universal Reality is forming Itself through the pattern of the thought or desire.

We should not deny ourselves the right to do this, and if we subject ourselves to the necessary conditions we will prove it! The right mental conditions or concepts are these: The universe is a perfect Unit; life is One; at the root all is One; it is many in the objective world because Unity or Oneness manifests in multiplicity differentiating Itself in variety. That which is One becomes many, but the many are still rooted in the One, without which they could not be. It is necessary then that the thought unite with the One, that is, it must recognize but One Power back of everything.

Since there is but One Power back of everything, whatever exists is this Power in some form, whether we call it good or bad. Hence we are healed by the very Law which makes us sick. If we believe that everything is wrong, everything will appear wrong and the Law will see to it that everywhere we turn things will be wrong. If we can bring our consciousness to a place where everything is conceived as fundamentally good and we perceive only harmony, we shall ultimately experience only that which is harmonious. Each lives unto himself and unto the Unity behind all things.

It is necessary that we recognize the Unity, Harmony, and Power back of all things, and then state that It is operative wherever and on whatever our thought rests. That is what a treatment does. A treatment thus becomes a spiritual entity, equipped with volition, propulsion, action, and a complete knowledge of how to manifest itself. No one knows why this is so, but it is so.

There is in the treatment just exactly as much and no more than we put into it. I do not mean put into it by force, by will, or by any compulsion, but by absolute conviction, by positive affirmation, by complete acceptance, and by true receptivity. The treatment is the nucleus, the seed, the idea around which the energies of Spirit play, just as the creative forces of the soil, sun, and air take the seed and produce a plant. So spiritual mind treatment is a concept through which universal Law flows, producing a form like the idea given It, just as the ground always gives us back a plant which is the logical outcome of the seed placed in the soil.

We involve the seed; nature evolves the plant. We involve the idea; the spiritual Power which surrounds us, operating on this idea, evolves the thing. But as we can only harvest what we plant, we can only take out of our garden what we put into it, so a spiritual mind treatment can only produce its logical correspondent.

It is necessary in giving a treatment to dissolve, within our thought, everything which denies the word that we speak. Nothing can neutralize our word but ourselves. When our word is spoken in harmony with the Truth it is linked with the inmutable Law of the universe. Hence a treatment seeks only to convince one's own mentality and never tries to convince anyone else.

In giving a treatment you are not holding thoughts, you are trying to convince yourself of the presence and the reality of the condition which you wish to bring forth. Always your treatment begins and ends within yourself, no matter what your word is spoken for. Because you are dealing with an intelligent Law, when you specify to yourself what your word is for the Law executes the word at the level of your recognition and acceptance of it.

We are surrounded by a receptive and creative medium which receives our thought and acts upon it. This is proved and may be announced as a definite principle. Because this is true our thought decides what is going to happen to us. Were we ever so religious, ever so desirous of doing right, and should still think destructively, we would be subject to destruction. The Law is an unfeeling thing, just as is the law of electricity, which will just as quickly electrocute a saint as a criminal because it neither knows nor cares about saints and criminals. The Law says this: "Here I am; you can never get away from me." "As a man thinketh in his heart, so is he."

It is not going to do any good to say, "There is nothing but plenty in the universe," and then go out and talk poverty. The Law is always right here and says, "Here I am. I am an immutable fact. I am an eternal presence. When you say 'Yes' I say 'Yes' and when you say 'No' I say 'No,' and when you say 'It is good' I say 'It is good.'" Or as Jesus said: ". . . as thou hast believed, so be it done unto thee." We must carry the science of our religion into everyday life—everywhere.

There is nothing harder than keeping the thought straight, and nothing else so desirable. It is not easy in our contacts with the daily world to keep our thoughts so clear that we never become unpoised, that we never accept anything which we do not wish to accept, that we always control the intellect so that the emotions cannot respond unless the intellect says to respond. But whenever we can do this our destiny will be in our own hands, backed by an immutable Power. But before we do this we must relate and harmonize ourselves with the Infinite. The Infinite is so constituted that It never fights Itself, hence we must not fight It; but we do fight It when we admit that anyone fights us. We oppose It when we admit that anything opposes us. We deny It when we admit that good is denied to us. The Law always stands by saying, "Here I am, continually reflecting into your experience exactly what you think into me."

We must take the Science of Mind into everyday life, and when we find ourselves confronted by discordant conditions we should never say, "Oh, what's the use, what's the use?" but rather say, "There is Something in me which is greater than this condition and It can dissolve it." We have the privilege and power to do this, and if we use this ability properly it will be productive of salutary results.

How do we do this? Very definitely. Very specifically. Always we bring our conscious thought to bear upon the specific condition which needs to be changed. For instance, if one were treating to heal himself of eye trouble his treatment would be so formulated as to bring out the realization that his vision is a perfect manifestation of a Divine idea. If, on the other hand, one were treating his business for activity, he would bring to his mental attention the realization that right where his business is there is a Divine Law of harmony, of plenty, and of continuous action.

In an iron foundry the liquid metal is poured into different molds and cools off in specific shapes. This is the way a treatment works. It always works from the basis that the cause of everything is an idea and that the thought is the mold into which our tangible experience is cast.

Hence it is necessary that a treatment be specific. All treatments are based upon the same principle but each treatment is a mold with a certain specific form. Consequently, in spiritual mind treatment the ideas incorporated must encompass the entire situation being treated. If the case is one of unhappiness we must make it clear to our consciousness that happiness is *real* and that unhappiness is a condition based upon a false premise. Back of unhappiness is the thought that there is not good enough, love enough, peace enough, health enough, nor understanding enough to go around so that as a result some of us lack or are short of the good things of life.

In the infinite nature of Spirit, and therefore back of everything, there is enough of peace, of good, of health, and of abundance to go around. Convince yourself, explain to yourself, what is wrong and say, "All of the abundance and peace there is is right here and flowing through me. I can no longer be unhappy." In other words, show yourself why you believe what you believe. By expelling or neutralizing false conclusions the newly established right ones will demonstrate themselves. The more completely your consciousness is in harmony with truth, beauty, peace, love, and righteousness the more power it will have.

There is nothing too great or too small for the action of Law. The same Power that swings the planets in space also creates the buttercup and the aroma of the rose. As Emerson said: "There is no great and no small to the Soul that maketh all, and whence it cometh all things are, and it cometh everywhere."

In spiritual mind treatment never try to make things happen, but *know* you are permitting them to happen and *feel* that they are happening. Imagine them to be happening, and during the process of the transition from the point where you are to the point where you would like to be, pay no attention to any discordant things which may occur.

The worse things seem, the more carefully you should go within yourself to declare the reign of God's Perfection. The worse the condition appears, the more certain you must be that you will accept nothing but harmony. This is the attitude that distinguishes the man who *knows* what he is doing in using the Science of Mind from the one who only *hopes* that something will happen. When a gardener goes forth to sow seeds he sows the kind he wants, and if other things come up during the process he uproots them and knows he is going to reap in due season a harvest of the things he has sown. He is working with definite laws. This is the right kind of faith; it is both scientific and practical.

In the use of Science of Mind one knows, with absolute certainty, that he is planting a seed—a constructive thought—in an absolute, causative Principle. When other things come up he says, "Those are the weeds, those are the negative thoughts," and he pulls them up— neutralizes them in his own consciousness. Then gradually that which was once a desire becomes an actual experience. He knows what he is doing, how to do it, and in doing it he realizes that behind and in his present act there is an eternal Intelligence from which he may draw greater and greater inspiration, knowledge, and power.

THE REDISCOVERY
OF HEALTH

The practice of spiritual mind healing is based on the theory that man's life is rooted in Divine Life and that through his mind he has access to the Original Spirit which animates everything. On first thought the possibility of any healing by this method seems rather vague, since both its principle and performance take place in an invisible realm. But, as a matter of fact, the technique of spiritual mind treatment in physical healing is both concrete and specific, for when one stops to consider the proposition he realizes that all causation is invisible. There are certain assumptions or faiths which we must accept in order to proceed with any activity in life. One general faith which all instinctively do accept is that *life* is in all animate things.

The physician to the physical body makes no attempt to create or coerce life; rather, he starts with the assumption that his patient already has life. His entire effort is to keep the body free for the expression of this life. The physician really treats the body as though it were an instrument through which life flows; in doing this he assumes that there is a Life-Principle already existent and perfect, ever striving for an adequate outlet.

The physician may not think of this life as being Spirit; he may call it nature. It makes no difference what he calls it; he knows that when the body is healthy the Life-Principle flows through it freely; and his business is to assist this circulation, to help the body throw off its impurities, to keep it from becoming congested, and to see that there is proper assimilation. When there is proper assimilation, circulation, and elimination, there is physical well-being.

When the physician proceeds in this manner he is cooperating with nature and its laws; he is, in reality, a copartner with the Originating Spirit. All true physicians understand and appreciate this position, and the layman can understand the work of the true physician only from this point of view. With this understanding in mind the spiritual practitioner cannot feel antagonistic toward the work of the medical practitioner.

When we analyze the methods and procedure of the psychiatrist we discover that his fundamental faith or assumption is not unlike that of the physician, for he also starts with the premise that nature is forever expressing itself through us; but the psychiatrist deals not so much with the body as with the mind, basing his work on the theory that many of our human ailments are the direct result of mental disturbances.

A mental disturbance or imbalance generally indicates some inhibited, misdirected, or blocked action in the conscious or subconscious part of the mind. It is the business of the psychiatric practitioner to restore mental equilibrium, with proper assimilation, circulation, and elimination. He is repeating the work of the physical practitioner, the only difference being that he is dealing with the mind directly and the body indirectly.

There should be no confusion between the general practitioner of medicine and the medically trained psychiatrist. One works with the body, the other with the mind, and since the mind and body are now conceded to be so knit together as to be inseparable, it follows that a good doctor of the body also needs to be a good psychiatrist, while a good psychiatrist needs to consider the body as well. The best results are obtained when the physician to the body is also a physician to the mind.

In analyzing the position of the spiritual practitioner we discover that his assumptions and faiths are almost identical with those of the physical and mental practitioners. He also starts with the assumption that life *is* and is forever seeking manifestation, but he calls nature and life God, pure Spirit—the intelligent Life-Essence animating everything.

He also realizes that the body cannot be well while there is poor assimilation, poor circulation, or a lack of elimination, any more than a stagnant pool can be pure; the pool is purified by running water. The spiritual practitioner knows that unless the assimilation, circulation, and elimination are well ordered, the body will become diseased. Hence his position should not be one of antagonism toward the other practitioners but should be one of cooperation.

The field of the spiritual practitioner lies in that realm of thought where pure ideas are introduced into the mind. In this he is a psychiatrist, since he seeks to straighten out his patient's consciousness. But it is not necessary that the spiritual practitioner have a thorough knowledge of human anatomy, medicine, and the variations of the process of thought, although it might be an aid to him if he did have familiarity with such knowledge.

The spiritual practitioner starts with the assumption that God is, and that man's life is rooted in pure Spirit. His whole work is in the field of mind and Spirit; in the field of mind since his treatment is a thing of thought, in the field of Spirit since his thought seeks to rise to a belief in and acceptance of Spirit as being the life of his patient.

The medical practitioner starts with the body; the psychiatric practitioner starts with the mind; and the spiritual practitioner starts with the Spirit. So interrelated are these three that no man can tell where one begins and the other leaves off. We shall understand the whole man only through our consideration of this threefold unity of body, mind, and Spirit.

The spiritual practitioner devotes his entire time and attention to building up a spiritual consciousness, a realization of a Divine Presence within his patient which is pure, perfect, and forever flowing. He seeks to impress upon his own mind that the life of the Spirit—filled with goodness, with peace, with perfection, and with pure being—now permeates, animates, harmonizes, and controls every atom, cell, and function of the person he is treating.

He knows in his own mind that this pure Spirit is forever flowing free and clear and has no congestion or impurities. He further knows that the Original Life-Force is now eliminating from his patient's mind every belief in or experience of anything which would impair or impede the Divine currents. He works in cooperation with both the physical and the psychiatric practitioner, for when the three shall work harmoniously together with one end in view—the well-being of the patient—they shall have arrived at the most effective method yet known for complete healing, for the making of a person whole again in every respect.

THE CONTROL
OF CONDITIONS

When we speak of using spiritual mind treatment for correcting undesirable conditions we are not suggesting that any mental or spiritual conjuring trick is involved, nor is the hope being held out that anyone, through imagination, will, or concentration, can bring into his experience that which is unlike himself. For instance, a man who knows nothing about music would be wasting his time visualizing himself as a grand opera singer. We must never forget that in dealing with spiritual and physical laws any energy must conform to the instrument through which it flows. This statement in no way can be construed as contradicting the limitless possibilities of Life nor the potential possibilities of man, but it is evident that whatever the Law does for us must be done through us. Hence it is necessary that we furnish adequate channels, as well as being receptive to It.

The facts involved in the effectiveness of spiritual mind treatment in material affairs are greatly misunderstood. Many believe that by thinking, willing, and wishing, by concentration, meditation, and prayer they can bring into their experience something which is utterly unlike themselves, but such is not the case. Yet it would be a mistake to deny ourselves the privilege of knowing that there is an intelligent Law which is accessible to us and which will react in our favor when we allow It to do so.

In everyone there is a unique possibility ever ready to become an expression of his individuality, and if he has not yet discovered his particular niche in the scheme of things he should work more for direction and guidance than for the fulfillment of some special desire. When the mental gate, which obstructs the flow of Spirit through the uniqueness of our individuality, is lifted, there will be an outpush which nothing can resist. Every man, then, should be willing to be himself, remembering with Emerson that "imitation is suicide."

In our spiritual mind treatments we need to affirm that that which most perfectly expresses us, that which will bring happiness, abundance, and peace into our lives will be made known. A treatment which embodies the idea of good and of abundance and which rests in faith will always be effective. The effective prayer is always "Thy will be done"; but we should know that the Divine can will nothing less than freedom, that limitation and lack must melt before It.

We should think of ourselves as happy and prosperous. The drag of the necessity of any limitation should be neutralized through the recognition of Life indwelling us and springing spontaneously into manifestation through our endeavors. And how can we assume such a mental attitude in honesty, in sincerity, and with conviction unless we are already convinced that whatever the nature of Reality is, it is always for and never against us? If we could sense that our place in the universe is Its expression of Itself through us, we would know that there is neither competition nor monopoly in right action. God makes no bargains and the Principle of our being argues with no man.

The originating Intelligence is a straight affirmation. To be forever fighting conditions and meeting emergencies in our minds is an obstruction to experiencing a greater good. There is a certain Divine freedom manifest throughout all creation, a certain flexibility in nature which we overlook. The Spirit cannot flow in freedom when our thoughts are rigid; then the gates of abundance are closed and our circumstances become cramped.

Unless we can sense a good which we do not see, and believe in a Power greater than our finite efforts, we shall tread around in a vicious circle of unattainment. When we are willing to let go and to receive into our intellects the new stimulus; when we have learned that the Law which creates and maintains all things is inseparable from our own thought, we are ready to demonstrate, and not until then.

When the Master Metaphysician said that *it is done unto us as we believe* he announced the law of mental equivalents. While there is a Power and a Presence in the universe which can and does respond to us, It can only respond *to* us *through* us. The Spirit cannot give that which we are unable to receive. It is infinite, forever flowing, and Its nature is to be always giving of Itself. Our receptivity to and embodiment of It automatically sets the gauge to our demonstration.

Our embodiment of It is more than a mere repetition of words. Anyone could stand in front of a paralyzed man and tell him to arise and walk, but it takes the consciousness of a Christ to know that the man will actually rise and walk. The words used in spiritual mind treatment have a power equal to the conviction behind them. Therefore it follows that a spiritual mind treatment must convince the mind of the one giving it; and, if it is to have any power, must find an embodiment in his mind through which the intelligent Law is set in motion finding an outlet and establishing a corresponding experience.

We cannot ponder this thought too deeply and everyone practicing Science of Mind should analyze it completely. The mind of man is the universal Mind individualized in and flowing through him. It is the original Creative Genius of the universe finding a fresh outlet through his mind, but how can It find an outlet unless there be first an inlet?

When a person gives a spiritual mind treatment, time is spent in bringing that assurance to his own mind, that conviction in his own thought, and that embodiment in his own spirit which shall thoroughly impregnate his own consciousness with the realization of the presence and the power of an active, intelligent, and creative Agency working through him.

To this universal Agent there can be no limitation. It is the sole and sovereign Agent of the universe and unless one believes this he cannot practice Science of Mind successfully; otherwise he has no principle and no power except that of the human will which always falls in its own tracks and dies for lack of nourishment.

There is no real mind or spiritual force outside of or external to the original Creative Cause. In no way does this make mere puppets of individual minds, but it does limit the activity of these minds—if this can be considered limitation—to their perception of Reality. There is plenty of freedom, however, in this concept since we are to recognize our own minds as outlets through which the original Mind works through our creative consciousness. Rather than a sense of limitation, this should give us a sense of freedom and unfold in our imagination a transcendent possibility.

The spiritual practitioner's work is quiet, within himself. He must remove every sense of limitation from his work, let his word loose as though it were an original Cause, unconditioned by any relative fact. There can be no sense of competition, monopoly, restriction, or existing condition imposed upon his word if it is to have power and effectiveness. So perfect and unified are the instinctive perceptions of his word as a subtle and natural Cause in the spiritual world that the mind cannot conceive of It in fragments or in parts but only in Its wholeness.

Our security lies in this sense of unity and of the inevitable outcome of good. No treatment can have power which supposes an opposite or which seeks through mental coercion to either restrain or compel. Hence it is written: ". . . not as I will, but as thou wilt." The will of the Infinite can be nothing less than goodness, happiness, and peace. Any denial of a condition in the treatment is for the purpose of eliminating a belief in the necessity of any opposite to the unitary Wholeness which is being proclaimed, to establish in our minds the recognition, the embodiment, and mental equivalent of our highest ideals.

It is impossible to practice this science either scientifically or effectively unless we are willing to subject our thought to this test. If the mind embodies goodness it can speak goodness; if it has an equivalent of peace it can give peace; if it has a sense of abundance it can demonstrate supply. But the moment it falls into the error of mental manipulation it has reduced itself to the level of wishing and willing and its power soon becomes exhausted, the fire dies out, and the ashes of hope lie dead and cold upon the altar of a broken faith.

ABUNDANT LIVING

The theory that we have the ability to change objective conditions through the creative power of our imagination rests upon the belief that behind the solid fact there is an Intelligence, a formless Energy, and a Law whose nature it is to manifest as form. This theory, coupled with the belief that our minds, our thoughts, are directly related to the infinite guiding and directing Intelligence, is the principle involved in the control of conditions through the creative power of our own mental action.

Experiences in the endeavor to prove this theory justify our acceptance of it. Whether or not we have been as successful as we would like to be in consciously directing our affairs through the creative power of thought, we may still rest assured that any apparent failure may be ascribed to insufficient knowledge of this Principle rather than to Its unwillingness to operate for us.

We should no longer ask ourselves whether or not there is such a Principle, but this: To what extent have we gained the ability to use It? The known laws of physical science will prove of little avail in this matter. Theological speculations are useless and philosophic discussions bear but little fruit. We are facing the problem directly as individuals—

do we or do we not believe? If we do not have a sufficient faith, how shall we acquire one?

Each man should be the master of his own mental household, although but few are, and "he that ruleth his spirit (is better) than he that taketh a city." The problem is one of *real* belief. If we can sense the fluidic nature of all that has solid form, that Energy becomes tangible according to a pattern, and that the solid form is an effect and not a cause, we shall at once know that in order to demonstrate we must more or less disregard the form and look to the Presence—spiritual Reality, Mind—in which originate the thoughts or ideas for the patterns of all that has form. We are too liable to be awed by the form and to stop at our point of contact with the tangible object. We go so far and no farther, refusing to look beyond to That which created it.

This intellectual obstruction is a lack of spiritual perception, a denial of the Creative Cause, and it results in limitation. The best practice for the conscious control of conditions is not the use of affirmations which declare that the All-Good is omnipresent, but is a quiet assurance in our own minds that the Spirit is both ready and willing to take full charge of our affairs, coupled with a persistent determination to believe that It is doing so.

But in so doing It must flow through our belief and must take the forms which our belief creates. The Spirit cannot give us something we do not accept and this accepting is a mental act. We must cause our minds not only to *believe* but to consciously *receive*, to concretely and definitely *accept*. Hence another proposition follows this one: the mind cannot accept what it rejects. The mind cannot affirm what it continues to deny. A weeding-out process is necessary, an uprooting and replanting, a cultivation of the creative soil of our imagination. The ground must be prepared for the new crop and we must wait patiently upon the Principle of Life to produce the new form. Meanwhile we should be careful lest, through denial, we affirm a belief which is the direct opposite of the good we desire.

The process is really simple. We must refuse to entertain doubts and fears and resolutely set our minds toward faith, acceptance, and receptivity. We must be patient with ourselves when we appear to fail, rejoicing when we conquer. There must be a flexibility of thought as well as a determination of purpose. In spiritual mind treatment we should turn entirely from the undesirable condition, and, looking through it, as it were, see the opposite outcome.

Each undesirable condition must be transmuted into a good one, and we must stretch the imagination to include the more, the greater and better things. Calmly persisting in the maintenance of this mental attitude, we are certain to win.

There can be nothing in the universe operating against our word except our own doubt. The Law cannot, because the Law is impersonal. God cannot, because God is the impulse which causes us to seek to express a greater, fuller life. Hence nothing can neutralize our work except ourselves. Whatever hinders, inhibits, or denies the reality of an omnipresent Good and Its eternal flow to us must definitely be erased from our thought.

We must consciously set the Good in motion, recognize and let It work for us. So long as a certain specific fear comes to our consciousness we should daily meet it, and, looking it squarely in the face, explain to ourselves why we do not need to be afraid of it. We should always be building toward the affirmative side of life, toward the recognition of an eternal and ever-available Goodness in the universe, ever manifesting in our lives and affairs.

A direct application of Science of Mind to the problems of the business world is both possible and practical. Business is a thing of thought followed by action. Without *thought* there could be no motive for action, and without *action* thought would remain unexpressed. Back of every enterprise there is some mind at work giving it the stimulus of its creative thought. This is a self-evident fact.

Often the mind which creates a business so endows it with vitality that the enterprise sustains itself long after the originating mentality has entered other fields of action. The thought has been so fertile that the business itself has become an entity in the minds of all engaged in it. But once let this mental pattern, this subjective action, cease to be and the business will fall apart like a chain of sand.

Business, like all things on this earth, is not an eternal verity. But, like most of the things with which we deal while in the flesh, it is necessary to the world in which we live. It is not a question of doing away with business, but of making it a success and a thing of joy.

Any activity which does not express a constructive program is wrong in principle and cannot be made right in practice. In the exchange of ideas in the world of affairs there must be both a giving and a receiving; the two should balance. We should not overlook the fact that the law of compensation is an eternal verity. In the use of Science of Mind one should wish to do only that which is right, and accept nothing less than a constructive program. Having complied with this program one is in a position to expect success and should use the Law for the direct purpose of bringing success into one's experience.

It is wrong to be unsuccessful, but success also means more than dollars and cents. Success means mental growth and spiritual attainment, and includes an abundance of those things which make living enjoyable. As the greater includes the lesser, so mental and spiritual growth includes material success, bringing with it personal happiness and temporal satisfaction.

We cannot avoid the Law so we may as well learn how to use It in the right way. The Law so works that as we believe so we shall experience; if we believe in our abundance we shall receive much, and vice versa. A small concept will provide a small container for the good we wish to receive. Great things are accomplished through great concepts. We wish to succeed and we have a right to be successful. But we can express Reality and partake of Its abundance only as we express freedom, not bondage.

Science of Mind connects Life with living, and spiritual Reality with what we are doing. We must remember that no knowledge is of value unless used. If we *know* a truth we can prove it, for that which we cannot prove we only suppose to be true. To the businessman investigating the possibilities of Science of Mind there must come a guarantee that its teaching is effective in the affairs of everyday life.

It is a mistake to suppose that some things are material while others are spiritual and that a sharp line can be drawn between matter and Spirit. Matter is Spirit in form; conditions, Spirit in many forms. Spirit expresses Itself in everything; there is no dividing line between form and substance. The best business methods evolved for the handling of affairs are the ones nearest the nature of spiritual Reality—God. One should not be engaged in anything that he feels could contradict that which is good. All legitimate business, constructively handled, is in accord with the highest good.

When we know that our business is an activity of the Spirit working through us we shall be viewing our business in the right light. When we are certain that the things in which we are interested are constructive we should go ahead with complete assurance of success. The only power there is is with us, for there is no power opposed to Spirit.

In a spiritual mind treatment for success we resolve things into ideas, conditions into states of thought, and act upon the premise that the thought is father to the thing. This method is both direct and effective and when rightly used becomes a law unto the thing thought of.

But in doing this we often contact obstacles, negative ideas in our thought which rob us of our good if we retain them. For instance, we sometimes come up against the thought of competition, the belief that there are too many people engaged in the line of business in which we are involved. Competition is a belief that there is not enough good to go around, and while believed in this thought manifests itself as limitation.

We must resolve and dissolve this thought into its native nothingness, for it has no validity in a limitless universe. God does not compete with anyone. Therefore we should not allow the thought to enter our minds that we are competing with anyone. We should never confine ourselves to watching what others are doing or how they are doing it, for when we do this we are limiting our own possibilities to the range of their vision. We must affirmatively guide our activities and not be bound by what anyone else thinks or does. We rob ourselves when we limit our good to the good of someone else, or refuse to admit a greater good than we have ever before experienced.

In spiritual mind treatment we are to think from the viewpoint of a limitless Power, letting It operate through our own minds. Spirit is not bound by anything that has gone before. It is always doing something in a new and better way. We are to let It conceive of new ideas through us and let the Law produce the forms in our experience.

In the business world everything is an exchange of ideas. The buyer wishes to purchase an idea, the seller has one for sale. Unless this were true nothing could be sold or purchased. Everything begins with an idea. These ideas exist in the One Mind and when one unifies with them they become a part of his experience. We *know* the ones who need our ideas will come to us, or we shall be directed to them. We abide in perfect confidence. Then some thought may come to us which says: Go to a certain person and talk the idea over with him. We must act on this thought, for this is the way the Spirit works. It is working through us and for us.

When an idea to act comes to the mind the act should follow immediately, but without hurry or worry, for confidence is the keynote to success. Business is built upon faith—faith in life, faith in people, and faith in oneself and what one is doing. Without faith there could be no business, no activity, no life—nothing.

If one is engaged in a business in which he has no faith he should get out of it and into something else to which he can give his entire faith and enthusiasm. He should expect success, think success, and talk success, refusing to listen to anything which contradicts success.

The outpush of Mind through human activities is the Self-realization of Spirit and when so understood this outpush becomes *invincible*. Ideas come from the great Mind through the human mind. *The two are really One.* But ideas can come *only to the mentality that expects them* and that opens its doors of thought to them so they can enter and pass through into expression.

Let the mind be open and receptive. Let us court the inner consciousness until its wooing draws from the higher field of realization an inspiration that is *real*. Conviction ever comes from this inner light.

We cannot convince another unless we are first convinced. The person who wishes to sell *must first sell himself to himself and his idea to himself*. His idea is then sold to the world for he is working in a field of unity.

Convince yourself first; the rest follows.

AN ANSWER TO
EVERY PROBLEM

It has been said that the only news we have from heaven has come through the consciousness of man, and this saying is true. The march of civilization, the advance of science, the creation of new and better concepts of God, are emanations of the original Intelligence through the intellect of man.

Since the dawn of human consciousness progress has rested in the mind of man. No new creation, no invention, no art, literature, or science has come from any other source. From this it would seem as though the mind of man were the sole agent, and yet, when we note that the same impulses and emotions are stirring different generations and races into action, when we perceive that a truth gained by the mind of one man may be instantly recognized and used by all, we are led to the deeper realization that there is an infinite Mind seeking outlet through all, operating in all and governing all. The reason why it appears as though the mind of man were the sole agent is that the mind of man is the highest form of intelligent outlet we know of for the universal Mind.

What beings there are beyond us in the scale of cosmic evolution we can only guess, but it seems logical to suppose the existence of beings whose consciousness transcends ours as ours trancends that of the tadpole or the mud turtle, but here in the life which we now lead, or in any life which we ever shall lead, the universal Mind proclaims Itself to us through us. Hence any question we shall ever ask, even though it be answered by God Himself, must be answered directly through the mind of man. Each individual gives voice to that which his own consciousness perceives, each has access to the same original Source, each goes as far as he can, and before and within each lies a limitless possibility of further evolvement.

The infinite Mind must contain an answer to every legitimate question. Infinite Intelligence knows and will willingly respond to any and every properly made request. We have immediate access to this Intelligence and in a very real sense the answer to every question is potential within us, because we are within It. We should learn to consciously draw upon It.

The reason no man has yet fully plumbed the depths of his own mind lies in the fact that his mind merges with the Universal and we can never encompass the Infinite. Herein is the possibility of everlasting unfoldment, the glorious concept of an eternal emergence in ever-widening circles. There is no circle so great but that another may be drawn around it. The questions which are unanswered today will be answered tomorrow. More questions will take their place and they in turn will be answered.

In seeking answers to our problems and questions we need to realize and know: There is an Intelligence in me which knows the answer to every question. There is nothing unknown to this Mind. *It has the solution to every problem.* This Mind is my mind. *It is now working in me, through me.* It is acquainting my intellect, my conscious mind, with the desired information.

The riddle of the universe is a paradox. The question is its own answer, for the mind that asks the question is also of the Mind that answers it.

There is a place in the mind which reaches and unifies with the

Spirit of pure Intelligence. Spiritual mind treatment is for the purpose of penetrating this inner intuitive perception, thus allowing it to descend into the intellect or conscious mind. The subjective state of our thought, being the result of our accumulated experiences, may or may not be in a state of peace. Hence it becomes necessary for the spiritual mind treatment to penetrate and permeate even the subjective currents of our thought.

When our treatment or prayer stops in the area of mere remembrances we simply rehearse our own accumulated experiences and those of the race mind. Hence our treatment may degenerate into a mild form of daydreaming, perhaps pleasant but generally unproductive. Treatment seeks to penetrate into the realms of the original creative Spirit, to communicate or blend its atmosphere in perfect unity with the original Source of knowledge.

Spiritual mind treatment differs from the average prayer in this: The average prayer *beseeches*, while treatment *acknowledges and accepts*. But effective prayer or treatment in its highest form is the simple and direct communion of man's soul or spirit with the Over-Soul or Spirit. There is no possibility of illusion in true prayer and treatment since it plunges completely through the present content of thought and is receptive only to the universal Mind. That such prayer and meditation find a corresponding response from some indwelling or overdwelling Intelligence is an undeniable experience. The greatest minds of the ages have proved this fact beyond any question of doubt and each one of us may prove it for ourself if we give proper time and attention to the subject.

As love alone knows love, and as that which is beauty in us responds to the beautiful around us, so the mind which sets its vision above the confusion of objective strife meets and unifies with a Presence which knows no strife. It would not be normal to spend one's whole time meditating and praying. The belief in the advisability of doing this is a mistaken idea and arises from one's attempt to separate oneself from the world in which one lives. Meditation should stimulate the intellect to renewed and greater objective action. Thus we should swing from prayer to performance, from meditation into action, from contemplation to accomplishment, until the time comes when thought gradually leads us to a place where we have a continuous sense of an overshadowing Presence and an indwelling Good, forever springing spontaneously into our experience.

If we find ourself surrounded by confusion we should meditate on peace until we feel a sense of peace. Then as the mind returns to its objective state it brings an atmosphere of peace with it which dispels the confusion just as light dispels the darkness. Thus our meditation becomes a practical thing; it has an actual value in everyday experience.

In giving a spiritual mind treatment we meditate upon the essence of pure Spirit and perfect Life until we sense a deep inner calm, until our mind becomes fixed in the realization that we are surrounded by perfect Good, by a complete and abundant Life, which our mind now contemplates as flowing through us or through the person whom we are seeking to help. Thus we join the atmosphere of our meditation with the object of our treatment. We withdraw from the finite and enter the realm of the Infinite, only to return again into the finite with an atmosphere of the Infinite. Thus the relative is expanded and enlightened with the essence of pure Being.

At all times we should be certain that in meditation we are not losing the self but that we are merging the lower self with the greater Self, and as time passes we should gradually come to feel that this greater Self is an inseparable companion, an ever-present and ever-available guide on our pathway of human endeavor.

"For God hath not given us the spirit of fear; but of power, and of love, and of a sound mind."

THINK YOUR
TROUBLES AWAY

FOREWORD

This Annual Edition of *Science of Mind* magazine is the third of these publications to bring together the miscellaneous writings of Ernest Holmes.

Once again the source of this material has been the early issues of *Science of Mind* magazine which started publication in 1927. For many years Dr. Holmes's writings which appeared in these issues have been unavailable to the general public. It is felt that they possess such a dynamic quality and spiritual insight that they should be brought to light, becoming a permanent and valuable contribution to the literature dealing with the Science of Mind.

Ernest Holmes was one of the great religious philosophers of our day, and his universal approach to the basic and innate spiritual yearnings of all men won him fame and worldwide recognition. His formulation of the teaching of the Science of Mind cuts across all religious barriers and greatly influences the lives of all who come to know it.

His fundamental philosophy is extremely simple, yet it has had a profound and tremendous impact on the thinking of countless people in all walks of life. He claimed no originality for his ideas, but said that they were a synthesis of the best yet learned in man's three great fields of inquiry: science, philosophy, and religion.

Many others have incorporated his ideas into their own way of thinking and teaching, but here we find in all their purity many of the basic
concepts which have changed and will continue to change the lives of
all those who discover them and use them.

WILLIS KINNEAR

Introduction

You are what you know, and the corollary of that is this: What you now know about yourself is also what you will become.

This idea may be more simply stated by the familiar expression "Thoughts are things," and there is more truth in this statement than you may realize.

You know that a thought always precedes an act on your part. Also you know that an idea is first formed in one's mind before some tangible manifestation appears, such as the making of a chair, the building of a bridge, the creation of a big corporation, or even the baking of a cake. Obvious illustrations to say the least. But, on the other hand, perhaps there is much more involved, much more resulting from your thoughts and your patterns of thinking than you are aware of.

Happiness stems from a way of thinking and not from any external factor. Your emotions and their resultant effects are not controlled by outward conditions, but by your inner direction of them. As much as you would like to believe that your state of health is determined by things outside yourself, you have now been told by leading authorities that even 100% of your physical ailments, in many respects, have their origin in the way you think.

It might be said that each thought you have, good or bad, is a seed that is planted in fertile soil and grows and produces fruit according to the basic idea imbedded in it. Regardless of the nature of your present experience in daily living, in some way or other you can trace that experience back to a thought-seed that you have planted and nourished within your own consciousness!

Yes, thoughts are things. So, if you find that your life is not all that you would have it be, it becomes necessary to change your patterns of thinking. You need to uproot those undesirable thoughts you have planted and replace them with others more to your liking.

This may sound simple, and it is. But in order to do this there needs to be an understanding of who you are, what you are, and the nature of the universe in which you live. The world in which you live does operate in a harmonious and lawful manner. And it is only by understanding the laws of life that you may be able to cooperate with them and use them to your advantage rather than disadvantage.

To make full and constructive use of the axiom "Thoughts are things" requires that you come to realize that there is a Power in the universe greater than you are, and that you can use It. This Power can and does always respond to you, but only in the manner in which you actually use It, not in the manner you would just like to have It respond.

The material in this volume can show you the way to so relate yourself to the great spiritual Power in the universe that you may come to think in a creative and constructive manner so that the things in your life are outward manifestations of your inner thoughts which you have learned to properly control and direct.

In this way you can come to experience more of the peace, perfection, good, beauty, power, and joy which reside at the center of that Divine creative Source of all things.

You have problems just like everyone else, but the solving of these troubles is a matter of the way you think. Wrong thinking created them; right thinking can resolve them and cause them to fade away.

W.K.

Part I

NEW FOUNDATIONS
FOR THINKING

For the most part you seem to be living in an age of turmoil. Both the external world and your inner world of the mind appear to be in a state of confusion. There seems to be a lack of stability, of what to think and what should be a proper reaction to things and events. But then most people have felt that way about the period in which they have lived.

However, throughout the ages there have been those who have found enjoyment, peace, and contentment in spite of the condition of the world around them.

What they have been able to discover you can discover. But the secret, if there is any, lies in the fundamental basic mental attitude you are able to establish. Your mind, needs a firm, intelligent, and emotionally satisfying concept of the nature of Life, and a recognition of your position in It and relationship to It.

It is your basic concepts in this respect that color all of your thinking, that determine the nature of your thoughts which become the things in your life, and enable you to adequately deal with all your problems.

In the ideas advanced in the following pages you can find a surety and a security on which you can build a better life.

A NEW IDEA

That we are entering a new cycle of experience is certain. It is impossible to pick up any periodical of the day without noting some evidence of the change of thought that is going on. We hear of the new psychology, the new science, the new religion, the new universe. What does this mean? and where is it leading us?

Has the faith of our forefathers been shattered on the rocks of a cold science? Has the shock which religion has suffered in recent years undermined our spiritual forces? Has our new philosophy solved the riddle of the universe? Are we lost in the fog of speculative theories? Is anything left that is certain? What can we believe? On all sides these questions are being asked, and whoever finds a reasonable answer will have the world for an audience.

There is no lack of interest. Life, hope, and love are still the dominant factors in people's thoughts. God may be a myth, but people still long for Divine guidance. Immortality may be an illusion, but people still hope that the future will not be an oblivion. Religion may be a mental hallucination, but people still have a mystic sense of Reality, an intuitive perception of Something higher. Aspiration may have turned into the ashes of dead hopes, but the urge to go on still pushes us forward. Science may have failed to find the ultimate Cause, but people still sense an invisible Presence. The age-old question, unanswered, still stimulates the interest: From whence the spirit—whither bound the soul? It is impossible to avoid the issue.

We are so constituted that we must go on. We cannot stop. People have always believed in some kind of God and in some type of savior. They still believe. The will to believe is our strongest passion, our greatest incentive, our constant source of inspiration.

Can we by searching find God? We have looked everywhere. The search has been intense, exhilarating, persistent. But have we found Him? Some will answer *yes*, and others *no*. Those who answer *yes* have the right to be heard as well as those who answer *no*. Both are sincere and each is motivated by the same purpose—necessity.

Anyone who doubts that the quest of man is after God is unacquainted with the human mind. The two great desires of man are for unity with the Spirit and for the realization of immortality. Beside these all other desires sink into utter insignificance. To question this is to admit a profound ignorance of the workings of people's thought.

Can such a universal demand be without a foundation in Reality? And if we have failed to find God or failed to realize the eternity of our own being, may it not be because we have failed to realize what God and existence mean?

God is not a person, yet God is more than a principle. The creative insistence of the universe, the emotional background of all incentive is God—the Urge and the act, the Thinker and that which is thought, the Conceiver and the conceived. Cause and effect are but two sides of the same coin. Who looks for God as a person must look into the personification. The Universe may be impersonal as law and as essence, but It is forever personifying Itself. It is revealed in creation.

Only the one who loves comprehends the meaning and the depth of love. Love declares itself through its personification. It is known by its works. It is as real as we make it. It is not a platitude, but a Divine passion. If we would know God as love we must become love. Those who have done this claim to know God as love. Dare we deny the validity of this claim? Can the coldly skeptical sense the Divine emotion of a love which proceeds from the fundamental unity and includes the entire creation as a manifestation of one central Cause? Could we love the individual unless we have some inner awareness existing prior to the advent of the individual?

The possibility of love existed before its expression or it never could have evolved. The greatest lovers have ever been the most God-like. If we would look for a God of love we must look long and deeply into each other. We must look away from the differences until we penetrate into the Unity of the Whole. Love alone reveals love. Hate but hides the gleam.

Depression and sadness do not reveal a universe of joy. We betray our spontaneity to the traitor of indifference and cry aloud that enthusiasm is dead and hope gone. The zest of life loses its keen edge to the coldly analytical. Mathematics may be necessary in computing distances or in counting marbles, but mathematics alone will never fire the heart of the average person with the joy of imagination. The laughter of the universe is not heard when the blood is cold. Warmth and color respond to their own and take no cognizance of their opposites. If we would know a God of joy, we must become joyful.

God is distant to the unbeliever, unknown to those who are not acquainted with Him. The Spirit may court us, but if we would be wed we must first be wooed. There is no marriage without both bride and bridegroom and mutual consent. The prophets of every age have declared the unity of God and man, but they have been among those who have "entered in." Dare we deny the reality of their experience, the truth of their message?

We would have peace, but we still persist in remaining in confusion.

The one is the opposite of the other. Cosmos does not affiliate with chaos. Some find peace while others find only confusion. We shall yet learn that each finds what he is truly looking for.

If we would find the more abundant life, we must live more abundantly. Life cannot be separated from living and whatever the nature of God or Life is, this nature must be one with our nature, else how could we be? When we enter into the spirit of livingness, we enter into the Spirit of God, for Creator and creation are one, Life and animation are latent in all things. When the creative power of our imagination stirs this latent energy into action there is a responding chord struck in our everyday experiences; we find that we are surrounded by Life. Truly did the great mystic proclaim that "he is not the God of the dead, but of the living: for all live unto him." If God is Life, and if Life is God, and if God and Life are one and the same thing, how can we expect to become conscious of immortality while we contemplate death? All are eternally alive unto the creative Spirit of the universe. The persistent urge to express is a continuous demand which the original Life makes upon us. It is God, the Essence, passing through the thinker into action.

How can we expect to find beauty if we contemplate only unloveliness? The God of beauty is understood by the artist who appreciates the beautiful and senses in all form some reflection of that universal Wholeness which finds harmony in the perfect adjustment of Itself to all of Its parts. Beauty, like greatness, is a thing of the soul, a spiritual quality, outlined in form, objectified in space. It is eternally imaged in the mind.

God must be Truth. The Universe could not lie to Itself. "Truth, crushed to earth, shall rise again." If we would understand God as Truth we must be truthful. The lie is a mask, a masquerade. The irresistible desire which all people have to find the good life arises from an intuitive perception which already knows not only that God is, but that God is present with men.

The kingdom of heaven must be a state wherein one senses his unity with Good, the unity of all people with Good. This kingdom is as distant from us as is our sense of isolation from it. It is as near to us as our belief and corresponding act will permit. The kingdom of heaven is not a place, but a state of consciousness. God is not a person, but an essence, and man proclaims that this essence and atmosphere is personal, and so it is, but in this way: personal *to* us *through* us.

Each person in this sense may approach ultimate Reality and say: "To me It is personal, through me It is personified." The sense of the necessity of some mediator between God and man finds its answer in the responsiveness of our own soul to the universal Perfection. The mediator is our own belief, our own thought, our own conviction, our own action. As the mind cannot isolate itself from itself, or separate itself from itself, so it cannot inject into itself a mind which is not itself, or which is unlike itself, or which is other than itself. Hence it is written: "I myself am heaven and hell."

The mediator or savior which all people have felt a need of is already within. The only thing standing between the essence and atmosphere of the Spirit and Its personification through man, and in creation, is recognition. The fruits of right belief have always fallen from the tree of faith.

We need have no superstition about the results of prayer, faith, or inner awareness. This is the way the Universe responds to us, and the response is in accord with Law, for the Universe is built on the action of immutable Law. How far or to what extent we may prove this depends upon our ability to believe and to receive.

A NEW FAITH

People are instinctively religious. By instinctively I mean that we are born with a religious sentiment. But many will declare that this instinctive religious concept is based on fear, that people have always been afraid of the unknown and have sought to propitiate it. Perhaps many of our religious ideas are the result of fear, but it is unthinkable to suppose that a sentiment which is universal in the human mind, and which rises in the intellectual scale with the evolution of the intellect, can be a delusion. After all, is it not true that instinct may be interpreted as one of the avenues through which the Spirit reveals Itself to us?

It is entirely possible, on the other hand, to say that many forms of religious worship are the result of mistaken concepts of the nature of Reality or God. It seems, however, a dangerous thing to take a man's religious convictions away from him unless one is in a position to give him better ones. It would be foolish to remove the underpinning from a house without first putting in a better one.

Fortunately our approach to Reality and to the religious sentiment need not rob anyone of his faith, but should give him a justification of it. I am not in sympathy with the idea that everything our forefathers believed was wrong. Neither am I of the opinion that we must believe exactly as they did. Any new form of religious belief will always be as nearly like the old as it possibly can be, but with the addition of new ideas. The transition is never too great. The impossible situation created in a nation like Russia today cannot last. We cannot compel a nation to become atheistic, because people are not atheists at heart. The heart already knows that some supreme Presence exists.

Not only do we instinctively believe and sense such a Presence and Intelligence, but everyone, insofar as he senses It and believes in It, finds a compensation for that belief in his own thought and he will not allow himself to be robbed of it. The religious sentiment itself will rise triumphant over any attempt to discard it. There is a Reality in this sentiment which we did not place there, but which we can draw upon. The problem which confronts the world today in the evolution of its religious concepts is not a problem of doing away with religion. Anyone who thinks he can do that does not think straight. It is not a problem of doing away with religion, but it may be a problem of doing away with certain dogmatic concepts which have been held by theology.

We cannot believe that God favors one nation or one person more than another. Such a belief degenerates into the worship of a tribal God. God is Light, and insofar as any man enters the Light, he will receive illumination. Thus the Spirit responds to each and to all at the level of the consciousness of each and all. Some psychologists will tell us that the apparent answer to prayer is the result of a subjective release in our minds when we pray. And I believe that in a certain sense they are right. Just as I believe that the confessional in the Catholic Church should never have been taken out of the Protestant Church, because it provides a release of the burdens of the soul. But there are many, on the other hand, who have not had any sense of the burden of sin. These people also have had some kind of response from the Universe which is difficult to explain on a merely psychological basis. Many believe that there is a communication of their own soul with the Over-Soul of the Universe. And we cannot brush aside their evidence or their experiences with a gesture of contempt.

The act of prayer is an attempt on the part of an individual to communicate with the Universal and to sense a reciprocal action on the part of the Universal. Now we can either do this or we cannot. If we cannot, there is no use trying. If we can, it is a healthful and happy exercise, both for the intellect and for the soul.

I assume that we can commune with the universal Mind and that It responds to us. If It can, then It must. I believe that it is Its nature to eternally express Itself through us, that it is Its nature to respond to us. It is Its nature to enter into us. The approach to Spirit, then, must be an approach to Something which desires such an approach, and to Something which responds to that approach. I do not believe that Spirit can refuse a man's approach to It. Spirit must respond if we approach It rightly.

It may be that our whole trouble is in the wrong approach. How does Spirit respond? If we are surrounded by an infinite Intelligence, how does this infinite Intelligence impart knowledge to us? It cannot do so externally, for the only way Intelligence can impart knowledge is by causing that knowledge to be known in our own minds. The only way that infinite Wisdom can become human knowledge is through an impartation of the infinite Wisdom through the human as knowledge.

Now, the Infinite is the sum total of all things, past and present, and must contain the potential possibility of every new thing and of all future knowledge. God, or the Infinite, contains within Himself or Itself all knowledge, all wisdom, and all instruments of knowledge and wisdom; hence, if the Infinite is one and indivisible, any instrument that It uses is simply some part of Itself.

How as individuals are we going to approach the Spirit unless we do so consciously? I cannot believe that there can be any formula given for this practice. The approach to Spirit should be direct and there should be an acceptance in the mind that there will be a direct response. Life and Intelligence is everywhere. There is no more or less of It here than there is in any place else in the Universe. There is no place where God is not.

A spiritual mind treatment—effective prayer—is for the enlightenment of the mind that the mind may directly receive; it is for the enlightenment of the consciousness that the consciousness may sense its spiritual existence. We all have a sense that there is Something bigger than we are in the universe. The average person at times senses himself to be an extension of It. I have never yet known anyone who did not at times sense a transcendent something. It is the Spirit in us, and our sense of this inner Spirit expands the consciousness, heals the body, and brings a betterment of circumstances in our experience.

The conscious approach to the Spirit is first a matter of faith. The mind cannot contain that which it rejects, it cannot demonstrate that which it refuses to accept, and I think right here lies perhaps the crux of the whole matter. The response of the Spirit to us must be equal to our faith in It. It is always reciprocal, always mutual; the response is by correspondence, as a man beholds the image of his face in a mirror. The Spirit is a mirror before which we hold our minds with all of their thoughts, beliefs, fears, and faiths. The mirror reflects back to us an exact likeness of that which is held before it. How then shall we generate faith? Here is where a knowledge of Science of Mind serves us. Faith is a mental attitude and can be consciously generated. The Spirit works by Self-pronouncement, never by denial. Its words are *Yea* and *Amen*. We must learn to live affirmatively. This is the secret of success in using the creative power of our thought affirmatively. At times we deny the necessity of the reality of that which ought not to be, and we make this denial in order that the mind shall the more readily affirm that which ought to be. The denial brushes aside a false affirmation. But more and more we shall learn to "believe" constructively, to think affirmatively. For our thoughts and beliefs constitute our prayers to the Spirit.

We should learn to live by faith, but we must first learn how to have faith. And if we shall strip the idea of all mystery we shall soon discover that faith is a complete mental acceptance, an unqualified agreement with an idea. We can consciously generate faith and progressively demonstrate the supremacy of spiritual thought force over apparent material resistance, but not while we concentrate on the material resistance and fear it. Hence we must overcome fear by the denial of its power. We must generate faith by the affirmation of its presence. We must have faith in faith, and overcome fear by the presence of faith.

Quiet the mind and definitely state that faith and understanding are present. Mentally state and spiritually feel that a conscious and constructive Presence pervades all life. Affirm that the Spirit wills to respond and that It does respond. Sit quietly and believe. Now state your desire as simply as possible, using only such words as have a real meaning to you. Never try to use other people's thoughts. You are alone with the Cause; see to it that no denial of this thought enters your mind. As simply as you can, create a definite acceptance in your mind that you are being guided into paths of peace and abundance. Feel a response in your thought. Feel that what you state is the truth about yourself. *Affirm that you accept and believe and receive.*

A NEW UNIVERSE

A pronouncement of one of our greatest modern scientific men, Sir James Jeans, was that we are coming to think of the universe as though it were an expression of an infinite Thinker, thinking mathematically. Coming from such a person that is a very interesting concept. What does such an interpretation of the universe mean from our point of view?

We believe there is a Spirit in the universe—an infinite, spontaneous, self-knowing Spirit. All religions believe this. Most philosophies believe it, and in the scientific world the opinion is divided. This infinite and spontaneous awareness we call Spirit or God—the universal Intelligence. We believe that there is also an infinite Law in the universe which obeys the will of this infinite Intelligence, a Law which cannot argue, which is intelligent, but unfeeling and unthinking. It is a Law which knows not why It does, but knows how to do what It does—an infinite Law which is mathematical in Its operation.

We very carefully differentiate between the Law, or the infinite Doer, and the Spirit, or infinite Knower. The knowingness of the Spirit we call contemplation or the word. That which the Spirit knows becomes the Law of Its action and this is the way Its Self-contemplation is manifest. The Law, being unfeeling, does not care if a man is a saint; It does not worry if he is a sinner. The laws of physics work alike for all men. Jesus, who was a profound thinker as well as a spiritual genius, announced this when he said: "Your Father . . . sendeth rain on the just and on the unjust." The Law operates according to the way It is contacted or used, and acts with precision but without emotion. But back of this Law there must be an infinite Emotion or else we could not have emotion; infinite Feeling, or else we could not have feeling; infinite Spirit or Being, else we could not be. The Spirit will never produce anything unlike Itself. Consequently, the very fact that we have warmth, color, emotion, and initiative, some powers which are conscious, and others autonomic, is all the evidence that one needs, if he be a rational and clear thinker. Back of everything is an infinite Mind or Knower!

Science is making a tremendous contribution in that it is deducing a scientific philosophy which will build up rather than destroy man's belief in God. Science has done another thing: it has theoretically dissolved the material universe. Science is sense, so it does not deny that any particular object or form, as such, is real. It has done away, however, with the material universe as a thing of itself and found that it is only energy and lines of force combining for the specific purposes of producing forms, all of which are temporary. It is interesting to note that the Bible affirms this position, saying that nothing is permanent in the objective world, that everything is in a state of continuous flow. Sir Oliver Lodge brought out this same thing by saying that the material form is always flowing and the apparent continuity of it is not occasioned by the flow, but by the mold which holds the flow in place.

Science teaches us that there is not an atom of our physical being that was in it even a few months ago. We can say this: We were born anew in this day and will be born anew in the next. A year from today, if we were to return to the same room we are now in, except for the mind that brings us here we would not bring anything with us in our physical bodies that we have with us right now. I do not see any reason, theoretically at least, why a person could not heal himself of anything, given time, if a new mold could be furnished. That is not just a metaphysical abstraction. The Bible says: "Things which are seen were not made of things which do appear." What we see comes out of what we do not see.

This is exactly the position that modern philosophers take; it is called the theory of emergent evolution, which means that when nature needs something, it demands it of itself, and out of itself makes it. So, in the evolution of the human being, when it was necessary for him to grasp, fingers were produced. Why, then, if it is necessary for you and me to know something we do not know, can we not—according to this theory of emergents—demand the information of ourselves and have it come to be known? The Bible says: "There is a spirit in man: and the inspiration of the Almighty giveth them understanding." Science, philosophy, metaphysics, and religion, viewed from the universal viewpoint, are all of much the same opinion.

We believe that when the human mind, individually and collectively, needs a new truth, out of the necessity of the desire comes the truth it needs. Everything we know in philosophy and science proves it. Out of the desire for a greater good come ways and means for creating the greater good; and if every person made a demand upon Intelligence for the solution to the present world problems, through the minds of those people who are our national leaders would come an adequate and happy solution. That is in line with what we know about the way Life works.

We must be practical; we must prove this modern philosophy, for unless we do it is worthless. We are conscious of certain needs. We need greater happiness, more love, wider friendships, deeper understanding, wiser counsel and advice, happier environment, a more tranquil mind, a healthier body. We say: "I have all these things; I am surrounded by friends, love, happiness, and abundance, my environment is right and harmonious," and this is what we call a spiritual mind treatment. By making these affirmations and believing in them, they possess the law of their own fulfillment out of the great universal Law. Our claim,

being one of faith and belief, would call forth or cause to be manifested
the answer.

Metaphysical practice is not the use of will power, nor is it an exercise to develop the will to the extent that one can concentrate on a given
thought or object for some period of time. That kind of will, though
popularly thought of as attending metaphysical practice, is contrary to
the way in which Life operates. We use the will merely to decide what
it is we are going to do.

Spiritual thought force is greater than any material resistance, because there is no material resistance to spiritual thought force. This is
the meaning of the new universe—the universe explained as a spiritual
system, a Divine order, a unitary and everlasting and indestructible
wholeness, so near, so close to us that every thought form carries with it
the cause of its own manifestation. So marvelous is that freedom which
Divinity has bequeathed to us that it becomes our very bondage when
we see it as bondage. It is our good when we use it as good. We have
reached the place in our evolution where we can consciously cooperate
and demonstrate the greater good.

Where is the individual's place in the universe? The universe cannot
be a joke, yet it cannot be overserious. We become too serious, too tense.
The universe is a joyous manifestation of some Self-sufficient Cause,
some universal Intelligence, some Divine and ever-present Will and
Purposiveness which appears to desire Self-expression that It may enjoy
what It knows Itself to be. Man is Divine because there is imparted to
him and incarnated in him some part of that indivisible Wholeness
which is what we mean by God or Spirit. Every individual is some part
of the universal Wholeness, yet each is unique in that no two people can
ever be alike, for Spirit is eternally individualizing, personifying Itself
in infinite variation while ever remaining a unity.

This is a stupendous concept, and when rightly understood will answer a great many questions. We wonder why there is suffering in the

world—an apparent negation. If a man does the best he knows, if he is as good as he knows how to be, why is it that what we call ill-fortune can come to him? I think that everybody somewhere along the line must ask that question of himself, but it seems that we are now beginning to find the answer.

If we are made out of this universal Wholeness, then we are some part of the Divine Being and Its nature is incarnated in us, with the prerogatives of that nature—the power to do, will, and choose, the necessity of being an individual with self-choice, in which case there must be a Law backing up our choice. Consequently, we can bring to ourselves what we call limitation by the very same Law that could bring to us freedom. If this were not true it would mean that there was a law of freedom and a law of bondage—two opposing forces, hence no Infinite or Eternal. Jesus understood this completely, for he said that when man is in league with this infinite Purpose and Will, then It is he; the two are one.

Self-realization comes to us, not by antagonizing or fighting other people's ways of believing, not by struggle or by strife, but by recognition; that is, by knowing the truth, by alignment with the nature of Reality which is wholeness and unity, goodness, truth, and beauty. Self-realization is not a struggle for personal attainment; it is not the setting up of adversaries to knock down. As we come to the recognition of what and who we are, we will see that we do not have to contend with anything on earth. We do not have to struggle to find a place for ourselves in the universe. In the sight of the Spirit, which is also in the sight of our own spiritual natures, we are part of Its expression, no matter where we are. Anything that expresses is the light that It expresses.

This should add a new dignity to our concept of ourselves; it should enable us to know that that eternal I Am in us will always remain infinite, unique, eternal, and yet, in Its oneness, the root of all life. No longer does a man need to feel himself to be a worm of the dust, a lost soul. There is just as much God in one man as there is in another. If it seems as though there were more God in one man than in another it is simply because some men have used more of this Divine gift.

It gives us a new sense of human values to realize that all humanity is Divinity waking up to Itself through self-discovery and self-realization. Plotinus said that all men have the kingdom of heaven within them. All men are of God. Emerson said that all men are a part of the universal Mind, and that all men are the inlet and may become the outlet to the same, and to all of the same. Which is what Jesus meant when he said: "I am the way." He did not mean the limited Jesus, but the limitless Christ. He was referring to the Divine nature of every man, that Divinity which we come to in our own natures, that which is called the secret place of the most High. "He that dwelleth in the secret place of the most High shall abide under the shadow of the Almighty." It means the Divine incarnation, that thing which quickens by Its glory every act of our human experience. The greatest evidence we have of Divinity is humanity.

All our study and concern with theories is only that we may prove and practice them. Practice, then, is the art and the act and the science (art because it is harmonious, a thing of perfect harmony; act because it is an aggressive, conscious thing; science because it is subject to exact laws) of bringing our thought consciously and subjectively to absolutely believe and accept and embody statements and declarations which affirm the great realizations of spiritual perception as now present in fact, in experience and manifestation.

Practice is not suggestion. We would not suggest that God be omnipotent. Practice is not a rite of concentration, because we could not concentrate God. We do not try to concentrate livingness; we try to center our attention upon it, that we may see that it is concentrated already. Practice is knowing the truth that the same pure Intelligence—the volition and will that created the universe—is incarnated in us right now. The spiritual mind treatment becomes a statement of our belief, an affirmation of our investigation, and the specific things we accept in our treatment externalize in exact mathematical ratio as the beliefs which deny them are dissolved from our consciousness.

We are not religiously superstitious. We say this: There is such a thing as Spirit. Spirit is intelligent; It is all-powerful. Spirit is really here; It does work, but It can only work for us as we let It. We only let It as we believe and embody It. Therefore, we will practice our belief. In such degree as we do this, we find that we are practicing self-realization, and this is the most remarkable thing that has been discovered: the power of spiritual thought force over apparent material resistance. The kingdom of heaven cometh not by external observation, but by internal recognition.

A NEW FREEDOM

In the rapid evolution of the thought of our times we hear a great deal about superstition and Reality. Some claim that the entire intellectual edifice upon which the religious thought of the world has been built is a false premise and that our acceptance of it is superstition. While others claim that the principal trouble with the world today is its lack of faith in some invisible Power of Good responding to the petitions of mankind.

Let us define superstition and Reality. By superstition we mean any belief which holds that there are powers, presences, or intelligences of a universal nature which respond more quickly to one person than to another. By Reality is meant the nature of ultimate Truth. It is self-evident that we know but little about the nature of Reality. The scientist finds everything culminating in laws, the philosopher in abstract ideas, the artist in pure feeling, and the religionist in absolute Being.

But these differences of understanding and approach to Life are not as far apart as they at first appear. The apparent gap comes rather from seeking to approach Reality from one direction only. An impersonal and impartial getting together might show that the nature of Reality starts in absolute Being, impulsed by pure feeling, giving birth to ideas which operate in accordance with immutable laws. Indeed, an analysis of the situation seems to evidence this type of Reality and this kind of Unity. If so, we should discover that infinite Person does not contradict infinite Law, that absolute Will does not necessarily deny spontaneous feeling, and that the universal ideal of Truth and of Beauty must necessarily give birth to that which is both truthful and beautiful.

But to return to the superstitious approach: It is one thing to believe in infinite Will and Person, and quite another to believe that the will of infinite Person is more solicitous for the well-being of one individual than for that of another. It is one thing to believe that the nature of Reality is such that It must respond to us in such degree as we approach It in Its true nature, and quite another to believe that by petition It will or can change Its nature.

For instance, if the nature of Reality is wholeness, perfection, and completion, any expression of Reality must be wholeness, perfection, and completion. It is certain that Reality could never change Its nature or Its expression. It would be futile to ask God to be God, to pray that the Spirit of perfection should enter our being and make us whole, but to seek, through realization, to enter into the nature of Wholeness would be a true approach to Reality.

Emerson tells us that any prayer for less than the all-good is vicious. By this he means that there is no isolated good, no separated good, no absolutely individual good. He does not mean that it is impossible to individualize good, but that the individual mind is already a part of the universal Wholeness, which truth, when discovered and embodied, leads to Its proper manifestation—the wholeness of the individualized life.

We are born with the instinct to believe, to have faith, to expect and to receive. Whether we say it has taken endless generations of experience to produce this instinctive belief, or that the instinctive belief appears with us and that it has taken endless generations of experience to understand the belief, makes no difference. Just as it makes no difference whether we approach Reality through the laborious method of induction or accept it by the intuitive perception of deduction, we arrive at the same conclusion. Reality, to be at all, must be all and must include everything. Its process and performance may be and undoubtedly are through the law of evolution or unfoldment, but the Thing unfolding can never be anything other than what It is—complete to begin with, complete in all Its processes, complete in everything It performs.

Prayer is transmuted from a material and a superstitious basis in such degree as it seeks, through contemplation, to recognize the inevitableness of man's Divine nature, the absoluteness of his real being—not a being isolated from but included in a universal Wholeness. This prayer can be scientific, artistic, philosophic, and religious at the same time: It can be scientific in that it should realize the necessity of compliance with universal Law. It can be artistic in that it senses the impulse of original feelingness as the motivating power of everything. It can be philosophic in that it recognizes the nature of Reality to be infinite Intelligence operating from abstract ideal to concrete performance. It can be religious in that it recognizes the necessity of an infinite Personalness, an infinite and absolute Being. "For in him we live, and move, and have our being. . . ." It can be dynamic and effective in such measure as it has absolute faith and conviction that when it is true to the nature of Reality, Reality responds to it. It is impersonal in such degree as it realizes that Reality imparts of Itself alike to each and to all. It can be personal in such degree as it realizes that the nature of the infinite Presence is to express Itself, to embody, to personify, to go forth into creation. Thus the simplest fact of life becomes exalted, the meanest person Divine, and all creation the body of the Infinite.

The practical application of this apparently abstract approach to Reality is very simple. One should feel that he and all people are Divine, all united in one common Mind, all moving to one common end, the manifestation of this infinite Mind. And yet, at the same time, each can feel that he is a unique, a particular individualization, rooted in the same Unity but manifesting a distinct identity—forever the same but yet forever different.

Through meditation and by contemplation we arrive at the essence of the power of prayer, which is identification. Jesus said: "The Son can do nothing of himself, but what he seeth the Father do: for what things soever he doeth, these also doeth the Son likewise." He also imposed this condition upon Sonship: the necessity of entering through faith and acceptance into the nature of Reality.

A prayer for an isolated good, for a good which is to be enjoyed by one and withheld from others, cannot enter into the nature of Reality to such a degree as would a prayer which includes the all-good, which at the same time recognizes the presence of an individual good. Viewed from the meditative and contemplative viewpoint, based upon this concept of Reality, affirmative in its acceptance and seeking to become an embodiment of the essence of its own realization, prayer will yet be discovered to be the most dynamic force there is in the lives of individuals and in the destiny of peoples.

A NEW LIFE

We sense in life a great mystery. There is not a normal-minded person who does not feel, for instance, that if there were something which could untie or loosen some other part of himself, there would result an entirely different manifestation of himself. I do not think anyone has ever lived, who has thought very much about the meaning of life and who has been willing to open his mind to interior convictions, who has not at times felt a bigger personality, a sense that this everyday individual is a projection of Something which stands back of it, projecting it. I do not mean the experience of a dual or a split personality. I mean, rather, the consciousness of a bigger self, the same self but more of it.

This is certain, the more deeply we penetrate the mind, instead of exhausting that which we are penetrating, the more we discover how much is left to be penetrated. We might have so much water in a reservoir and when we use it, it is gone; so much money in the bank and when we draw it out, it is gone; so much food in the larder and when it is eaten, that is the end of it. Everything in the objective world begins and ends in the duration of time. But when we enter the subjective world, the spiritual world, or the thought world—all of which mean the same thing—when we enter ourselves, we discover ourselves to be an inexhaustible reservoir. Why is this unless there really is an inexhaustible self which we all may feel?

The great problems which confront humanity today are not economic, not political. The problems of the day are those which deal with the soul and with the spirit. In saying this I do not belittle the economic problems, I do not belittle the international problems, but they are effects of man's mind. They are not causes. No government ever ran itself. No system of thought ever devised itself without the instrumentality of mind, of soul, and of spirit. Therefore, the things that we do, the things in which we are objectively interested are effects of our interior selves.

The real questions to which people are seeking answers are not like this: Shall I regain a lost fortune? For it does not make a bit of difference whether any of us regains a lost fortune. The questions which people are asking today are: What is worthwhile? What is it all about? Why am I? What am I? What, if any, is the reality of my own life, the integrity of my own soul? Is there any continuity of my own consciousness? Am I simply a happening in a universe which is chaotic, meaningless, destitute of intelligence and purposefulness, lacking in program and progress?

Today we are finding a transition in the race thought greater than at any other period in the entire history of the human race. The crumbling and the downfall of empires, the breaking up of established systems of thought, the changing of institutions, all conspire to cause the individual to look into his own soul.

This contemplation, this inquiry as to what it is all about, is producing a rapid evolution in our thought. Religious systems are changing. People are asking whether or not the church shall ever survive, whether or not any human institution can survive the terrific shock of recent years.

This inquiring attitude is a healthy mental state. The world, spiritually speaking, is in better condition than it has been because out of all this controversy, this mental turmoil, there will come some kind of an answer. That answer which is to satisfy the new order must do four things. It must satisfy the intellect, therefore it must be intelligent. It must satisfy our factual findings, which means that it must be scientific. It must satisfy our emotions, therefore it must be artistic. It must satisfy our cosmic sense, that is, the sense of bigness which the soul has, therefore it must be spiritual. The new answer must also provide a bridge between the intellect and the emotion.

Science and philosophy are things of the intellect. Religion and art are things of the feeling and of the emotion. Every religion which has ever been devised, crude as it may have appeared to a more cultured form of worship, has been an attempt to interpret in an objective manner that mystical sense which all people have. All the symbologies of the ages have been some attempt on the part of the intellect to interpret a spiritual sense which is instinctive in human thought.

We are on the verge of the greatest spiritual renaissance the world has ever known. Each one is seeking to reinterpret life to himself. There are certain things we must *know* about ourselves. Throughout all the ages there have been certain people who have plunged beneath the material surface and found a relationship of the individual to the Universal. We have called such people illumined. Always there have been people who, like Walt Whitman, have announced: "I . . . am not contained between my hat and my boots." That is either true or else it is not true. We will never know whether or not it is true by listening to what somebody else tells us about it. Nothing can save the world from the terrible dearth of peace which is prevalent today but the soul itself. We may look about us for saviors but we shall not find them. We may listen to sages and can interpret or misinterpret what they say, but we will never find any satisfactory answer outside an immediate personal spiritual experience.

What is a spiritual experience? A spiritual experience is a certain interior awareness through which the soul becomes conscious of itself as being in unity with the Universal and with all other selves. We all have had such experiences in varying degrees, but is it possible for the average individual to have a satisfactory spiritual experience, so that he may *know*, so that he can speak as one having authority? The most pathetic spectacle in the world is a man who is not sure of himself. The most unhappy person in the world is the man who does not believe in himself. The most impossible mental state is that which does not know that good must come to all alike, at last.

We believe that there is in the Universe a limitless, all-knowing Intelligence with the infinite capacity to know and to be—an infinite, intuitive, instantaneous Power. It is impossible for the finite to grasp the full meaning of God. This infinite Being is, or has within Itself, what we may call an infinite personalness. This does not mean that God is a person as we think of a person. It does not limit the idea of Infinite to think that the Spirit has the elements of infinite personalness and the fact that It has produced personality is proof that It is possessed of these elements.

It is the nature of this infinite Being to express Itself. That is, It has infinite intelligence and feeling; It is an infinite artist and an infinite thinker. It is infinite feelingness; It has infinite personalness. It is the abstract essence of all concrete personality, the abstract essence of the possibility of the feeling of every artist. It is pure Intelligence—the abstract essence of the answer to every problem for It has no problems.

It is an infinite Will, not as we understand will, but an infinite Will from the standpoint and basis that It is infinite in Its capacity to know and to project. Therefore, the Truth or Reality is never a fragment. It is always a totality. That is what we mean when we say God.

This Infinite was, is, and is to be. I realize that the concept that I have given could produce absolute philosophic materialism because I could turn around and say that this Infinite has no beneficent purposefulness, that It is just blind, mechanical Mind. This may be an intellectual and a philosophic concept, but it does not satisfy us, mainly because we recognize ourselves as warm, pulsating, colorful beings.

We long for human love and understanding and Divine relationship. The intellect, trained in things intellectual only, turns upon itself and destroys itself. We have witnessed such a turning in the world in recent years.

We wish to know if there is in the Infinite anything that knows us. We say: Does God know me? Every person is going to ask that question sooner or later. Either there is no Power, no Intelligence, nothing in the Universe that knows me or cares what happens to me, or else there is such a Power. We can no longer believe that we can pray to some God who will bless us but not bless our neighbor, simply because the neighbor does not believe as we believe. We know that whatever this Infinite Thing is, It is not a house divided against Itself. It is you and It is me, and It is all. But does It know you, me, and Itself?

I believe that the infinite Mind knows us but I do not believe that It knows us apart from Itself. I think Mind does know us but It knows us as a part of Itself; It knows us within Itself, not as separate or isolated. We are part of Its Self-knowingness. Therefore, I believe that our self-knowingness, what we know about ourselves that is really true is our consciousness of God at the present level of our evolution.

In saying this I hasten to add that I do not believe I am God. There is a great difference between saying I am God and saying God is me. Ice is water. All ice is some water, but not all water is ice. So we might say of the life of man: All of the life of man is some of the Life of God; some of the Life of God is all of the life of man; but man is not all of the Life of God. It is my conviction that whatever my life is, is God. There is no difference between my life and God in essence; the difference is in degree. Consequently, if that infinite I AM in me and in all men is God, it accounts for the fact that in moments of illumination we are able to see that Thing back of us. That infinite Thing knows me at the level of my ability to know It. Its Self-knowingness is me and my self-knowingness is It.

There is an infinite Intelligence which gives birth to our own minds, and if our own minds are in league with It, then we arrive at the reason for the power of thought. The practical application of this metaphysical idealism is right here. But there is likely to be great misunderstanding about this. Mind is the thing that creates. My mind is the Mind of God functioning at the level of my perception of life. Therefore, to me my mind must be as God. It is the only thing that could interpret, understand, accept, or reject. Because of this, thought is creative. If this is true, and if this mind of ours does partake of that universal Wholeness and is creative, then we are bound by our own liberty, and bondage is an expression of freedom—man's freedom under the infinite Law of all life.

I believe that each one of us in turning to the great inner life is turning to God. He who penetrates this inner life will find it to be birthless, deathless, fearless, eternal, happy, perfect, and complete. Gradually there dawns in his consciousness a sense that God, or the Infinite, is flowing into everything that he is doing. As individuals we must re-educate our minds, realize that we have as an ally a Presence and a Law in which the past, present, and future, and all people whom we call living and dead, live and move and have their being, forever unfolding.

Part II

THE CREATIVITY
OF THOUGHT

Whether you realize it or not, whether you believe it or not, it is demonstrable that your thoughts are creative in and of your experiences.

This being the case, what your patterns of thought have been becomes a matter of great importance. In all likelihood you have been creating, without being aware of it, through the process of thoughts becoming things, many situations and conditions in your experience which are definitely not too desirable.

Any attempt to fully ascertain just why thoughts are creative is impossible. It is known and has been proved that they are. To go beyond this would be to penetrate the very nature and mystery of Life Itself. Although man's understanding of Life is increasing, the finite could never encompass the Infinite.

So there is a need to accept the fact that thoughts are creative, then proceed to think in the most constructive manner possible.

The following pages provide many valuable suggestions, ways and means, for the beneficial use of your power to think creatively. In your own mind lies the key that will open the door to the wealth of good things in life you desire, and remove from your experience all unlike them.

YOUR UNLIMITED POSSIBILITIES

The possibility of this modern age existed at the time of prehistoric man. If there had been anyone then who knew how to build a gasoline engine and knew how to get gasoline, he could have had an automobile, so far as the Universe was concerned. In the evolution of his thought man provides avenues through which infinite potentialities can come into being. Man does not create anything except the form, the shape, and the use. Everything else already is in nature, and awaits man's discovery.

That is just as true when it comes to the use of Science of Mind. That is why I have often said that the practice of Science of Mind does not involve concentration or will power, as people think of those things. If it did, you could not use it. It is most amusing, but very pathetic, to see people concentrating on something, willing, trying to compel something to be. It does not work that way. The individual is merely providing the avenue through which That which is may express Itself through the terms of Its own nature. We do not will that electricity shall light a room; we provide ways for it to light the room.

The sooner we realize that this is true about the use of Science of Mind the quicker we will demonstrate its effectiveness. Nobody understands exactly what mind is. I don't myself. I just know enough about it to know that it is, and something about how it works. How it works is the most marvelous thing in the world; it is the greatest discovery that was ever made by man; it taps the greatest resourcefulness that has ever been tapped; and it works whether we believe it or not. The thing, first of all, is to believe it does. Some people can believe it does just because they are told it is true. And that is fine. It makes no difference how we believe it, or for what reason, but belief is essential. There is no approach to its use without belief.

If one can accept it in the simplicity of a childlike faith, that is marvelous. But if a person cannot believe with that childlike simplicity, he is not hopeless either. I have found that the people who come disbelieving and unbelieving and contradicting and arguing, provided they have good intelligence, eventually have the best understanding. Conviction is what we need above everything else in the Science of Mind. I do not care if a man is the best philosopher who ever lived, or the most highly trained scientist or psychologist or religionist, there is nothing in the use of Science of Mind that will contradict any positive fact he knows. Therefore, we need not be afraid to approach the man who is full of "common sense." When he begins to understand it he will believe it.

We start with the premise that absolute Intelligence is fundamental. Just as I know I exist, and I respond to you and you respond to me because of our intelligence, Intelligence must recognize and must respond to Itself. The only way in which Intelligence can respond to Itself is by corresponding with Itself. That is why the ancients taught that Life responds to us as we respond to It.

Suppose we approach the use of Science of Mind with the desire of demonstrating success—and I am thinking of success from the broad-gauged viewpoint. A successful life must be happy, must be sure of itself, must be adequately provided for in what we call the material things, surrounded by as much beauty as it can appreciate, friendship which every normal person craves, and the experience of happiness and joy.

There is no such thing as a successful person unless he is absolutely certain of himself and of his destiny. There is no successful life without the complete conviction of the eternality of one's own consciousness.

We must approach this understanding with belief, conviction, and flexibility. We are not flexible enough with life; we fight it too hard. It may be true that up to certain periods in our evolution we made progress by fighting, but after we have reached certain levels we shall make more progress by acquiescence. The Universe does not strain. It produces of Itself in peace.

We are surrounded by pure Intelligence and we are a part of It. Intelligence responds to us directly, specifically, concretely, and personally. God is Universal, Life is Universal, but at the point where the consciousness of man contacts It, It becomes personal. Therefore, when we approach this Principle of Life we should approach It not as something distant and far away, or something to which we petition. Jesus said: "Ye shall neither in this mountain, nor yet at Jerusalem, worship the Father . . . God is Spirit: and they that worship him must worship him in spirit, and in truth." He was talking to every living being. Therefore, it is not necessary that we go to some hallowed spot, to some sacred precinct, for Spirit is within us. We never can find Reality outside ourselves. Consequently, the one wishing to demonstrate a specific good must turn to his own mind and his own thought because his own mind and his own thought constitute the place where he is an individualized center of God-Consciousness.

All we have to do is to state our desire, believe it, and let it alone. The hardest thing any man has to do is to learn to trust the Universe. We might say it should be the easiest thing to do, but it is not. We like to dabble with our request, pull our prayer back, give our spiritual mind treatment and then steal it back to see if it is taking root. In the last analysis a man must convince himself that he is in league with the only Power there is.

Someone will say, "Why is the world situation as it is today, and how can it be worked out?" It would work out this way: Everything is the result of intelligence and thought. All human conduct is a thing of thought acting itself out. Shakespeare said: "The thought is ever father to the act." When the majority of the mentality of the world agrees about anything, that thing always happens. If the majority of the people in the world were honest-minded, we would not have dishonesty. We will have what we call corruption and graft in public places until the minds of the majority of the people are honest, which time will not be while I would take advantage of you, or you would take advantage of me. But when that point in mind is reached we will not have any more dishonesty.

The Universe springs to the response of the individual thought. But meantime there is no law in the Universe that says you and I as individuals have to wait until all the rest of the world catches up. "A thousand shall fall at thy side, and ten thousand at thy right hand; but it shall not come nigh thee." I believe that is true, otherwise we should be subject to a fate over which no individual would have control. The greatest power on earth today toward the stabilizing of the world is the individual, like you and me, who is thinking constructively.

We must come to the consciousness that Spirit wants to respond and does respond, and then we must accept It and accept It intelligently. What I mean by accepting It intelligently is this: If you will notice, you will see that everything in nature is definite. Nothing is chaotic. A seed always produces its kind. Even when there are definite combinations of specific things, the thing produced by the union of these two is another specific thing. This law of physics is also one of the greatest laws of metaphysics.

What we put into a spiritual mind treatment we know will come out of it, but we do not have to make the result. When we say we must put into a spiritual mind treatment what we want to come out of it, many people think that we must inject a positive force and energy against a reluctant force of nature and compel it to work. That is not so. If we put into the ground a corn kernel, we get corn. We do not have to make the corn come out of the soil. In fact, we could not do it. We only have to make it possible for the corn to be produced. If we had to put into our thought the force to make that thought effective or creative, we would be lost, for we would not know how to do it.

The one giving the spiritual mind treatment believes there is a Power and a Presence that responds to his thought. No matter what all the world believes, no matter what anyone says, he must believe that this Power directly and specifically responds to his word. As Jesus said: "Heaven and earth shall pass away, but my words shall not pass away." That is a conviction! First of all we must have that same conviction, and if we do not have it now, we must get it in the best way we can. I am not interested in the way. I am interested only in the fact that the way we choose shall finally get us to the conviction. We are to approach this Presence simply and directly and easily because It is right here within us. We can never get outside ourselves; we shall always be interior in our comprehension. I am here and It also is here.

Having reached this conviction, we state what we would like the Principle of Life to do for us. We do not wish a good for ourselves that would not be good for other people. But good is right; good cannot do evil. Abundance cannot hurt anybody. It is not going to hurt the rest of the world for you and me to have plenty. It is not going to hurt the rest of the world for you and me to be happy. Others around us need not think as we think; we do not have to watch the other fellow. There is nothing for us to watch but ourselves. We will never see anything or experience anything else but ourselves.

We believe all good is available to us. As much of that good comes to us as we are able to perceive. Therefore, in our spiritual mind treatment we must definitely remove the thought that the good we desire is not for us. Good always exists and disregarding anything to the contrary we can experience it. Everything that we do and say and think is based upon the infinite availability of goodness, truth, and beauty. Therefore, everything that we do and say and think should prosper. Our thought must come to believe it, affirm it, state it definitely and with faith until the mind comprehends what it means and is fully convinced of its own statements.

Then a thought comes to the mind which says: "But you haven't anyone to intercede for you, no influential person to make it possible for this good to come to you." Right here is where the mind must be alert and say: "This word has nothing to do with influential people. This word out of itself makes what it states." A spiritual mind treatment becomes a mental entity in a spiritual world just exactly as the kernel of corn is a physical entity in the creative force of nature which we call the soil.

The word which we speak in our spiritual mind treatment is complete and sure, and has the means and processes of producing itself at the level of our recognition of it. Consequently, as our recognition of our word becomes greater, the result in our experience becomes broader. We should work consistently and definitely to convince ourselves that we are happy, surrounded by an environment of goodness and truth and beauty, of friendship, of everything that makes life worthwhile. Our good is at hand. This is the day in which it is received, if we accept it.

When doubts, fears, and contradictions come up in the mind, we must consciously and definitely cast them out. We must remember that a thought is a thing. A thought that doubts good neutralizes a thought that affirms good, and vice versa. It does not matter what has happened or what condition exists. We must still affirm with an ever-growing conviction the active presence of good in our experience *right now*. We are dealing with absolute, unconditioned Causation right now, and in such degree as our concept embraces this conviction, we are able to demonstrate the condition we desire and eliminate our problems and troubles.

USING
SPIRITUAL POWER

L et us define spiritual Power as the dynamic quality of that invisible essence of life, intelligence, and law which we call God or First Cause. The conscious use of this Power comes from the recognition that It actually exists, really responds to us; that we can directly contact and definitely use It. That there is such an invisible essence of life is evident throughout all nature, the visible side of which but proclaims this invisible essence. Objective nature, our own bodies included, is a phenomenon of the invisible Cause which we call Spirit.

Man is an incarnation of this invisible Cause, not by choice but rather by the Law of Life. As man touches his own thought, he touches It. He touches It with power, not because he wills this power to be, for *this power is*. This is the nature of the Universe. As Hegel said, the Universe consists of will and representation. This will is intelligent knowingness; its representation is creation. The will of Spirit, or the universal Will, must be goodness, truth, and beauty. As we imbibe Its nature, we come into Its harmony. The Divine does not come to us bringing an olive branch of peace with which to allay our confusion. The Divine knows no confusion. It persists in remaining true to Its own nature. The will of God *is* peace. Only the finite is confused; the Infinite remains certain of Itself. As we enter the atmosphere of peace our confusion vanishes. This is not done through objective power, nor by might, but through a realization and an embodiment of that Presence which transcends confusion. The spiritual Presence in the universe is real and dynamic. It surrenders Itself to us in such degree as we comply with Its nature. Our consciousness is so at one with the universal Law of Cause and Effect that when we know confusion we become confused; when we know peace we become peaceful.

Life never expresses by external impartation but always by a process of interior awareness. The very breath we breathe is God. We are not evolved from that which is unlike Spirit to that which is like Spirit. We are evolved *within* Spirit, by, from, and of Spirit. Hence, the very ignorance of the Law of our own being, while such ignorance continues, produces bondage. It is not as though there were a power of good on one side and a power of evil on the other. There is but one ultimate Power. This Power is to each one what he is to It. "With the pure thou wilt shew thyself pure; and with the froward, thou wilt shew thyself froward." The Divine exists to each only as a measure of his own belief.

The question arises whether any limit can be placed upon the possibility of the conscious use of spiritual Power. Theoretically it would seem impossible to place such limit. The only limitation would be that of belief and understanding. The Spirit Itself, in Its original state, must be ever-present with us. It refuses to change through any process of time. It refuses to be divided. Consequently, the eternal Wholeness Itself is immediately at the point of our perception—*all of It*. The question would not be, how far can Principle allow Itself to be used? but rather, how greatly can we understand It? Since Its whole purpose must be that of Self-expression, It must be Its nature to represent Itself spontaneously through our will, through our imagination, fulfilling our intentions, desires, or plans, for in so doing It finds Self-expression. The only limitation being that we must approach It in Its own nature.

In such degree as we are in alignment with this nature, Its power must be ours.

If we could strip the mind of fear, superstition, and all sense of separation from this Divine Presence, approaching It quite simply and directly, we probably would be surprised at the results which would follow. How can we approach this Principle of our being other than directly through our own thought, and through a great simplicity of thought? What can a spiritual mind treatment, which is the conscious use of spiritual Power, be other than a direct statement of our desire and a simple acceptance of that desire? Since we are desiring, accepting, or rejecting at all times, whether we are conscious of the process or not, we are using this spiritual Power at all times. It is not alone in the moments of conscious self-contemplation that we use spiritual Power; it is in every moment of the activity of our thought.

Whatever condition we impose upon this Power causes It to appear to us as though that condition were real. There was once a man in America who healed many thousands of people through prayer. This man believed that God wished him to go barefoot, consequently he wore no shoes. It was necessary for him to go barefoot in order to arrive at certain conclusions in his mind. The Infinite did not impose this condition upon him. Could he have believed that God desired him to wear satin slippers, his healing ability would have been the same. Whatever this spiritual Power is, It works according to an exact Law of Its own nature. One of the accusations placed against Jesus was that he ate with publicans and sinners, that he allowed an evil woman to anoint his feet with rare ointment. How could such a man be holy? Yet he exercised a spiritual Power transcendent of objective limitations and proclaimed that it was through his belief that he did this.

Today we are seeking to make practical use of spiritual Law as well as of other laws. In order to do this we must maintain a spiritual freedom of the intellect; the mind should be free from dogmatic theological bondage, and we should come to believe that we can approach the Spirit both consciously and directly. Whatever spiritual Power is, It must operate through our minds, and It must do so according to our belief that It can do so. We should not waste time trying to discover what spiritual Law is, since no one knows, nor does anyone know what any law is— only what it does. We do know this, however, that in using spiritual Law the one having the greatest faith obtains the best results. It works best when we use It in a straight affirmative manner. Any method of procedure that conducts the mind to this place of faith is good. If the mind finds itself already there, then no method is necessary. If we really believed that we are surrounded by a spiritual Presence which responds to our word, that when we speak our word into It our word tends to take form and objectify, then we should have the essence of the whole matter.

The Universe is so organized, is of such a nature, that we reach this straight affirmative factor is such degree as we sense the supremacy of Good, the necessity of Good overcoming all evil, the availability of Good. The universal Mind is centered in Itself, knows nothing outside Itself, nothing different from Itself. It knows no separation. In such degree as we are conscious of this unity of Good, we are conscious of that truth which makes us free. Spiritual Power is latent within us but unless consciously used appears to have no existence. It is through our minds that we till the mental soil, cultivate and imbibe the Spirit, seize the affirmation of spiritual Power, and march with a surer tread.

Like other laws, spiritual Law should be aggressively used. As we come to see that spiritual Power is the use of a natural Law, the whole thing will become more simple. We shall no longer separate matter from Spirit, but will realize that we are living in a spiritual Universe right now, the Law of which is order and harmony, the Life of which is consciousness, and the Presence of which is both peace and perfection. It is said that God is Love, Reason, Beauty, Truth, and Wisdom—the essence of all salutary attributes and qualities—but if we are looking upon life with sadness, doubt, and fear, then to us God becomes these things, for if Spirit should proclaim Itself It would be compelled to say: "I look at you as you look at me." This is why the enlightened have said that God's only language is *Yea* and *Amen*. This *Yea* is incarnated in us and our own *Amen* decides the form it is to take.

The transcendent powers of the human mind proclaim the Divinity of man. The more completely one penetrates the mystery of his own mind the more he must come to realize that he is not studying a human mind at all, but that, through the avenue of what he calls a human mind, he is penetrating an infinite sea of Intelligence. When we turn to that inner self we are turning to the Infinite. It is not our external personality but this inner Principle operating through us which gives us the power to stand and to walk, to think and to be. We must realize that there is no matter opposed to Spirit, no material universe separated from the spiritual Universe. All is One. We are not turning, then, from the human to the Divine; the Divine is but turning to Itself, giving expression to Itself. The *self* comes bearing its own gifts.

We lack the experience of consciously using spiritual Power because we have not tried definitely to demonstrate that we already have this Power and can use It. We must prove to ourselves that the power of our own word, spoken in harmony with the great Cause, is the law unto the thing whereunto it is spoken. When a majority realize this the thought of the world will be revolutionized and its objective manifestation will produce a greater freedom for all.

We neither fast nor feast to arrive at spiritual Power. Spirit is already in the loaf of bread. We are not spiritual because we refuse to eat it. Spirit already occupies all space, the loaf of bread adds nothing to It. The apparent power from fasting is not in the abstaining from food, but rather in the fact that the hunger for an idea is greater than the hunger for food. Some have fasted and obtained. Some have feasted and obtained. Both were right. Some have prayed without ceasing. Some have not prayed but have contemplated the inner Presence. None of these methods changes the eternal verities of our being. But, if any one of these methods causes the mind to more greatly believe and to more completely receive, that method is right for the one using it, no matter what name it may go by.

The Spirit knows Itself and knows us as Itself. It is only as we know It that we know ourselves. It is only as we embody this knowledge that we have real spiritual Power. What difference, then, whether we pray, sing, feast, fast, or dance? Only let us be sure that we arrive at our destination. And what is this destination? It is that place in our minds where we no longer doubt, where there is no opposite to Good, where God is all, but where God is natural, spontaneous—the interior awareness of our own thought. There will never be anything external to this inner knowingness.

The mind must definitely see what it wishes to experience and as definitely repudiate what it does not wish to experience. This repudiation is either through denial or by the nonresistance of nonrecognition. In the midst of confusion we must be peaceful; in the midst of fear we must be fearless; in the midst of doubt we must be certain. We must be poised and confident. We must expect the good and inwardly know that we receive, disregarding any apparent contradiction in our objective world.

Demonstration will be as perfect as is the subjective embodiment of thought. If we realize that form is Spirit in manifestation, that the father of any specific form is a subjective idea, and that we can consciously create subjective ideas, then we shall have a correct method for effective practice. The one wishing to make direct and conscious use of spiritual Power should first believe in spiritual Power and in the creativeness of his own thought. Then he should compel his mind to act as though his belief were true. When the subjective state of our thought, which is the inner mind, completely accepts an idea that is in line with the nature of Reality, then we shall demonstrate that idea in our experience.

All have spiritual Power but only a few consciously use It. As time passes larger numbers of people will come to make conscious use of this Power until finally a majority of the race will be guided by that inner inspiration which guides men's feet aright. Then many of those questions which are now so perplexing in the social and economic order will be permanently answered.

YOUR WORD
IS LAW

The Universe is not only a spiritual system, It is an orderly system. We are living under a government of Law, always, whether we deal with the mind, the body, or the Spirit; whether we are dealing with physics or metaphysics. Although the Law is subject to the Spirit, this does not mean that Spirit is capricious and may create a Law only to break It. Instead, Law is always subject to Spirit, in that It is Spirit's servant, just as all the laws of nature are our servants and obey us insofar as we understand them and properly use them. The Spirit, being omniscient, understands and properly uses Law, which is part of Its own nature. Hence, Spirit never contradicts Its own nature, is always harmonious and complete within Itself, and exists in a state of perpetual perfection. While It always acts in accord with the Law of Its own Being, Its own Being is perfect and It never contradicts Its own Law. The Law is a willing and obedient servant; the Spirit is a gentle taskmaster.

We are of like nature to this supreme Spirit. We exist within It, having arrived at a state of consciousness whereby we can consciously approach It, believe in It, receive It. In recognizing Spirit we may use the Law which is Its servant, hence that Law becomes our servant.

We are intelligent beings living in an intelligent Universe which responds to our mental states. So, insofar as we learn to control our mental states shall we automatically control our environment. This is what is meant by the practical application of the principles of Science of Mind to the problems of everyday living. This is what is meant by demonstration.

Naturally the first thought of the average person is that he would like to demonstrate health of body, peace of mind, prosperity in his affairs; to neutralize a circumstance which is unhappy or to attract to himself some good which he has not been enjoying. Such a desire is natural and in every way normal, and the possibility of such demonstration already exists within the mind of every living soul. Every man has within himself the power to consciously cooperate with the spiritual aspect of his existence in such a way that it will create for him a new environment and a greater happiness. But the greatest good which this philosophy of life brings to the individual is a sense of certainty, a sense of the reality of his own soul, of the continuity of his own individualized being, and the relationship of his apparently isolated self to the great Whole.

The greatest good that can come to any man is the forming *within him* of an absolute certainty of himself and of his relationship to the Universe, forever removing the sense of heaven as being outside himself, or the fear of hell or any future state of uncertainty. Man is a part of Life—some part of the eternal God. Man is forever reaching out, forever gaining, growing, expanding. The Spirit is forever expressing Itself through him.

Such an understanding teaches us that there can never come a time when we shall stop progressing; also that age is an illusion and that limitation is a mistake, that unhappiness is ignorance, that fear is uncertainty. We cannot be afraid when we know the truth, and the greatest good accompanying such an understanding of truth will be the elimination of fear. This understanding will rob man of his loneliness and give him a certain compensation in that sense of security which knows that

Spirit responds by corresponding, a peace without which no life can be happy, a poise which is founded on this peace, and a power which is the result of the union of peace with poise.

We can be certain that there is an Intelligence in the universe to which we may come, which will inspire and guide us, and a Love which overshadows. God is real to the one who believes in the supreme Spirit, real to the soul which senses its unity with the Whole. Every day and every hour we are meeting the eternal and ultimate realities of Life, and in such degree as we cooperate with these eternal realities in love, in peace, in wisdom, and in joy, believing and receiving, we are automatically blessed.

It is not by a terrific mental struggle or emotional effort that we arrive at this goal, but through the quiet expectation, the joyful anticipation, the calm recognition that all the peace there is, and all the power there is, and all the good there is, is Love—the living Spirit Almighty.

A spiritual mind treatment is a definite act of the conscious mind, setting the Law in motion for the idea specified in the treatment. The one giving the spiritual mind treatment believes that his word is operated upon by an intelligent, creative Agency which has at Its disposal the ways, the methods, the means, and the inclination to make manifest his treatment at the level of his faith in It, creating those circumstances which would be the logical outcome of the ideas embodied in his treatment.

If we wish to demonstrate supply we would not say, "I am a multimillionaire," but we would seek to realize that infinite Substance is limitless supply. We would say, "I am surrounded by pure Spirit, perfect Law, Divine Order, limitless Substance which intelligently responds to me. It is not only around me, but It is also in me; It is around and in everything. It is the essence of perfect action. It is perfect action in my affairs. Daily I am guided by Divine Intelligence. I am not allowed to make mistakes. I am compelled to make the right choice at the right time. There is no confusion in my mind, no doubt whatsoever. I am certain, expectant, and receptive."

As the result of statements such as these we re-educate our mind, re-creating and redirecting the subjective state of our thought. It is the subjective state of our thought which decides what is going to happen to us and because the subjective state of our thought often contradicts our conscious desires, a sense of doubt arises.

When we affirm the presence of good, any sense of doubt is but an echo of previous experiences; it is the judgment according to appearances which we must be careful to avoid. For, unless we are conscious that we are dealing with a transcendent and a creative Power, how can we expect to demonstrate at all?

We must never lose sight of this Power. The demonstrations produced through the scientific use of this Power in spiritual mind treatment are the result of the operation of the Law which is in no way limited to any present existing condition or circumstance. Evolution itself should prove this to be self-evident, and the one seeking to use this Power intelligently and constructively must have some sense and some inward conviction that he is dealing with an immutable, creative Law.

Why these things are so no one knows, but experience has repeatedly proved that we can use this Law. It is never a question as to whether the Law is able or willing, but rather a matter of our conviction that It does respond. The beneficial action of the Law in our lives is conditioned only by our unbelief.

The Law is both able and willing, and we might say that the only limitations It imposes upon us are these: The Law cannot do anything which contradicts the Divine nature or the orderly system through which the Divine nature functions; It must always be true to Itself. The Law cannot give us anything we cannot mentally and spiritually accept. In these two propositions we find the only limitations imposed upon our use of the creative Law.

But these are not limitations at all, for we do not wish anything contrary to the Divine nature, nor can we expect either Spirit or Law to make us a gift we do not accept. There is really, then, no limitation outside our own ignorance, and since we all can conceive a greater good than we have so far experienced, we all have within our own minds the ability to transcend previous experiences and rise triumphant over them. In order to accept our greater good we must raise our mental equivalents to reach the level of the good desired.

ACCEPT THE GOOD
YOU DESIRE

The study of Science of Mind does but little good unless we make definite use of it. Science is the knowledge of laws and proximate causes. The technique of any science constitutes what we know about the principle of that science and our ability to definitely use it. A scientific truth can be demonstrated insofar as we understand it. If any particular theory cannot be demonstrated it is still in the realm of a speculative or theoretical science and may or may not be true. When a theory is proved to be true it should be accepted, and an intelligent and comprehensive way of approach to it should be given to the world. All people interested in that science should know that if they use its laws in a certain way they will be able to demonstrate its principle.

It is such an approach to religion that the world needs today, for all people are instinctively religious. Most normal-minded people believe in some kind of a universal or supreme Intelligence. Different people have different concepts of this universal Intelligence and react differently to It. We all feel that if we could only understand this God, this supreme Intelligence, and come into close enough relationship with Him or It, our troubles would cease to be. This has been the insistent urge, the dynamic vitality in all religions, because religion has ever been a way through which the human has sought to approach the Divine. Most religions have taught that faith in God produces definite results in human experience and it is interesting to note that in some measure they have been justified in their belief in the power of faith.

This at once suggests a "universal something" operating in and through all religions, for all have taught the possibility of communication with God, with the supreme Being; all have taught some form of prayer, and all have been justified in their teaching since through prayer and communication each has been able to demonstrate to its devotees that they are dealing with Reality. To those who no longer are interested in differences but in likenesses, who are no longer interested in negations but in the broader affirmations of life, there at once comes this thought: prayer and communion, stimulated by faith, have tapped some universal Essence which has an actual existence and which responds alike to each and to all.

Without having the slightest superstition about the unique personality of Jesus as a man, I do feel that he either knew something we do not know, or he more completely believed something that we only *think we believe*. We accept theoretically what Jesus taught because it is beautiful, it soothes and calms us. His teaching has given the Christian religion the vitality that it has had; that vitality was injected by a few simple flashes from the thought of this remarkable man. Always there have been a few who have seemed to enter into his teaching, to accept it. Their lives have been attended by a spiritual and a mental magnificence which is marvelous. In going back over the teaching of Jesus, most of which has been superstitiously interpreted to a still more superstitious listening ear, what do we find? A most simple teaching—believe, and it shall be done unto you. What shall be done? The thing that we believe in, be it heaven or hell!

Jesus taught an absolute and exact equivalent and correspondent to the belief. When his disciples tried to believe—and how hard we all have tried—and were unable to do what Jesus had done, they came to him and asked: What is wrong? He answered: Have more faith. He told them to bring the boy to him and he would show them again. And they brought the one who was obsessed to him and he said to whatever was wrong with him: I command you to come out of him. And the boy fainted, becoming as one dead, but Jesus took him by the hand and raised him up and he was healed. Wonderful!

The thing that Jesus had done no other person could have done for him. He believed what he taught. We do not. We should not condemn ourselves, however, for our unbelief, but should seek to develop a greater faith. If one had the faith one could say to a mountain: "Be thou removed!" and it would be done. If we could only have faith it would be done unto us as we believe. This calls for a deeper search into the meaning of belief and faith, and when we are willing to take these two ideas, belief and faith, lay them on the operating table of the mind, dissect them and see what they are, we shall find that they are very simple; they are psychological, mental reactions of the mind to itself.

It must be that Jesus had convinced himself that the Universe responded to him, and that there was no lingering doubt. He came into such alignment with this universal Something that there was no longer any question in his mind about Its responding to him in the way he wanted It to. He said to the man whose servant he had healed: Go home, and when you get there you will find your servant well. That Thing which responded to him never seemed to fail. This Power did not say to him: "Now, Jesus, this man is really sick, he really has a cancer and it has been pronounced incurable." The Power responded to the great faith of this remarkable spiritual genius. It always responded to him since he never doubted It and because he lived in harmony with It.

There have been many others who have tried to believe. People have tried many ways, means, and methods—esoteric, occult, mystical. Most have failed. Occasionally someone has attained while the rest have proclaimed in awe: "This man has found the secret. If he would only tell us." And when he does, they say, "Oh, no, that could not be it, he doesn't want to tell us." And then they offer him a great price to be told what the secret is. They will seldom believe the answer. It is too simple; it could not be anything so simple as *belief* and *faith*, built upon assurance that Spirit responds to the mind of man *according to his acceptance.*

And so the endless chase for the secret goes around and around and around. The secret is belief and faith; expectation and acceptance, anticipation and recognition of the response of spiritual Law, Law operating through our belief in It. But how can Law respond while we deny the principle governing It? Can the mind accept that which it rejects? can it contain that which it pushes away from itself? Can any amount of intellectual endeavor do other than guarantee the maintenance of the convictions that the mind has affirmed?

We must return to a basis of absolute and utter simplicity. The way to use Science of Mind is to use it. The way to think about it is to believe in it. The way to demonstrate it is to act as though it were true and to stop acting as though it were not true. We must teach our minds to accept the idea that faith deals with the original Cause, the First Cause, the Thing that creates and sustains everything; to believe and understand that this Cause is immediately accessible, immediately flowing into our consciousness through the creative use we make of It.

We must give up our *unbelief* in order that we may entertain our *belief.* The one who does this the most effectively is the one who is not afraid of the external experience which contradicts his inward affirmation. He may acknowledge the condition, but he is at the same time conscious that the Power he is using is greater than the condition. The Power to do this already lies within every man's mind. It is already in you and in me, in Its fullness.

We must train the mind to believe. One of the first things that we must come to realize is that the Universe is not divided against Itself. The good we can experience is equivalent to as much good as we can conceive. Our well-being corresponds to as much well-being as our

Part III

THOUGHTS BECOME THINGS

There is a time for learning and absorbing knowledge. But then there must also come a time when such knowledge as you have learned must be practiced—put to practical use—or else it is of no value.

Faith without works is dead. Similarly, without properly applying the ideas you are absorbing your life will remain barren of the greater good you say you desire. Your thoughts do become things, so guard them carefully. Many valuable and practical suggestions are to be found here, but they have to be put to use before they will mean anything to you. In spite of how often or how much you may desire to turn to another for help in the matter of improving your life, in the last analysis there is only one person who can make you think the way you should, and that person is you.

A new experience in living, free from troubles and problems, lies ahead of you if you will but take the time and make the effort to do some proper thinking about them. Follow the suggestions for doing this that you will encounter, but remember they are but suggestions. You will have to take them, absorb them, and make them your own ideas before they will be of value to you. Then you will be able to loose the splendor that lies within you, and in so doing find yourself surrounded by all those things that make life worthwhile.

YOUR SPIRITUAL
ADVENTURE

One of the greatest, if not the greatest, endeavors we could possibly undertake would be the discovery of the infinite creative potential that resides in our minds. In undertaking this discovery there are several specific ideas which can be followed and which, if properly used, may be productive of concrete and tangible experiences in our daily lives.

Suppose we wish to embark on a voyage of friendship. Suppose I am an individual, typical of countless other individuals, who is very sensitive, very confused; whose experiences have been such that I feel everything is against me and nothing is for me. Nobody loves me; no one considers me. I am quite conscious that once in a while I am asked to a party through some spirit of altruism on the part of another, and being conscious of this fact I am doubly miserable. I am that individual whom the world has apparently turned against, who hasn't a friend. Now I begin to embark on the voyage of friendship. The first thing I must do is to become friendly in my own thought. Not anywhere else but in my own thought. So I must begin in my own mind and say, "Everything is One. I have no enemies. I am one with all good. All good is one with everybody; therefore I am one with all people. Wherever I go, whenever I go, I am meeting friendship, love, kindliness, and consideration."

He who would have friends must be a friend to everyone he meets, must sense and know that everyone he meets is a friend. Whoever does this will find friends everywhere he goes. How long will it take to bring about such a desired result? It will take just as long as it takes. How will he know that his work is complete? When the demonstration is made. One is not healed until one is healed.

Suppose we wish to demonstrate peace. Absence of peace denotes fear. What is it that people are afraid of? Only a few things, and in the long run only one thing. We are apparently afraid of physical suffering, being misunderstood, lack, poverty, and the uncertainty of the future. But these are all the offspring of one central fear, which is that we are not sure of the *self* and the continuity of the *self*. I say in all seriousness that the starting point of spiritual understanding, and whatever goes with it, is the solid establishment, without superstition but by reason and such intuition as we have, of the actual *beingness* of the *self*. That is why a great Teacher said: "For what is a man profited if he shall gain the whole world, and lose his own soul? . . ."

Our soul is lost when we are confused or in doubt. It is lost when we are unhappy. The starting point, then, is one's conviction of one's being as a manifestation of God. A man cannot assure himself of the Reality of his own being until he assures himself of the Reality of all people's being. We are conscious of the real self which is established in perpetual peace in such degree as we become conscious of the Universal Self in which all other selves exist. "For in him we live, and move, and have our being. . . ."

To be conscious that one is poised in the Eternal, that the outcomes of evolution are certain, that the continuity of one's own soul is secure, that all is working together for good, is what produces peace. There is no happiness, without peace, no true fulfillment of life, no real joy in living. Peace is the pearl of great price for which a man will sell all that he has in order that he may possess it. Peace cannot arise from doubt or fear, but comes only in quiet confidence and perfect trust. Peace is not in the wind or the wave, but in the "still small voice." Peace is not to be found in the future nor can it be dragged out of the past. Today we need to establish it as a mental and spiritual quality. It has nothing whatever to do with externals. We must arrive at the place of peace in the midst of apparent confusion or not at all. Not by the contemplation of the confusion, but by the recognition of peace itself, shall we arrive.

Self-treatment to know that "I am the principle of peace within me, which is God, the living Spirit Almighty," is desirable. In spiritual adventures of the mind we consciously use our thought to set creative Power in motion and then await with expectancy the desired result. We are, in a certain sense, experimenting not with Mind Itself, but with our own thought in seeing what use we can make of the creative power of Mind. This creativeness we do not inject into Mind; it is already there, a natural Law in the Universe.

We should each picture ourself and think of ourself as we would like to be. We should do this without contradicting the good of others, without seeking to coerce others. We should do this in as absolute a sense as possible, that is, we should withdraw from any contemplation of the relative facts in the case and think only of the desired outcome as being established in Mind. Mind finds Its own avenue and outlet and releases Its own energies for the purpose of Self-expression. Whether we think we are dealing with our individual mind or with the universal Mind, we are dealing with the same thing. What we call our individual mind is merely the place where we, as an individual, use the creative power of Mind.

Therefore, to "be still and know" means to get quiet in our own thought, to become conscious that the creativeness of the universal Mind is immediately present with us, to believe that whatever is in accord with Its fundamental unity is responsive to us; to believe that Its responsiveness is mechanical, exact, that any of us, no matter who he is or where he is, has immediate and complete access to this ever-available Power; to believe that It is omnipresent and come quietly to It, stating our proposition in complete trust—this is correct practice.

This great adventure which the mind makes in the realm of Spirit is perhaps the most fascinating thing we can do. We must be careful to differentiate between this form of practice and mere daydreaming. In daydreaming a person sits around longing for things, picturing himself as being something that he knows he is not, letting his imagination run wild, soaring, as it were, into realms of fancy. But in scientific spiritual mind treatment he does not do this. He takes a proposition which his mind can encompass, such as realizing that he is surrounded by friendship, right opportunity, and abundance, and compels his mind to accept this idea as now being a fact in his everyday experience. Consequently, his work is intensely practical, and although he is an idealist, he is scientific in his application of this universal Principle of Mind to the problems of everyday life.

What can be more practical than to set our mental and spiritual house in order and then, insofar as possible, let it produce for us the necessary things of life, the beautiful things of life? What can be more practical than to gain the ability to demonstrate in our experience that we can consciously call on a higher Power to do our bidding whenever our will is in conjunction with Its will, with the understanding that Its will never limits our real good?

YOU LIVE
YOUR IDEAS

When a man compares himself with others, he is prone to create within himself either a superiority or an inferiority complex. But when he identifies himself with the Universal, and all selves with the Universal, there comes a sense of unity with the Whole and he feels himself to be neither superior nor inferior. He sees himself and all creation as some part of God.

It is this identification of the individual life with the Universal that produces a true humanity. Righteousness and virtue cannot compare themselves with unrighteousness and vice. The Spirit knows Itself through Self-recognition. The devil is unknown to the great God. Good is positive. Evil is a denial of this good. The two do not meet. We should learn to identify the self with its Source, and this is the true office of prayer.

Cause and effect are inseparable partners, and when the self identifies itself with the Law of love and wholeness, through spiritual mind treatment, a corresponding effect in the outer life follows. This effect is an answer to prayer. Jesus called it a sign following those who believe.

A spiritual mind treatment or prayer should not be a petition. It should be a recognition. Most of our prayers are petitions, unconscious admissions that the soul is still passing through the travail of birth. We are not yet completely born into a consciousness of the heavenly kingdom. So we pray that God will make the crops good, that He will cause the rain to fall, that He will save the soul of some sinner. But whenever anything is wrought by prayer we shall find affirmation and belief— more affirmation than negation. God cannot work by negation.

Great religions are sustained by their affirmations and according to the universality of such affirmations they live and prosper. When the disciples of Jesus asked him to teach them how to pray he answered: "After this manner therefore pray ye . . ." and he taught them a prayer of affirmation. The method Jesus used was recognition, identification, unification, and then authority. He recognized a Presence and a Power greater than the human mind, but he did not recognize this Power as separated from, or apart from, the human mind. He placed it in the human mind—"Our Father which art in heaven." And he said that the kingdom of heaven is within. Jesus recognized the immediate presence and availability of Good and he relied on this Good in every emergency.

All great souls have sensed that the universal Spirit is greater than the human mind, but they have also known that this Divine Presence is one with the human mind. The kingdom of heaven is within. God is in His kingdom. The access to this kingdom is immediate and it will spontaneously flow through every man's consciousness.

Prayer, an act of the mind, is a recognition of the Divine Presence as universal Life, Energy, Power, Intelligence, and Substance responding to us. We need not feel that we must encompass the Infinite, for if we could encompass It we would exhaust the Infinite's resources and, being immortal, we should be condemned to an eternity of boredom. The Infinite will always remain Infinite, but It will always be revealing Itself to us in ever-widening circles of experience.

Through recognition and unification with Divine Intelligence the mind is directed; it comes to understand what the specific laws of na-

ture are relative to any definite thing. The man of science is, symbolically, on his knees, listening greatly to the inner self, for it is through
this individual self that we reach the universal Self. Those who have
wrought marvelous things by prayer have been those who could stand
still and listen. We talk at God too much, and seldom reach a place
where we can relax long enough to let the great Self speak to us. God
cannot listen to that which is contrary to the Divine nature. A prayer
should be a mental and spiritual state of acceptance in the individual mind.

Where is the darkness when the light enters? Where is the lie when
the truth is told? It is not, or it is as though it never were. It was only a
supposition. The world has yet to understand that there is a great difference between a false belief and Reality, and that whenever Reality enters, the false belief tends to sink into its native nothingness. Jesus
understood this, hence he told his disciples when they prayed to affirm
the Divine Presence, to recognize It and unify with It: "Our Father
which art in heaven, Hallowed be thy name"—a recognition that the
kingdom is come. Great souls have listened to the Spirit; they have lived
the good life of the Spirit, and the illumination of their consciousness
has been a beacon light to future civilizations.

Prayer starts with this identification, this recognition of the Divine
Presence, overdwelling and indwelling: "It is no longer my human will,
but Thy Divine Will." True prayer does not affirm: "I will do thus and
so." Who by affirming that black is white will change its color? We cannot expect any prayer to be answered if its answer requires the denial of
any law of nature or a contradiction of the true nature of the Divine
Being. But we can and should expect an answer to any prayer which is
prayed in accord with the nature of Reality. In such prayer a definite,
cosmic Force is set in motion through our faith, belief, and conviction.

It is because of this that the religions of the world have had their
power, for with all great religions has come a spiritual conviction, an
acceptance of an overshadowing Presence, and a desire to enter into

harmony with It. Religion is not a thing of itself, but is an approach to the Thing Itself.

The Infinite does not contend with anyone or against anything. How seldom, then, are our prayers in accord with Its nature. We do not know the possibilities of the Divine Law, nor should we feel discouraged if we do not ourselves measure up to our highest sense of Its possibilities, but we should learn to have faith and to accept a continuously expanding good.

By certain laws of our own nature we may be limited and bound. By a greater understanding of these same laws we are free. The first steam-driven ship to cross the ocean carried in her hold a book, written by the scientific men of that day, explaining just why it was that a boat could not be driven by steam.

We do not know the possibilities of man, and while we cannot believe that prayer will change the Divine nature, we can believe, without violating our intelligence, that prayer might awaken a deeper Divinity, a greater possibility, and bring into our experience a greater good. But the only evidence we have of our faith and its validity is in the result obtained.

We do not have to say that people are not sick in order effectively to give a spiritual mind treatment for their recovery, but how can we doubt that there is a Power inherent within all people to heal? How can we place any limitation on Its capacity or willingness to act in our behalf? The contemplation of the Divine Life, awakening within us a recognition of and a receptivity to Its influx, is the greatest single curative agency known to the mind of man.

We do not know what the energies of Mind and Spirit are. We do not even know what Consciousness is. Causation will not stand too close an intellectual scrutiny; It avoids the issue and, remaining true to Its own nature, argues with no man. All we can say of It is that *It is*. That the impulse of the Creative Genius starts in pure Intelligence, we must inevitably conclude. That Consciousness is back of all that lives, seems to be self-evident. That the universal creative Mind projects Itself upon the screen of Its own experience through the contemplation of Itself, I accept. That man is of like nature to this Mind is the teaching of the great of the earth.

Why, then, should not a man of the perception and spiritual intuition which Jesus had, living as he did in harmony with the Universe, declare that all things are possible to him who believes, if his belief is a true belief and in accord with the Universal purposes. Laying aside all differences of opinion, all theological controversy, and all philosophic abstractions, and coming down to the simplicity of the thing, we must learn to believe, to have faith, and to accept, knowing that as we do this we are entering into that Power which is not bound by any existing circumstances or conditions whatsoever.

We should learn to identify ourselves with right action, with pure Life, with perfect Intelligence; to unify ourselves with Good, and to contemplate right action as now being apparent in our affairs. It matters not what has gone before, for if we introduce a higher state of consciousness it will be made manifest in our affairs.

Well did Tennyson say that "more things are wrought by prayer than this world dreams of." Prayer contradicts no scientific fact, affirms no impossible state of being, contradicts no law of nature, but rises gently to the comprehension of the Divine Presence as an agency of good, of right action, and of immediate availability.

It is our privilege to prove our faith through our demonstrations. This we shall do through the contemplation, in our own minds, of the Divine Presence. Our life is created by our ideas, so in actual practice we must turn resolutely from the condition which obstructs and contemplate its opposite, affirming the presence of the desired result even in the midst of confusion, assuring ourselves that the Divine Presence is the Law unto our faith, bringing immediately into our experience the healing of our body, the beautifying of our circumstances, and peace to our mind.

THINK EFFECTIVELY

There is a great desire in the minds of all of us to feel and believe that each has within himself a principle, or a consciousness, or a way of arriving at peace, joy, and plenty. I am not going to say that it is possible to demonstrate a spiritual tone while we do those things which contradict the truth we seek to demonstrate. On the other hand, I do not wish to compromise our belief because we believe, and rightly, that there is a Principle which if correctly approached and embodied will work for our good.

There has been throughout the ages enough experience to prove this, whether we consider part of that experience as the answer to prayer or merely a psychological reaction. Prayers have been answered, of that there is not the slightest question. Many prayers have been answered, and many prayers have not been answered, in the experience of the human race.

We are confronted with a fact and not a theory. We seek to find a theory that will fit the fact. We must first have the fact and then evolve the theory. It is a wrong method to start with a theory and try to compel the fact to fit it. Such theory has been held among many right-minded, religious people. These people have tried to explain this and they have said, "Sometimes God feels that it is good to answer our prayers and at other times He feels that it is good to let us suffer a little longer." This has been a very sincere thought. Personally, however, I do not believe that it is a true thought. I do not believe that God wills suffering to any living soul at any time for any reason. It cannot be that way, for if God desires us to suffer, then it is certain that we are going to suffer and all the prayers, wit, and science, and all of the philosophy and religion will not stop that suffering because what Omniscience wills, It decrees, and what It decrees is inevitable.

The answer to the question why some people have their prayers answered and others do not is not in the will of God but in the act of man. That which is Life can will only life. That which is Freedom can will only freedom. That which is sufficient unto Itself can will only self-sufficiency. We need not bother as to whether or not the will of God is that we shall suffer. The poor do not suffer any more than the rich, but they suffer in a different way. The ignorant do not suffer any more than the intellectuals. From the popular concept, the bad do not suffer any more than the good. It cannot be that limitation and suffering are imposed upon us by the Deity. They are the result of ignorance. Insofar as we express ourselves rightly, in accord with the Divine harmony, the Divine Self goes forth anew into expression through us; we are avenues through which God comes more completely into fruition.

The Apostle James said: "Ye ask, and receive not, because ye ask amiss. . . ." I do not feel, as many people do, that a prayer for a personal good is asking amiss. But if our prayer is for a personal good which we would refuse to others, it is a prayer based on the belief that the Universe is divided against Itself. Such a prayer cannot disturb the infinite Unity and Harmony. But to suppose that one serves the Universe or society any better by denying himself good is to suppose that there is not enough good to go around. When we pray amiss it is not that we pray for individual good, but it is that the prayer contradicts the universal Good, the Divine Harmony. If we exist, we exist for the purpose of self-expression, fullness of expression, joy, and completion. We exist "to glorify God." But God is glorified only as God is expressed.

I do not think we need to have any theological tremblings as to whether or not we have suffered enough. We have suffered more than enough, so far as I am able to deduce. It must be that we are not quite in accord with the fundamental harmony of Life. I know someone will say, "Well, we have no right to ask for an individual good while there is want in the world." There has always been want in the world and there will continue to be until the majority of people think right and act right.

We may look at this proposition from the materialistic viewpoint and say that there is no beneficent God, no final Power or Mind in the Universe which cares. Or we may look at it from the standpoint of a sense of religious restriction and say that God does not want us to have plenty. But we will find that both points of view are wrong. As religionists, we cannot conceive that there is an infinite God who creates a world and countless numbers of people but fails to create at the same time the way for those people to express life. Since limitation cannot be part of the Divine scheme, we must arrive at the conclusion that the Universe is not against us; we are against ourselves.

Still there is the question: Why is it that some people's prayers are answered and some are not? The answer is in the prayer. There are times when our prayer is in accord with Reality and that prayer is going to be answered. In such cases prayer is always answered, whether it is prayed in the name of Jesus Christ, or Buddha, or disregarding all methods, it is a direct statement to God. If a man embraces these three concepts—the unity with Good, the belief in Good, and the receptivity to and mental equivalent of Good—his prayers will always be answered.

When a man says, "If you are doing the will of God you will prosper," he is right. But I would say to him, "How do you know what the will of God is?" The only way we can know what the will of God is is to understand the nature of the Universe in Its final integrity. It is Unity. Its purpose is to project life and more life. Consequently we must be in unity with Its Oneness, Its Life. It is ever present. We must feel that It is ever present. It is eternal. We must feel that we are eternal. We must believe that It is in us as we are in It. If we expect the Truth to make us free, we must understand what the Truth is and how It works. We must not expect God to give us anything that He would withhold from anybody else.

The Universe must be a unity, a harmony. If It is a unity, It has to be a harmony, and if harmony, It has to possess beauty and balance. The average person believing in good, willing everyone good, need not be afraid that his prayer is selfish. There would have to be something of a universal essence in his nature. If I cannot go into a Catholic church and kneel and pray, or into a Buddhist temple, I am unfortunate. The same heart beats in every man's breast. We must come into a Universal sense of things. Our own good is good for the world. If we feel that way, why should we feel that God desires to withhold any good? How can we *really* live while we feel that there is anything in the universe that is not included in the great universal Wholeness of things? Spiritual thought penetrates the past and future and finds the present but a continuity of experiences threaded on Something which of Itself is changeless. The will of God is obeyed when we are in unity.

And the next thing is belief. Jesus said: "When ye pray, believe that ye receive. . . ." He was announcing a Law which has an analogy in the physical life—when we wish to harvest crops we plant seeds. The physical universe in the last analysis is a mental and spiritual thing. It is Mind in action.

God is a universal Presence and a universal Responsiveness. God creates by Self-knowing. God does not doubt His own Self-knowingness. That is why it is that if we wish to use the Law of Mind we must not only unify with It but we must believe It. We must unify; we must believe; we must receive. We must receive into the mind because the mind cannot contain what it rejects. A thing, so far as the mind is concerned, cannot be true and false at the same time. I cannot speak a lie as though it were the truth. I cannot say, "I believe" and by saying it, believe. But if I really believe, I know that I believe. I cannot say, "I receive," if there is a doubt. We are trying to analyze the things necessary to assure the answer to prayer. What we know, we can prove. We want to know by having lived and proved.

We must believe; we can receive only an equivalent of what we believe. I am not in sympathy with people who say that everything is all right when it is not. The man who is confused cannot demonstrate peace while he remains confused. It is only as he drops his confusion and enters into a state of peace that peace abides in him. We must embody. Can anything emanate from us unless it is first in us? We must expect to be able to demonstrate or have our prayers answered today according to the degree of life we embody today. But we are ascending, enlarging, expanding all the time. Out of the experience of today we will know a greater good tomorrow and so there will always be expansion.

The Universe never disputes, contradicts, or denies Itself. It is not alone what the intellect announces, what the mouth speaks, or the conscious thought thinks. In the last analysis, it is our whole inward thought—what psychology calls the subjective state of our thought—which decides. And this is where the practice of Science of Mind comes in. If we say, "I guess God did not want me to have that good thing for which I prayed," this is the reason it is not always done at once. If the subjective state of our thought denies what our objective thought says, it neutralizes that objective thought.

In the old order of thought we had what was called "praying through." This does not mean praying through God, but through our own minds. It means praying until our conscious thought believes and our subjective thought no longer denies—praying until all doubts are removed. We do the same thing now, but we do not call it that. It is "dressed up" a little differently and it seems more intelligent, we think. When we say, "We treat," what do we mean? Spiritual mind treatment is a mental adjustment; it is doing something to the mind so that the mind no longer denies or refutes the idea which it embodies in a treatment.

A person should feel that he is surrounded by a creative Mind which receives the impress of his thought and acts upon it. He is in this Mind and this Mind is in him. The power by which he thinks is this Mind in him. His mind is not another mind, but that One Mind manifesting as the individual, as himself. Each of us, as an individual, evolving into reason and freedom, is continuously using that Mind at the level of our consciousness.

The greatest thing that has ever come to the world in the entire history of its evolution is the conscious recognition that there is a creativeness in our own minds which uses a Creativeness that is infinite; that each man in the integrity of his own soul can enter this universal Goodness and take from It as much as he is now ready to receive.

BUILD A NEW LIFE

The past is gone, yet the experiences of the past are written in memory, and memory contains the accumulated knowledge of the individual and of the race. We continuously depend on this source for information, for inspiration and guidance. Could memory be entirely extinguished, both in the mind of the individual and of the race, the entire background of our life would disappear, the stream of consciousness would be abruptly severed. No greater catastrophe could be imagined. It is inherent in our nature that memory and experience shape and mold our lives toward greater attainment and eternal progress.

Hence the time past is giving birth to the present time in which we recognize, understand, and experience the activities of everyday life. Recognition, experience, and activity slip away into the past, ever building a more substantial foundation upon which in time, now only anticipated, we shall rear a more noble edifice.

Could the expectation of the future be removed from the enthusiasm of our vision, all efforts of today would be futile. Life has instinctively provided that there shall ever be held before our waiting thought a goal, not too easily reached. Symbolically, the face of progress is ever toward the future, facing the light of the goal before it, while casting its shadows behind.

Since it is impossible for anyone to rob himself entirely of memory, it behooves all to guard carefully the experiences of the present that when they do become memories they shall be happy ones. It is a well-established fact, according to the known laws of the mind, that if one is retaining unpleasant incidents in his memory they can be neutralized through the power of his own word and his imagination. This is the secret of the confessional and of psychoanalysis—to remove the stain, the hurt, and the condemnation from the past, leaving in their place the gentle urge of better purpose and a sense of the Divine forgiveness.

If we are carrying about in our memory that which does not measure up with harmony, we should consciously discharge it, knowing that though all of us have made mistakes there is still no power in the Universe which wishes us ill. It is impossible to draw a fair estimate of the life of the soul from the short-range experiences of a few years. We are eternal beings on the pathway of experience for the purpose of gaining true individuality; even our mistakes are a part of our evolution and should be so considered. Let our present experiences be of such character as to harm no one and help all. Then shall the past be a beautiful memory, the present a glad hour, and the future a joyful expectation. All souls are eternal, all men are Divine, and in the long run good shall come to all.

From the viewpoint of infinite Mind it must be that what we call the past, present, and future are one. The Omega must be potential in the Alpha. Thus it is written: "I am Alpha and Omega, the beginning and the end"—he that was and he that is to come. The potentiality of our lives must have been forever in the Divine Mind, so as individuals we should forever expand, continuously growing into the likeness of that Divine Spirit inherent in all men. Could our eyes completely penetrate the spiritual realms, and could our imaginations rise by pure intuition to the comprehension of Reality, we should, no doubt, perceive what the illumined have seen and sensed: that there is very little between us and heaven, and that this is entirely bound up in our own concepts.

This intangible Thing which refuses analysis, this subtle Presence which can be neither caught nor bound, the Life Principle and the intelligent Consciousness within us, partakes of the nature of eternity and cannot even conceive of Its own birth, nor can It possibly experience, even in Its own imagination, any reality to Its passing. Thus can eternity be crowded into a day or a day stretched forth into eternity.

In the study of Science of Mind we learn that the sequence of the creative order is: first, Intelligence; next, the movement of Intelligence as Law; then, manifestation of Itself as creation. Whatever the nature of the physical universe is—and no one *knows* what it is—it is certainly not an illusion. Creation, or visible form, is necessary to the life of the Spirit, for without it the Spirit would be unexpressed. As time is a creature of eternity, so form also is the creation of time, and both time and form are forever necessary to self-expression, whether considered from the viewpoint of the individual or the universal Life.

Let us never think of creation as an illusion, or of things as being evil in themselves. The illusion is never in the *thing* but always in the way we look at it. The infinite variations of life, the eternal manifestations of creation, though in changing forms, *all* point to the fact that the Infinite clothes Itself in form in order that It may enjoy Its own Being. It must do this through the power of Its own imagination backed by the Law of Its own word. There is no other possible conclusion at which we can arrive.

Man as the complement of the Spirit is of the image of the Father; partaking of the Divine nature he must also have an inherent power within which is creative. This creative power immanent in man is not placed there by the disposition of his own will nor through the imagination of his own thought, but should be considered rather as the nature of his being. In other words, we should not attempt to explain why ultimate truths are true; they are true because they are true. Having discovered them there is nothing left other than to accept and utilize them.

If there is any truth relative to the individual life which is of greater importance than this, it is that the thought of man deals with a creative Agency or Power. From this he can never escape. Our word, our thought, our imagination are all creative. We did not hang the stars in space nor set the lofty peaks overlooking the sea, but we *have* imagined unhappiness and we *do* experience in life the outward manifestation of our inward convictions. Thought is an actual force dealing with a potential creative Power in the Universe of which only this can be said: It is.

Our thought operates independently of conditions, and has the possibility of transcending circumstances as they now are and causing new ones to be created. However, we should bear in mind that the creative Power is only set in motion by our thought. The Power Itself belongs to the Universe, and no man made It. All that we can do is to accept It, believe and use It. But while we continuously remold thought according to the pattern of ancient ideas, we remain bound by previous opinion, bias, and prejudice. We must do something to break down the walls of experience and expand the vision of the soul. Here our imagination comes into play, enabling us to conceive a greater good.

Neither the will nor the intellect is creative; they simply decide what the thought, the emotion, and the imagination shall respond to. The one who would rise above previous conditions, transcend intolerable limitations and create a better situation for himself must deliberately turn, in his imagination and thought, from the old order, and with a calm but flexible determination, endeavor to contemplate only the good, the beautiful, and the true. He should refuse to admit into his consciousness any controversy or argument, compel himself to know and to accept that in the apparent isolation of his own soul, from the genius of his own thought, he is molding an individualized destiny out of the Essence from which all form emanates.

Suppose we could reach the place where we no longer contemplated adverse conditions, opposing forces, or divided power of good and evil. Would we not be at peace, our minds tranquil? Could we ever again be afraid? We lack peace because we have torn the Universe into pieces and set one part against another. The din and roar of the human conflict has so filled our ears with discord that we no longer hear the heavenly voices. Our eyes have become so blinded by self-grief and self-inflicted wounds that we do not even behold the harmony in nature. *Power* cannot come out of confusion. *Power* is the child of peace and poise, the union of which must forever give it birth.

Let us contemplate strength and forget weakness; let us meditate upon peace and poise, forgetting the confusion. The first step toward this goal is a realization of the integrity and the eternality of our own being, and of that universal Wholeness from which we spring and *in* and *by* which we live. From such contemplation comes the establishment, not of a self-centered life, but of a life centered in the eternal Self—not egotism but egoism.

What if our immediate universe does tremble to its very foundations? What if the "slings and arrows of an outrageous fortune" are apparently directed toward us, shall not our armor of faith shatter them in dust at our feet? Who can measure life by *one* experience, or estimate the possibilities of the soul by the slight observations of any *short* period of time? The soul knows no limits but finds itself eternally merged with the One whose only answer to man is *Yea.*

Abundance is a state of mind. The Universe abounds with good. The Universe must be a self-sustaining and self-perpetuating spiritual order amply able to provide for Its own needs, and adequately able to express Its own inherent desires. Man is some part of the Universe. Why, then, is he limited unless it be that he has contradicted the fundamental principles of self-existence, and, in ignorance of his true nature, repudiated the greater claim which he might have made upon the Universe?

Prosperity is a state of mind; activity is also a state of mind; and the law of compensation is an invisible but infallible government of Divine order. It is done unto us *as* we believe, but belief is largely subjective and we are all more or less marked by the grooves of experience, a large portion of which has been adverse. Those who wish to demonstrate the effectiveness of spiritual mind treatment must *claim and know*, in their own thought, that there is a Divine Intelligence directing them and providing the ways and means for their thoughts to become things.

All thoughts of doubt and fear must be resolutely banished from the mind. We must learn to build upon faith, live in a state of conscious receptivity and enthusiastic expectation. Let us no longer limit the future possibility of eternal progress in our own lives and affairs. We are living in a spiritual Universe and we should always remember that the Universe responds to us as we respond to It.

LIVE CREATIVELY

A great many people are in some degree destroying their happiness because they have inner desires to create that are unexpressed, and these desires stifle them, congest them emotionally and physically, and make them unhappy.

There is a great deal of physical starvation in the world today, but there is a great deal more mental and spiritual starvation than anyone realizes. It takes only a short while to starve to death physically, but think of the people who have plenty to keep the body going but who are starving the mind and the spirit, year after year.

Back of every man's life there is a natural desire to express, to accomplish constructively. It does not matter what the accomplishment is. To the universal Desire Itself the creation of an empire involves no more than the building of a bridge; It does not know that one is great and the other small. All this inner Urge knows is what It feels, and It feels Itself to be. Because It feels Itself to be, It knows It has to express, and because It knows It has to express It beats against our consciousness, and that expression fulfilled is what we call self-expression.

A man who is self-expressed is always happy. He is not afraid of his stand, no matter what it is. This Urge does not know any comparison.

If It did It would be confined by finite limitations. It just knows Its necessity to express. We feel this impulse. Even a child feels it. A child wants to do something, but the parents squelch that desire. After a while the child is inhibited and if unable to express his desire secretly will have a sense of having been repressed. Of course, on the other hand, we know that we cannot allow children to do exactly as they want to do. Therefore we say that there must be a balancing. The child must express but he must do it constructively. A child can be very easily taught what is constructive.

We are all just children of a larger growth, a greater experience, and sometimes a deeper perception. When we find that we have this perfectly normal desire to express, we must decide what we are going to express. The intellect must consciously determine to what the emotions are going to respond. The well-balanced man is the man who has struck a good balance between his intellect and his emotions. We find people giving vent to extreme emotional expression, who think that thereby they are being modern and up-to-date, but who, as a matter of fact, are merely chaotic. We misconstrue what Truth is because of our desire to express a thing as we want to do. There must be a conscious direction of that inner creative urge to express into channels which are happy, constructive, and in all ways profitable. We are not to "bottle" a desire to express, calling it evil or bad; we are to more greatly express and direct it in a constructive manner.

We are to view this great creative urge of Life as the eternal sun which shines beyond and through the mist and the cloud of uncertainty, that sun in whose beams we may bask at will. Every form of creation— the creative arts, the accomplishment of any purpose in life, the good that we do to each other, the kindly smile, the peaceful thought— is some part of that great Divine expression which balances and equalizes and makes sane our everyday life. When it comes to the art of spiritual mind treatment we shall find that it is this Creativity which is the Power that projects the word into form.

"Not every one that saith . . . Lord, Lord, shall enter into the king-dom of heaven. . . ." He who enters into a state of wholeness and com-pletion is in a holy state. He who would know goodness, peace, and happiness must so enter into this native state of wholeness that he will find his prayer to be backed by conviction, his treatment filled with faith and feeling, and back of his whole outlook on life, perfect certainty. Such a man no longer walks the earth as downtrodden, dis-consolate, and afraid. He knows that heaven is here, that God is his host, and he has further learned the great lesson which all people must learn, that he is today potentially a perfect and Divine being. We do not have to acquire Divinity; we have to reveal that Divinity which ever indwells us.

Love interprets Itself to everyone who knows love; comes to everyone who senses love; personifies Itself in forms which are human, in experi-ences which are Divine. We know that as we experience this indwelling Divinity, It becomes real. It is not an illusion; It is the great motivating Power of the universe. We touch It, revealed through this man, this woman, this child, and because they reflect that Love to us we "fall in love" with that person. It is God expressing through us. So we touch a Cause and we feel through that Cause a Divine and cosmic Reality.

As the unreality of the temporal is rolled away, the temporal does not pass from existence, it is translated into a new form; it comes as a Divine awakening. And looking at each other we see no longer the finite broken upon the wheel of circumstances, impoverished and sick, but we see back of the form that glorious Presence which tells us that gods are convers-ing with gods. The more universal a man becomes, the more sane he becomes, and the more he is able to appreciate the individual.

In learning to express Life, to give release to the Divine creative urge within us, we ultimately have to face the undeniable truth that thoughts do become things in our experience. What we need to do is to have our thoughts so conform to what we consider the nature of Spirit to be that nothing unlike Its inherent Good can become a part of our daily life.

The process of doing this through the practical use of Science of Mind is actually very simple. We train our minds to believe that there is a spiritual Presence within us which guides, controls, comforts, and heals. We put gently but firmly out of our minds those thoughts which deny this belief and persist in this belief until finally it becomes a part of our nature to believe that the Spirit through our minds responds to us and that we are daily re-created in the image of Perfection. We guard our thought against negative statement, against unbelief, until gradually we are living on the affirmative and constructive side of life.

There is no one living who cannot practice this simple method of spiritual healing. Do not refuse any good or comfort that can come on the physical plane. But realize this: There is That which transcends the physical, which is the builder, creator, sustainer, and arbiter of all that is. There is also that Thing in each one of us which is transcendent. As we learn to listen to this inner Presence, getting our impulse from It, we shall create our prayer, our spiritual mind treatment, after the perception received from It, and our increased awareness of Perfection will restore our body and affairs after a Divine pattern. So let each of us endeavor to heal himself and help to heal others of infirmities, troubles, and problems, not becoming discouraged, but always realizing that the possibility is here, that "there is a Divinity that shapes our ends,/ Rough-hew them how we will."

YOUR GREAT
EXPERIMENT

One does not need to be unique to experience a higher degree of spirituality. However, there have been people, of all religious faiths, who have had spiritual perception, realization, or experience that has far transcended the ordinary experiences of daily living. These people, regardless of how crude or exalted their outward form of theology may have been, have at times so experienced God that God, to them, was real. This is what inner awareness is.

Those who have had such illuminating experiences of inner awareness have told us that they have been able to perceive that there was an absolute correspondence between the visible and invisible worlds. In other words, with the broader, deeper vision of spiritual perception they have been able to recognize that for every objective manifestation in the physical world there is what we may call today a subjective, or unseen, correspondent in the spiritual world. This would imply that what we actually see is but a reflection of an invisible image. This has been an experience common to all the great mystics who have so greatly influenced the course of religious thought.

The great spiritual geniuses of the ages have recognized that there is an invisible correspondent, or pattern, which is being reflected into what we term objective form. The objective form thus becomes not a thing in itself but exists as a reflection of a Cause which in Itself is intangible and is encompassed by neither time nor space. The tangible form is a reflection of Reality—the ultimate Cause and Source.

There does not appear to be anything in modern science or metaphysics that can, with any degree of validity, disagree with this viewpoint. In fact there is much today that confirms it.

The great problem of modern philosophy—and it was the problem of ancient philosophy—is the query as to how we get our images of thought. The great tendency of modern science is to reach out into the Invisible where there are adequate mental causes for this objective world which we call physical. Modern science supposes a certain hypothetical and theoretical Force of alleged motion and movement which no one knows anything about. This hypothetical and theoretical, but apparently mathematically conceived, operative Thing is what we call God or infinite Intelligence. Because we are intelligent, this infinite Intelligence must be the Source of our intelligence. The mind we use is the Mind of God functioning at the level of our conception of It. This is what Jesus meant when he said: "I can of mine own self do nothing . . . the Father that dwelleth in me, he doeth the works."

Now if there is a spiritual or a mental correspondent in the invisible world for every objective fact—from the greatest poem that was ever written, the greatest song that was ever sung, to the newest invention— then it naturally follows that not only must there be an invisible prototype or likeness of all that is which becomes visible according to Law, but also, if we can consciously create a prototype, according to the same Law that prototype will project itself into our environment. This is the practical angle of this very idealistic concept of the Universe.

Why, then, should not we be able to consciously create an image of thought and know that this same Law will cause it to be tangibly reflected in our environment? But, if the mind never gets beyond the place where it is controlled by its response to its physical environment or past memories, then the images it casts will be limited by these ideas. Therein lies one of the apparent mysteries of the philosophy of Science of Mind, but one we can solve by experiment in our own lives.

For the most part we are hypnotized from the cradle to the grave. Why do we cry and laugh in the theater? Because we allow ourselves to be subject to the emotional reaction of what we witness. A person is a great actor, or a great orator, who is able to cause us to so react, but the influence is more or less hypnotic. In calmer moments we would say, "This is all a show; it is not going to affect me," and it would not.

If we could always let the intellect decide consciously what the emotions should respond to, we would save ourselves most of our emotional strain and, in all probability, many of our ailments would be practically eliminated because they seem to result from some form of tension or mental disturbance. We experience the physical correspondents of our patterns of thought, the prototypes we have created.

Nothing in this world can possibly happen by chance because the Universe is a thing of law and order. Hence, there must be a definite subjective cause for every physical effect. It does not matter whether a person is a materialist or idealist, this is a situation that does exist and sooner or later one will come to learn the practical aspects of it in daily living. Jesus said: "As thou hast believed, so be it done unto thee. . . ." And to make it more emphatic, in the story of the Prodigal Son he taught what has been called the "reciprocal action" between the Universal and the particular. There is this Thing in the Universe which turns to us as we turn to It, through absolute correspondence.

Why, then, should we not consciously and definitely turn to It and provide for the action of the Law by mental images, spiritual realizations, or images of thought that shall no longer produce discord and disharmony? This is what spiritual mind treatment is. If a man turns to the creative Spirit within him, which does not foreordain limitation, lack, evil, or destruction, and creates in his thought through interior awareness, through spiritual perception, a mental equivalent of a better physical good, he is practicing the Science of Mind.

It is necessary in this world that we have the things that make us comfortable in this world. It is not only necessary, it is also right. But if we continue to maintain in our minds thoughts which are uncomfortable, it does not matter how good we are, they become the law of our lives. The Law of Mind is no respecter of persons. It does not say, "This man is good, I will honor him." The Law only knows us by reflection, by correspondence. It cannot know us any other way. So we bring what we call good or what we call evil upon us by the very Law of our being which is a Law of reflection.

Where are we going to get the ability to make our thoughts become the things we want, to create a happy situation, unless we can come to believe in spiritual equivalents? We shall never discover the Principle of Life by dissecting a corpse. We shall not find the spiritual Principle by dissecting any objective facts. Who by searching can find God? It is rather through that still, small voice, that inner perception, that interior awareness—"Be still, and know that I am God. . . ." If we wish to demonstrate a greater abundance it will not be done by continuing to think about lack. It is not easy to think happiness when we are unhappy, but we become the servant of our thoughts. As Tagore said: "The slave is busy making whips for his master." Our master is the Law of Cause and Effect. It serves us and then compels us to serve It as we have believed. It is at the same time heaven and hell; It is at once love and hate, freedom and bondage, because of Itself It is one Law, ready to take any form our thoughts establish for Its action.

Watch the life of a man who believes in God and the life of one who does not. The man who has a spiritual conviction lives in a different world from the one who does not have such a conviction. Unfortunately, too often our spiritual convictions come from theological dogmas and have a certain amount of sting in them, but even then they are better than none. There is no man on earth who is so forlorn as a materialist. There is nothing in the world so sad as unbelief.

How shall we find the equivalent of certainty? By so contemplating the eternal verities that doubt disappears. We shall find the equivalent for life and immortality by so dwelling on the idea that the Principle of Life cannot conceive death until the intellect perceives it and the mind accepts it. We go about seeking the fulfillment of joy, of peace, of certainty, and of security. This is what all the world wants, but we think these things are objective. They are not. Real as they are, they did not create themselves. They are but effects of a spiritual cause, which is an idea created by an act of the mind.

When all the world shall know that there is nothing to be afraid of, fear will disappear from the human mind forever, and not until then. But we cannot wait for that time. We must definitely and deliberately decide whether or not we are going to be afraid of anything. That is our decision; no one can make it for us. Nor is there any power in heaven or any belief in hell that can withhold the result of our decision from us.

We must right now develop this interior awareness, this spiritual perception which is a very real thing. If we embody the idea of confusion, we shall become confused, and if we maintain the idea of unhappiness, we shall become unhappy. But if we entertain the idea of peace long enough, we shall become peaceful. When we *know* freedom, freedom is ours. It so happens in our lives that as we gradually discard and do away with discord, harmony then sits like a wreath of benediction on our brows. Can we, in the midst of the crowd, as Emerson said, keep "with perfect sweetness the independence of our solitude"? As we walk on the sidewalks of the city, can we stop seeing that which we no longer wish to experience and mentally embody only those ideas which we wish to experience? That is what practice is.

Spiritual mind treatment is for the purpose of consciously creating those states of mind which we should like to see tangibly manifested in the objective world. If we want to be prosperous, we must think nothing but success, no matter how much failure appears. If we want to gradually gravitate into the atmosphere of friendliness and love, we must know that the Universe is our friend, and if some person appears not to be friendly, we must utterly disregard it. We can convince the mind that our unity with Spirit is absolute, therefore we are *now* unifying with our good forevermore.

Our mind is an experimental laboratory. In it we can definitely prove for ourself, by specifically repudiating certain negative thoughts and dwelling on their opposites, that the eternal verities are real and ever present; that life is good, happy, complete, radiant, strong; that all the good there is is right here. Our mental equivalents, our spiritual concepts, our interior awarenesses are causative prototypes in the mind. They are not illusions, and our dynamic acceptance of them as realities causes the great universal Law to project a likeness of our acceptance on the screen of our experience.

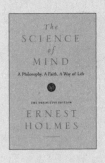
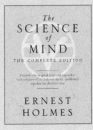

A Treasury of Inspiration and Guidance

A New Design for Living

978-1-58542-814-4

Love and Law

978-1-58542-302-6

The Hidden Power of the Bible

978-1-58542-511-2

The Essential Ernest Holmes

978-1-58542-181-7

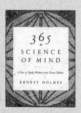

365 Science of Mind

978-1-58542-609-6

Prayer

978-1-58542-605-8

Simple Guides for Ideas in Action

Creative Mind   978-1-58542-606-5

The Art of Life   978-1-58542-613-3

Creative Mind and Success   978-1-58542-608-9

This Thing Called You   978-1-58542-607-2

Discover a Richer Life   978-1-58542-812-0

Living Without Fear   978-1-58542-813-7

Coming Soon

Questions and Answers on the Science of Mind

Think Your Troubles Away

It's Up to You

Mind Remakes Your World

**TARCHER
PENGUIN**

For more information:
www.penguin.com
www.tarcherbooks.com
www.scienceofmind.com

If you enjoyed this book, visit

www.tarcherbooks.com

and sign up for Tarcher's e-newsletter to receive
special offers, giveaway promotions, and
information on hot upcoming releases.

TARCHER
PENGUIN

Great Lives Begin with Great Ideas

New at **www.tarcherbooks.com**
and **www.penguin.com/tarchertalks:**

Tarcher Talks, an online video series featuring
interviews with bestselling authors on everything from creativity and prosperity to 2012
and Freemasonry.

If you would like to place a bulk order
of this book, call 1-800-847-5515.